VOCABULARY POWER

BUILDING A MORE POWERFUL VOCABULARY

Contributing Editor
Sharon Shirley
Branford High School
Branford, Connecticut

*A **Get Smart Book**® from*

WEBSTER HOUSE
PUBLISHING LLC

Ridgefield, Connecticut

Library of Congress Control Number: 2004100352

ISBN: 1-932635-05-X

Printed in the United States of America

10 9 8 7 6 5 4 3 2 1

For additional information about Webster House Publishing LLC titles or Get Smart Book® titles, contact us on the Internet at *http://www.websterhousepub.com*, or write to Webster House Publishing LLC, Box 294, Georgetown, CT 06829.

Contents

Introduction

"I don't know what you mean by 'glory,'"
Alice said.

Humpty Dumpty smiled contemptuously.
"Of course you don't till I tell you. I meant 'there's
a nice knock-down argument for you!'"

"But 'glory' doesn't mean 'a nice knock-down
argument,'" Alice objected.

"When I use a word," Humpty Dumpty said,
in rather a scornful tone, "it means just what I
choose it to mean, neither more nor less."

"The question is," said Alice, "whether you
can make words mean so many different things."

"The question is," said Humpty Dumpty,
"which is to be master, that's all."

Lewis Carroll
Through the Looking Glass

Humpty Dumpty's position is evidently quite defensible
among the logicians, but not, unfortunately, in the world. We are
quite aware of our present need to improve written and spoken
English, and we try to repress the Humpty Dumpty within us,
especially when it comes to words.

Using words precisely clarifies a thought, makes a letter
convincing, impresses a listener. We must be familiar with the
meaning of a word before that word comes naturally to our tongues
or pens. If we have the slightest doubt that we may not know
the meaning of a word, we should look it up immediately. This
Vocabulary Power is a handy book for just this need: immediate
reference at the desk, computer, or, worktable. It contains more than
3,000 essential words as well as 500+ words for those of you
studying for the SATs or PSATs.

Writing is hard work, and we tend to be lazy about looking
up words. We say to ourselves that the sentence sounds correct,

the spelling seems all right, and chances are the receiver at the other end of the line (the reader) won't catch our error anyway—a dangerous assumption. The receiver at the other end of the line may be a schoolmate, a boss, or a jealous friend who might like nothing better than to catch us with the wrong word or an incorrect spelling.

Many people enjoy gloating and saying, "Edward never could spell *existence*" or "June will never be able to distinguish between *effect* and *affect*." We should do everything in our power to avoid such criticism, especially since we have become so conscious of good English.

The first step to remedy our laziness is to have a reference book handy at all times. The advantage of this book is its size and convenience; it can fit anywhere without cluttering or getting in the way. It will also be a time-saver, and you will be able to use this book instead of a bulky dictionary.

The second step is to become more closely attuned to the signals in our own mind. If we feel the slightest uneasiness with a word, we should pay attention. Our unconscious may be telling us that we have a mistake in front of us that our conscious mind has not picked up. Then we should look up the word. It is important to get in the habit of looking up a word even if we are sure we know the meaning. We may be surprised to find that we have misused the words for years. It is better to look up words than to trust in our own habitual usage.

The third step (or state of mind) is not to be frustrated by lack of retention. You should look up the word again and again until you have mastered it. This seems odd, but the mind plays tricks all the time. Some big words will be retained immediately—spelling, meaning, and all; other, simpler words might cause us problems for a long time. The mind will continually forget how to spell a word, for it is often confused by similarities in sound.

For instance, people often misspell *grammar* because they confuse it with *hammer*; *existence* may be misspelled as *existance* because of words like *distance* that sound nearly the same. These confusions can be sorted out by constant referral to a reference book. We should never become discouraged because that will accomplish nothing more than laziness; the mistakes will remain uncorrected.

We often misuse words that are close in meaning because we have not taken the time to think them out. A classic example is the difference between *infer* and *imply*. We *infer* or come to a conclusion about something from the evidence offered by someone else. We *imply* or give an impression to someone else by offering them evidence. The two words depict exactly opposite actions, messages being carried in opposite directions.

A fourth step or word of advice has to do with the process of enlarging your vocabulary. This often brings to mind a crash course, lists of words, definitions hurriedly learned, numerous multiple-choice tests. Such an effort may well be counter-productive and leads more readily to the kinds of confusion that have caused the trouble in the first place. The best way to enlarge a working vocabulary is slowly, a word at a time.

Part of the effort may be to retrieve, from a kind of limbo, words that we read and understand (or think we understand) but do not use naturally. To use a word in speech or even in our own writing is to be familiar with it. We become familiar with a word by being sure of its meaning, by looking it up.

You should also remember that an enormous vocabulary must also be a useful one. The best writers do not employ overwhelming numbers of learned words to impress us; they use the exact and often the simplest word to enlighten us.

Using this book

The book is divided into sections. The first section, with which you should become familiar, is about prefixes, suffixes, and roots. These are the building blocks of words, of vocabulary; and a strong knowledge of the material in this section can help you deduce the meaning of a word without having any previous idea of what the word means.

The second section is the vocabulary list, with more than 3,000 words. Don't study them all at once. Pace yourself. Read through a section of the alphabet, perhaps. Or you may just want to check a word you've encountered in your reading. To make this an easy learning process, we include the parts of speech, definitions of the word, and a sentence so that you can understand the word in context.

The third section of the book is for those of you planning to take the PSAT or SAT exam. Since these exams require a strong knowledge of vocabulary, we had our experts analyze previous exams and extracted 500+ words that will be helpful when you take these exams.

The fourth section of the book is an extensive list of abbreviations. It's ideal for anyone who has to write a letter, an essay, a report, or any other kind of written material.

Following this section is a list of chemical abbreviations. It's a great reference for those studying — or just reading about — chemistry.

Finally, the last section is just a list of humorous plays on words. Nothing to study. Nothing to learn. But we hope these little tidbits put a smile on your face.

If you are persistent and confident, you will gradually enlarge your useful vocabulary, and there is pleasure in this. There is pleasure in knowing for its own sake; there is pleasure in realizing the practical advantages of increased word power in your business and personal relations.

Prefixes, Roots, and Suffixes

The English language is a rather complex collection of words derived from a wide variety of other languages and their particular rules. The origins of many English words date back to the Ancient Greek and Roman times. Many other words are creations of modern times for modern purposes. The language has been made even more complicated by the way different groups of English-speaking peoples in different areas of the world have contributed to and modified the language over time. Because of these and other influences, the English language has more words than most other languages, and many of those words have similar, and often the very same, meanings.

As humans, we have the capability to become lifelong learners, and we can continue to develop and expand our individual vocabularies throughout our lives. We can incorporate vast numbers of words into our own internalized dictionaries and make distinctions between many of those words that are similar to each other. In this way, we continue to become more adept at articulating our thoughts through conversation and writing. Also, knowing more words makes it easier to understand what others intend in their speaking and writing. In sum, a strong vocabulary is the sign of a strong communicator.

Many people equate a strong vocabulary with intelligence. While the ability to use words well may be a sign of one form of intelligence (linguistic), the true genius of those who have strong vocabularies comes from their consistent efforts to increase and use their own vocabularies, not solely from any particular talent to do so. There are several tools available to help everyone expand his or her own personal vocabulary. For instance, some people make it a practice to look up in the dictionary every new word they encounter. They then review it and use it repeatedly until it becomes natural to them. Others play word games, such as in the *Reader's Digest* or newspapers (crossword puzzles, acrostics, riddles), or use tools such as a vocabulary building word-a-day calendar.

One of the best ways to improve your vocabulary is to read. You must do so actively, meaning that you think about what you are reading and work at making sense of it as you go along. When you come across a word you do not know, look it up. If there is no dictionary readily available, study the context. What do the words around the one you do not know tell you about what the word could mean? What does the topic of the paragraph and writing as a whole indicate about the possible meaning of the word? Many times, using the context can help you get the gist of what the word means.

Another tool that can help you to determine the meaning of a word is an appreciation of how to find and interpret root words, along with a strong understanding of the meanings and purposes of prefixes and suffixes. By understanding the root, or core idea, of a word and applying the meanings of prefixes (which appear before the root) and suffixes (which appear after the root), you can literally take a word apart and figure out its meaning by putting the meanings of its pieces back together. For instance, look at the word "extraction." The prefix is "ex," the root is "tract," and the suffix is "ion." If you know what each of these means, you can determine the meaning of the word "extraction."

Prefix	Root	Suffix
ex-	tract	-ion
"out"	"to pull"	"the act of"

Using the meanings of the prefix, root, and suffix of extraction, you can figure out that the word "extraction" means "the act of pulling out."

Take a look at another example. The word "endangerment" can be broken into the prefix "en," the root word "danger," and the suffix "ment."

Prefix	Root	Suffix
en-	danger	-ment
"in"	"exposure of risk or harm"	"the state of being"

Using the meanings of the parts of the word set forth in the chart, you can determine that "endangerment" means "being in the state of exposure to risk or harm."

To use this skill, you need to have a strong knowledge base of root words, prefixes, and suffixes. Below are lists of each, along with their meanings and sample words in which they appear. These lists are not comprehensive, but if you take the time to learn them well, you should be able to figure out any number of words that you might otherwise not know.

As you are reviewing and learning the partial words on the lists, try to come up with examples of your own for practice. Learn the examples too, because if you can associate the word part with the example, you will be more likely to remember it when you need it. You can also make a notebook in which you start collecting new words. Once you have collected a few words, test yourself by breaking the words apart into their prefixes, roots, and suffixes and figuring out the meanings. Then, check yourself using the lists provided here or in a dictionary.

Finally, when you are working with vocabulary, and the tools you have do not seem to be working, listen to your instincts. Go with your intuition about what a word means when the other tricks are not working quite right for that particular word. Often, something about the word will be familiar to your brain, whether you are consciously aware of it or not, and your guess will likely be on target. Of course, the more practice you have with discovering meanings through context or by breaking them down into prefixes, roots, and suffixes, the better at guessing you will be. Trust yourself, but work hard at giving yourself a strong foundation on which to place that trust.

Table 1.1 Common Prefixes and Meanings

Prefix	Meaning	Examples
a-, an-	without	amoral = without morals
ab-	away from	abnormal = away from normal abscond = run away
ad-, at-	toward, to	address = to guide toward attract = draw to
ambi-	both, either	ambidextrous = both hands
ambul-	about or around	ambulatory = used for moving about
ante-	before	antecedent = before in time
anti-, ant-	opposite, opposing	antipathy = opposite of feelings
arch-	first, chief	archbishop = chief bishop archetype = original pattern
auto-	self, same	autobiography = self living story autopilot = self pilot
be-	thoroughly	bemuse = thoroughly confuse beloved = thoroughly loved
bio-, bi-	life, living organism	biology = study of living organisms
co-	together	coauthor = author together
contra-	against	contradict = speak against
de-	down, from, off	degrade = put down in rank deflect = push away from
di, dia-	through, across	diagonal = through angles
dis-	not, un	disbelief = no belief disentangle = untangle
e-	away	evade = move away
en-	in	engage = in obligation
equi-	equal	equidistant = equal distance
eu-	good, well	eulogy = good words euphoric = feeling of well-being

Prefix	Meaning	Examples
exter-, extra-	outside of	external = outside extraordinary = outside of ordinary
geo-	earth	geology = study of earth geography = to describe earth
hetero-	different	heterogeneous = different kind
homo-	same	homogeneous = same kind
hyper-	excessive, excessively	hyperactive = excessively active
hypo-	below, under	hypoactive = under active
il-, im-, in-, ir	not	illogical = not logical improper = not proper infinite = not finite irrational = not rational
intra-	within, into	intravenous = within veins
inter-	between, among	international = between or among nations
mal-	bad, badly	malnutrition = bad diet
mega-	great in size, very large	megalopolis = very large city
micro-	small	microorganism = small organism
mis-	wrong, wrongly	misread = wrongly read
mono-	one, single, alone	monochrome = one color monotheistic = believe in one god
multi-	many	multidimensional = many dimensions
omni-	all	omnipresent = all present
neo-	new, recent	neonatal = newly born
non-	not	nonessential = not essential
ob-	in the way	obstruct = to be in the way

Prefix	Meaning	Examples
pan-	all, general	pandemic = all people
ped-	child	pediatric = medical treatment of children
per-	through	pervade = to pass through
peri-	around	perinatal = period around child birth
post-	after	postdate = date after
poly-	many	polytheistic = believe in many gods
pre-	before	prevent = come before
pro-	for	protest = state for
re-	again	readjust = adjust again
retro-	back, backward	retrospect = look back
se-	away	secede = pull away
semi-	half, partial	semicircle = half circle
sub-, sup-	under, below	submarine = below water
super-, supra-	over, above, beyond	supernatural = beyond nature supersonic = above sound
syn-	together, similar	synchronize = together in time synonym = similar word
tele-	distance	teleport = move in distance television = broadcast from a distance
thermo-, therm-	heat	thermometer = heat measure hypothermia = below normal body heat
trans-	across, beyond, through	transatlantic = across the Atlantic transdermal = across skin
ultra-	exceeding	ultraviolet = exceeds violet
un-	not	unlimited = not limited

Table 1.2 Common Root Words and Meanings

Root Word	Meaning	Example
agri, agro	field	agriculture = culture of a field agrobiologist = one who studies field growth
anthro	human	philanthropy = love of human kind
aqua, aque	water	aquatic = in or of water aqueduct = water pathway
aster, astro, stell	star	asterisk = star-like symbol astronomy = study of stars stellate = shaped like a star
audi	to hear	audience = listeners
bene	good, well	beneficial = functions for a good result
biblio	book	bibliophile = lover of books
breve	short	abbreviate = shorten
cap	take	captive = one who is taken
-cede, -ceed	go before	secede = go apart exceed = go beyond
chrono	time	synchronize = together in time chronological = in order of time
circum	around	circumnavigate = travel around
clud	keep	include = keep in
cosmo	world	cosmography = science of the world
cracy	government	democracy = government of the people
cred	to believe	credit = belief incredible = not believable
cur	run	concurrent = running at the same time

Root Word	Meaning	Example
dem	people	demography = study of people endemic = in a group of people
derm, derma, dermo	skin	epidermis = outer skin
dexter	hand	ambidextrous = possessing ability to use either hand
dict	to say	edict = statement dictate = say aloud
duc	to lead, bring, take	reduce = take down
frat	brother, sibling	fratricide = murder of brother
gram, graph	write	telegram = write across distance graphite = substance for writing
gress	path, way	regress = backward
hydro	water	dehydrate = water level is down
ject	to throw	eject = throw away
junct	join	conjunction = act of joining together
lat	side	latitude = extend from side to side
lev	raise	levitate = to raise into the air
lith	stone	lithology = study of rocks
loc	place	locator = one who finds places
logo	thought, word	dialogue = words between two people
manu	hand	manual = operated by hand
meter	to measure	diameter = measure across
mit	send	transmit = send across emit = send away
morph	form, shape	amorphous = without shape

Root Word	Meaning	Example
mortis	final, death	mortal = subject to death
nym	word, name	synonym = similar word anonymous = without having a name
path	feeling	apathy = without feeling
pedo, ped	child	pedagogue = teacher of children
pel	to drive	repel = drive away
pend	to hang	depend = hang from pendulum = hanging device
philo, phil	love	philanthropy = love for humans
phob	fear	hydrophobia = fear of water
phon	sound	phonetics = representing or being a sound
pod	foot	podiatrist = person who cares for feet
port	to carry	import = carry in
press	push	express = push away impress = push in
pseudo	false	pseudonym = false name
psycho	mind	psychogenesis = beginning of the mind
sanct	holy	sanctuary = holy place
scope	see	telescope = see from afar
scrib	to write	subscribe = write underneath (sign)
son	sound	sonorous = full of sound
soph	wise	sophomore = wise fool
spect	look	introspection = act of looking in
theism	belief in god(s)	monotheism = belief in one god atheism = belief in no god

Root Word	Meaning	Examples
tox	poison	toxic = relating to poison
tract	to pull, drag, draw	extract = pull out
vent	expose to air	ventilator = thing that gives air
vert	to turn	revert = to turn back to
vinc, vict	conquer	invincible = cannot be conquered victorious = one who conquers
voc	call	evoke = to call out
vocat	call	convocation = act of calling together

Table 1.3 Common Suffixes and Meanings

A special note about suffixes: Suffixes add to the meaning of a word, but they also change the part of speech of the word. Very often, the suffix changes the word from a verb into a noun or adjective, or from a noun into an adjective or verb. This chart shows the part of speech the word will be changed into when that suffix is used.

Suffix	Part of Speech	Meaning	Example
-able, ible	adjective	capable of being	manageable = capable of being managed vendible = capable of being sold
-ac, -al	adjective	of or relating to	parental = relating to being a parent
-age	noun	connected to action or result of action	frontage = connected to the front carriage = thing that carries
-ance, -ent	noun	state of being	deliverance = state of being delivered

Suffix	Part of Speech	Meaning	Example
-ant, -ent	noun	thing or one who does	servant = one who serves deterrent = something that deters
-ary	adjective	relating to	complimentary = related to a compliment
-ate	adjective	become like	obstinate = to become in the way
-er, -or	noun	person who does	teacher = person who teaches regulator = person who regulates
-er	adjective	more	friendlier = more friendly
-est	adjective	most	friendliest = most friendly
-ette	noun	little	luncheonette = little place to eat
-ful	adjective	full of	bountiful = full of bounty
-gram	noun	record	cardiogram = record of heart activity
-graph	noun	recording, recording tool	cardiograph = records heart activity
-ial	adjective	of or relating to	partial = part of
-ic	adjective	being like something	toxic = relating to a poison
-ier	adjective	more	fancier = more fancy
-iest	adjective	most	fanciest = most fancy
-ing	verb	to be in the process of	acting = to be in the process of acting
-ion	noun	condition or result of act or process	vacation = result of vacating
-ise, ize	verb	to cause to be	empathize = to cause to feel
-ish	adjective	to be like	childish = to be child-like

Suffix	Part of Speech	Meaning	Example
-ism	noun	action or trait	fatalism = to be fatalistic hypothyroidism = to have the trait of a low thyroid
-ist	noun	someone who is or does	biologist = person who studies living organisms
-ive	adjective	performing or acting, relating or belonging to	pensive = act of thinking consecutive = relating to togetherness
-less	adjective	without	childless = without children
-logue, -log	noun	speech, discourse	monologue = speech by one
-logy	noun	study	toxicology = study of poison
-ly	adjective	having the characteristic of	happily = having characteristic of happiness
-ment	noun	state of	pavement = state of being paved movement = state of moving
-oid	noun	resembling	humanoid = resembling a human
-ory	noun	place for	laboratory = place for lab work
-ology	noun	study of	anthropology = study of humans
-ous	adjective	full of	ardurous = full of ardor (passion)
-phile	noun	lover of	audiophile = sound, music lover
-phobia	noun	fears	hydrophobia = fear of water
-phone	noun	sound; device	telephone = sound over distance

3000+ Words You Should Know

A

abnormal
adj ab-nor-mal: unusual, irregular

The *abnormal* way in which he behaved bothered his parents.

abode
n a-bode: residence

He moved his *abode* to the other part of town.

abolish
v a-bol-ish: to put an end to

They tried to *abolish* the long lunch hour.

abominate
v a-bom-i-nate: to hate

I *abominate* having to eat celery.

abortive
adj a-bor-tive: ineffectual, unsuccessful

They made an *abortive* attempt to capture the radio station.

abrade
v a-brade: to rub off, wear away by friction

Sandpaper is used to *abrade* a rough surface.

abridge
v a-bridge: to shorten

The book was *abridged* and did not contain all the information.

abrogate
v ab-ro-gate: to annul or abolish

Congress has the right to *abrogate* laws with the consent of the chief executive.

abrupt
adj a-brupt: sudden, quick

He made an *abrupt* departure from the party.

abscond
v ab-scond: to steal off to avoid some penalty

The teller *absconded* with the bank's funds.

absolve
v ab-solve: to forgive

She was *absolved* by her father.

abstain
v ab-stain: to refrain voluntarily from some act

Alcoholics must *abstain* from any indulgence in alcoholic drinks.

abstemious
adj ab-ste-mi-ous: moderate, especially in eating and drinking

The *abstemious* eater is seldom overweight.

abstruse
adj ab-struse: hard to understand, abstract

The *abstruse* style of the artist confused the viewer.

absurd
adj ab-surd: ridiculous
> He wore an *absurd* jacket to the party.

abundant
adj a-bun-dant: more than enough
> There were *abundant* baskets of fruit for the guests.

abusive
adj a-bu-sive: insulting, attacking
> His language was *abusive*, and he was asked to leave.

abut
v a-but: to touch, as bordering property
> When estates *abut*, borders must be defined properly.

abyss
n a-byss: bottomless pit
> The *abyss* was deep and treacherous.

accede
v ac-cede: to give in to, agree
> I will *accede* to your wishes if you cooperate.

access
n ac-cess: admission
> He received *access* to the files from his boss.

acclaim
v ac-claim: to approve, applaud
> He *acclaimed* their new production.

acclaim
n ac-claim: loud approval
> The audience's *acclaim* was overwhelming.

acclimate
v ac-cli-mate: accustom to a new environment
> Visitors to the desert have a hard time *acclimating* themselves to the variations in temperature.

acclivity
n ac-cliv-i-ty: upward slope
> He viewed the great *acclivity* with dismay as their car chugged along.

accolade
n ac-co-lade: an award or praise
> He accepted the *accolade* modestly.

accomplice
n ac-com-plice: a partner
> They were *accomplices* in the crime.

accord
n ac-cord: an agreement
> All of the members of the council signed the latest *accord*.

accost
v ac-cost: to greet, aggressively
> The boy was *accosted* by a beggar on the country road.

accouchement
n ac-couche-ment: confinement for childbirth
> They waited impatiently during her *accouchement*.

accumulate
v ac-cu-mu-late: to collect, gather
> He *accumulated* a large assortment of stamps.

acerbity

n a-cer-bi-ty: bitterness, sourness

The *acerbity* of her wit won her many enemies.

acme

n ac-me: highest point

The *acme* of the skyline was the radio tower.

acolyte

n ac-o-lyte: an assistant, especially in a religious rite

The youth was anxious to serve as *acolyte* to a priest.

aconite

n ac-o-nite: a type of poisonous plant

The *aconites* include wolfsbane and monkshood, which figure in many mystery stories.

acoustic

adj a-cous-tic: pertaining to hearing

The *acoustic* qualities of a room may be improved by insulation.

acquiesce

v ac-qui-esce: agree, submit

He was forced to *acquiesce* to his boss's demands.

acquit

v ac-quit: to declare innocent

The jury voted to *acquit* the defendant.

acrid

adj ac-rid: sharp, bitter

The drink left an *acrid* taste in his mouth.

acrimony

n ac-ri-mo-ny: harsh or biting language or temper

His *acrimony* resulted from years of disappointment.

acronym

n ac-ro-nym: word formed from initials

Radar is an *acronym* for radio detecting and ranging.

actuary

n ac-tu-ar-y: an expert who calculates insurance risks

The *actuary* plays an important part in establishing insurance premium rates.

actuate

v ac-tu-ate: to put into action, incite

The machine was *actuated* by an electric starter.

acumen

n a-cu-men: sharpness, insight

His financial *acumen* helped make him rich.

adage

n ad-age: a proverb, a saying that has been in long use

"A stitch in time saves nine" is an old *adage.*

adamant

adj ad-a-mant: inflexible, hard

A man must be *adamant* in his determination to succeed.

adapt

v a-dapt: to change

He was able to *adapt* himself to the warmer climate.

adduce
v ad-duce: to bring forward as a reason or example
In their defense they *adduced* several justifications for their actions.

adept
adj a-dept: highly skilled
She was *adept* at skiing.

adept
n a-dept: an expert, one who is skilled
He was considered an *adept* in their field of art.

adequate
adj ad-e-quate: sufficient
The drink was *adequate* and quenched his thirst.

adhere
v ad-here: follow, stick to
He tried to *adhere* to the rules.

adipose
adj ad-i-pose: fatty
The doctor removed the *adipose* tissue from around the heart.

adjacent
adj ad-ja-cent: alongside of, near to
She lived in the *adjacent* building.

adjourn
v ad-journ: to postpone, discontinue
They were unable to *adjourn* the meeting for him.

adjunct
n ad-junct: something added to
The building was an *adjunct* to the school.

adjure
v ad-jure: to charge or command solemnly
The witness was *adjured* to weigh his words carefully.

admonish
v ad-mon-ish: to warn
The child was *admonished* by the man and told not to mistreat the dog.

adroit
adj a-droit: skillful
The child's *adroit* piano playing made the audience cheer.

adulation
n ad-u-la-tion: extreme praise
The movie star was not used to his fans' *adulation*.

advent
n ad-vent: arrival
With the *advent* of winter, I start to wear mittens.

adverse
adj ad-verse: unfavorable
The movie received *adverse* comments in the papers.

advocate
v ad-vo-cate: to speak or write in support of
They tried to *advocate* a new rule in the Congress.

advocate
n ad-vo-cate: one who pleads in support of something

He was an *advocate* of free speech.

aesthetic
adj aes-thet-ic: pertaining to the beautiful

Modern design seeks to produce machines that have *aesthetic* as well as functional appeal.

affable
adj af-fa-ble: sociable, courteous

The dog was *affable* and liked by the neighbors.

affidavit
n af-fi-da-vit: a sworn statement in writing

An *affidavit* may serve in place of a personal appearance.

affiliate
v af-fil-i-ate: to connect with, to join

He planned to *affiliate* himself with the other team.

affiliate
n af-fil-i-ate: one who belongs

He was elected an *affiliate* of the firm.

affinity
n af-fin-i-ty: attraction

He had an overpowering *affinity* for chocolate.

affirmation
n af-fir-ma-tion: solemn avowal

Quakers and others may testify in court on *affirmation*.

affirmative
adj af-fir-ma-tive: agreeing

He was *affirmative* in his decisions.

affirmative
n af-fir-ma-tive: an experession of agreement

I will vote in the *affirmative* for that measure.

affluence
n af-flu-ence: wealth

They had achieved their *affluence* by hard work.

affluent
adj af-flu-ent: abundant, wealthy

The United States is an *affluent* nation.

affront
v af-front: to insult

He *affronted* the girl by slamming the door.

affront
n af-front: a deliberate insult

The way he acted was an *affront* to his father.

agenda
n a-gen-da: schedule of events, list

His talk was to be the first on the *agenda*.

agglomerate
v ag-glom-er-ate: to gather into one mass
> It was necessasry to *agglomerate* all the minerals into one product to produce the necessary weight.

aggravate
v ag-gra-vate: to annoy
> His leg *aggravated* him throughout the race.

aggregate
v ag-gre-gate: to collect
> He was able to *aggregate* a large collection of art.

aggregate
n ag-gre-gate: a total
> The *aggregate* of all his holdings was immense.

aggressive
adj ag-gres-sive: quarrelsome, forward
> The child was too *aggressive* to play with the others.

aghast
adj a-ghast: frightened, surprised
> She was *aghast* at her child's behavior.

agile
adj ag-ile: nimble
> The *agile* child climbed the bars.

agitate
v ag-i-tate: to disturb, shake
> The washing machine *agitated* the clothing in the final cycle.

agnostic
n ag-nos-tic: skeptic
> He was an *agnostic* when it came to believing in God.

agony
n ag-o-ny: great suffering, pain
> He was in *agony* after the accident.

agrarian
adj a-grar-i-an: having to do with land
> *Agrarian* reforms were one of the first measures proposed in the economic rehabilitation of land.

agronomy
n a-gron-o-my: the science and practice of crop production
> Many positions in *agronomy* are offered by the federal government.

aigrette
n ai-grette: feathers worn as a head ornament
> Laws had to be passed to prohibit the wearing of *aigrettes* in order to preserve the birds.

ajar
adj a-jar: opened slightly
> The door to the office was *ajar*.

akimbo
adv a-kim-bo: position with hands on hips
> He stood *akimbo*, his elbows touching the sides of the hallway.

akimbo
adj a-kim-bo: position with hands on hips
> He posed in an *akimbo* stance to have his picture taken.

alacrity

n a-lac-ri-ty: cheerful briskness

The *alacrity* shown by the new employee gratified the manager.

albino

n al-bi-no: white, without pigment

Albinos are extremely rare.

alchemy

n al-che-my: medieval chemistry

A goal of *alchemy* was the transmutation of base metals into gold.

alcove

n al-cove: small room or nook

The *alcove* was cozy and warm.

alibi

n al-i-bi: excuse

The police did not believe his *alibi*.

alibi

v al-i-bi: to offer an excuse

She tried to *alibi* herself out of trouble.

alien

adj al-ien: foreign

She was an *alien* agent.

alienate

v al-ien-ate: to estrange, make inimical or indifferent

One purpose of the offer to the East was to *alienate* the Western nations.

align

v a-lign: adjust

They were able to *align* the wheels to stop the shake.

allay

v al-lay: to pacify, calm

Therapy will often *allay* the fears of the neurotic.

allegation

n al-le-ga-tion: assertion without proof

He was unable to prove his wild *allegations*.

allegory

n al-le-go-ry: a story that teaches through symbols

Animal fables are usually *allegories* of human behavior.

allegro

adj al-le-gro: fast, quick (in music)

The conductor asked them to play the *allegro* movement.

alleviate

v al-le-vi-ate: to lessen, make easier

The morphine helped to *alleviate* the pain.

alliance

n al-li-ance: a union

They created an *alliance* of automobile workers.

allocate

v al-lo-cate: to distribute or assign

The new serum was *allocated* among the states by population.

distribution

...cy quickly used up their *allotment* of sugar.

alloy

n al-loy: a mixture of metals

The truck was made from a new *alloy*.

allude

v al-lude: to mention indirectly

He *alluded* to their previous conversation.

alluring

adj al-lur-ing: attractive, tempting

She was *alluring* in her new dress.

alluvial

adj al-lu-vi-al: left by departing water

Alluvial deposits are marked by stratified rock.

aloof

adv a-loof: at a distance but in view

At the party, she remained *aloof* and stayed in the corner.

aloof

adj a-loof: withdrawn, distant

The others considered her too *aloof* to be their friend.

alter

v al-ter: to change

The new hair color *altered* her appearance.

altercation

n al-ter-ca-tion: a quarrel

After the *altercation*, the crowd went home.

alternative

adj al-ter-na-tive: choice

The *alternative* means of transportation was to take the train.

altruistic

adj al-tru-is-tic: unselfish

He displayed his *altruistic* nature by giving away all of his dinner.

amalgamate

v a-mal-gam-ate: to combine

The scientist was able to *amalgamate* the chemicals into a new substance.

amass

v a-mass: to accumulate

The snow *amassed* on the ground after the storm.

amatory

adj am-a-to-ry: pertaining to sexual love

The *amatory* emphasis in films disturbed some groups.

ambergris

n am-ber-gris: intestinal secretion of the sperm whale

A great prize of the whaling expedition was a quantity of *ambergris*.

ambidextrous

adj am-bi-dex-trous: able to use both hands equally well

Ambidextrous tennis players have a great advantage.

ambiguous

adj am-big-u-ous: unclear

They did not understand her *ambiguous* instructions.

ambulatory
adj am-bu-la-to-ry: moving about, able to walk
> *Ambulatory* patients require organized activities to speed their recovery.

ambush
n am-bush: a trap
> The soldiers were caught in a well-planned *ambush*.

ambush
v am-bush: to attack from hiding
> The Indians were able to *ambush* their enemies.

ameliorate
v a-me-lio-rate: to improve
> He was able to *ameliorate* the patient's pain.

amenable
adj a-me-na-ble: open to suggestion
> He was *amenable* to any proposition.

amend
v a-mend: to change, to improve
> Make sure to *amend* the contract with the new rules.

amenity
n a-men-i-ty: pleasantness, courteous act
> One must observe the *amenities* in dealing with strangers.

amicable
adj am-i-ca-ble: friendly
> The new neighbors were extremely *amicable*.

amnesty
n am-nes-ty: pardon
> The president granted *amnesty* to the rest of the men.

amorous
adj am-o-rous: loving
> She was extremely *amorous* to her husband.

ample
adj am-ple: large, roomy
> He had an *ample* suitcase to carry all of his belongings.

amplify
v am-pli-fy: to increase
> The guitarist *amplified* his music electronically.

amputate
v am-pu-tate: to cut off
> The leg had to be *amputated* due to the infection.

amulet
n am-u-let: magic charm
> She wore the mustard seed *amulet* around her neck.

ancient
adj an-cient: old
> She purchased the *ancient* table at a good price.

anecdote
n an-ec-dote: interesting story
> He kept them amused with witty *anecdotes* all evening.

anguish
n an-guish: great pain
> The *anguish* he suffered from the death of his friend stayed with him for many years.

animate
v an-i-mate: to give life to
  He was able to *animate* the characters on film.

animate
adj an-i-mate: living, active
  He grew extremely *animated* when he spoke.

animosity
n an-i-mos-i-ty: anger, extreme hatred
  He showed his *animosity* by cancelling her contract.

annex
v an-nex: to join or add
  Argentina tried to *annex* the Falkland Islands.

annex
n an-nex: something added
  They built a new *annex* to the hospital.

annihilate
v an-ni-hi-late: to destroy
  They were all *annihilated* in the savage attack.

annual
adj an-nual: yearly
  It was an *annual* picnic for the employees.

annul
v an-nul: to cancel, make void
  The marriage was *annulled* after only a few months.

anode
n an-ode: a positive electrode
  The wire was connected to the battery's *anode*.

anon
adv a-non: soon, shortly
  He will be arriving *anon*.

anonymous
adj a-non-y-mous: without a name
  The book was written by an *anonymous* author.

antagonist
n an-tag-o-nist: opponent
  The two *antagonists* met in the middle of the ring.

anthracite
n an-thra-cite: hard coal
  Anthracite is mined in many parts of the world.

antidote
n an-ti-dote: a remedy
  They immediately gave the child the *antidote* for the poison.

apathetic
adj ap-a-thet-ic: indifferent, uncaring
  She was *apathetic* about going to the show.

aperture
n ap-er-ture: opening
  The wider the *aperture* on a camera, the more light can enter.

apex
n a-pex: highest point
  The man was at the *apex* of his career.

aplomb
n a-plomb: poise, assurance
Although he was young, he faced the audience with *aplomb.*

apogee
n ap-o-gee: the highest point
The space capsule began to descend after reaching its *apogee.*

apothecary
n a-poth-e-car-y: druggist
He purchased pills from the town *apothecary.*

appalling
adj ap-pall-ing: horrifying
The child's behavior was *appalling* to her mother.

apparatus
n ap-pa-ra-tus: equipment
The magician unloaded his *apparatus* backstage.

apparel
n ap-par-el: clothing
They gave their old *apparel* to the charity.

apparition
n ap-pa-ri-tion: ghost, phantom
The children were frightened by the *apparition* that appeared in the room.

appease
v ap-pease: to satisfy, allay
The child *appeased* his aunt by being attentive.

append
v ap-pend: to attach
He *appended* the paragraph to the end of the story.

appraise
v ap-praise: to estimate
He was unable to *appraise* the value of the ring.

apprehend
v ap-pre-hend: to capture
The robber was *apprehended* trying to escape.

appropriate
adj ap-pro-pri-ate: suitable
She wore an *appropriate* dress for the party.

appropriate
v ap-pro-pri-ate: to seize, steal
He *appropriated* the candlestick from the museum.

aptitude
n ap-ti-tude: ability, talent
The *aptitude* that he showed on the test was remarkable.

aqueous
adj a-que-ous: watery
The ship sunk to its *aqueous* grave.

archaic
adj ar-cha-ic: old fashioned
It was an *archaic* style of dance.

arduous
adj ar-du-ous: difficult
It was an *arduous* climb up the mountain.

arid
adj ar-id: dry, barren
> The *arid* desert showed little animal life.

armada
n ar-ma-da: fleet of ships or planes
> The American *armada* approached the enemy's coastline.

armistice
n ar-mi-stice: a truce
> Both sides signed the *armistice* aboard the battleship.

arouse
v a-rouse: to awaken, stir up
> He was *aroused* by the sound of the marching band.

arrogant
adj ar-ro-gant: haughty, proud
> The man's *arrogant* behavior embarrassed his wife.

artificial
adj ar-ti-fi-cial: not natural
> The food contained *artificial* coloring.

ascend
v as-cend: to rise, climb
> The old man *ascends* the stairs slowly.

asphalt
n as-phalt: tar-like substance
> His shoes stuck to the hot *asphalt*.

assault
n as-sault: an attack
> The *assault* upon the fortress was unsuccessful.

assault
v as-sault: to attack
> He was *assaulted* in front of his own house.

assert
v as-sert: declare, defend
> He *asserted* himself in the new job and eventually was in complete command.

assiduous
adj as-sid-u-ous: persistent
> He was *assiduous* in his attempt to learn chemistry.

assimilate
v as-sim-i-late: to absorb, digest
> The newcomers were quickly *assimilated* into the neighborhood.

assume
v as-sume: to take for granted
> The man *assumed* that his friend would come back.

assure
v as-sure: to make sure of
> He tried to *assure* himself that she was on the way.

astonish
v as-ton-ish: to surprise, amaze
> He was *astonished* at her ability at the piano.

astute
adj as-tute: shrewd
> She was an *astute* judge of human nature.

atone
v a-tone: to make up for
> In church, he *atoned* for all his sins.

atrocious
adj a-tro-cious: cruel, horrible
He committed an *atrocious* act against the enemy.

attain
v at-tain: to reach
He was able to *attain* the fifth level of karate.

attest
v at-test: to certify, verify
I *attest* that she was present during the accident.

attire
v at-tire: to dress
She liked to *attire* herself in jewelry.

attorney
n at-tor-ney: lawyer
They hired a young *attorney* to handle their case.

auction
n auc-tion: a public sale
He bought the photograph at the recent *auction*.

auction
v auc-tion: to sell publicly
I was able to *auction* off the old car.

audit
v au-dit: to examine and check
The CPA *audited* his bank statements to find the error.

audit
n au-dit: an examination of financial records
The IRS requested an *audit* for the previous year.

auspicious
adj aus-pi-cious: favorable
It was an *auspicious* day to begin his new job.

austere
adj aus-tere: harsh, stern
The winter in Canada is extremely *austere*.

authentic
adj au-then-tic: reliable, genuine
The painting was *authentic* and signed by the artist.

auxiliary
adj aux-il-ia-ry: helping
They joined the *auxiliary* police squadron.

auxiliary
n aux-il-ia-ry: an adjunct organization
She was a member of the Ladies' *Auxiliary*.

avarice
n av-a-rice: greed
She objected to his *avarice* in business.

avert
v a-vert: to turn away
He *averted* his eyes away from his mother.

avid
adj av-id: eager, greedy
She was an *avid* reader and took out many books from the library.

aware
adj a-ware: watchful, realizing
He was *aware* of the other people looking at him.

awe

n awe: feeling of wonder, fear, and reverence

He was in *awe* of the president.

awry

adj a-wry: twisted, amiss

As soon as he heard the squeak, he knew something was *awry*.

axiom

n ax-i-om: rule, established principle

He lived by the *axiom* "Do unto others..."

azure

adj az-ure: sky-blue

Her coat was *azure* in color.

B

babble

v bab-ble: murmur

She could hear the children *babble* as she walked in the room.

badger

v badg-er: to annoy, tease

The little girl always *badgered* her brother.

badger

n badg-er: a burrowing animal

The mascot of the university is a *badger*.

baffle

v baf-fle: to confuse

They tried to *baffle* him with too many clues.

baffle

n baf-fle: screen to deflect sound, light, gas, etc.

He removed the *baffle* from the furnace to allow it to give off more heat.

baleful

adj bale-ful: destructive, deadly

The *baleful* glance of a witch was feared.

ballad

n bal-lad: song

She sang a sweet *ballad* to her husband.

banal

adj ba-nal: ordinary, trite

The poem was a *banal* example of his work.

baneful

adj bane-ful: actively evil

The ex-convict exerted a *baneful* influence on the other members of the group.

banish

v ban-ish: to exile, send away

He was *banished* from his homeland forever.

banquet

n ban-quet: formal dinner

They wore tuxedos to the *banquet*.

banter

n ban-ter: genial teasing

The *banter* between them was purely innocent.

banter
v ban-ter: to tease, joke
 The children were *bantering* with each other in their room.

barbarous
adj bar-ba-rous: uncivilized
 The tribe's *barbarous* customs changed little over the years.

bard
n bard: poet
 Shakespeare was known as the *Bard* of Avon.

baroque
adj ba-roque: highly ornate
 Baroque decorations are characteristic of the last century.

barren
adj bar-ren: empty; fruitless
 His house sat on a plot of *barren* land.

barter
v bar-ter: to trade
 She tried to *barter* with the salesman for the ring.

bastion
n bas-tion: a fortress, protected place, stronghold
 The restaurant was a *bastion* of old world charm.

baton
n ba-ton: staff, stick
 The drum major passed the *baton* to the person who marched by her side.

bawl
v bawl: to cry out
 The child began to *bawl* when the music started.

bazaar
n ba-zaar: an exchange market place in the East
 The *bazaar* is the center of political, social, and business life in many countries.

beckon
v beck-on: to call, signal
 He *beckoned* his son to join them.

bedlam
n bed-lam: uproar, confusion
 The *bedlam* of the pots crashing in the kitchen disturbed his sleep.

befuddle
v be-fud-dle: confuse
 His explanation only *befuddled* her.

begrudge
v be-grudge: to envy, to give reluctantly
 He didn't *begrudge* his friend the extra money.

beguile
v be-guile: to mislead, deceive
 Where he found himself weak, he would *beguile* the opposition into applauding his propositions.

behemoth
n be-he-moth: large animal
The elephant was a *behemoth*, bigger than any he had ever seen.

belabor
v be-la-bor: to work diligently on, to argue to absurd lengths
The attorney *belabored* the point until the jury was bored.

bellicose
adj bel-li-cose: warlike
He was extremely *bellicose* in front of the men.

belligerent
adj bel-lig-er-ent: warlike
The two dogs began to grow *belligerent* toward each other.

bellow
v bel-low: to roar loudly
The newborn *bellowed* as he entered the world.

bellow
n bel-low: a bellowing sound
The *bellow* was heard throughout the city.

benediction
n ben-e-dic-tion: blessing
They received the *benediction* at the local church.

benevolent
adj be-nev-o-lent: kindly
The *benevolent* old gentleman came to all the parties.

benign
adj be-nign: favorable, not malignant
The tumor was *benign* and did not require removal.

bequeath
v be-queath: to leave to, to give
He wanted to *bequeath* his money to his children.

berate
v be-rate: to scold harshly
She continued to *berate* her children for their error.

bereaved
v be-reaved: to be deprived of, usually by death
The widow was *bereaved* by the death of her husband.

beret
n be-ret: flat cap
He wore the *beret* at an angle.

berserk
adj ber-serk: in a frenzy, crazed
The father went *berserk* when he opened the telephone bill.

beseech
v be-seech: to beg, plead with
I *beseech* you to come back home.

besiege
v be-siege: to attack
They were *besieged* by black flies while they ate.

bestow
v be-stow: to give
He *bestowed* dozens of gifts on his visitors.

bevy

n bev-y: small group

She went to the movies with a *bevy* of friends.

bias

v bi-as: prejudice

The man was *biased* and changed his wife's viewpoint.

bicker

v bick-er: to quarrel, argue

They continued to *bicker* in front of the company.

biennial

adj bi-en-ni-al: happening every two years

The *biennial* board meeting convened.

bigot

n big-ot: a prejudiced person

Her neighbors considered her a *bigot*.

bind

v bind: to hold, fasten

They used the rope to *bind* the packages together.

biped

n bi-ped: a two-footed animal

Those paw prints were made by a *biped*.

blanch

v blanch: to whiten, bleach

The sun *blanched* the laundry hanging on the line.

bland

adj bland: agreeable, smooth

He preferred to eat *bland* food.

blatant

adj bla-tant: noisy, obvious

It was a *blatant* attempt to be noticed.

bleach

n bleach: a chemical for removing color

He used a brand-name *bleach* to take out the stains.

bleach

v bleach: to whiten, to use bleach

She was able to *bleach* the shirts to make them brighter.

bleary

adj blear-y: dim, blurred

After many nights without sleep, he was *bleary* eyed.

blemish

n blem-ish: stain, spot, flaw

The *blemish* first appeared on her cheek and then spread to the rest of her face.

blemish

v blem-ish: to spoil by a flaw

The painting was *blemished* by the use of poor lighting.

bliss

n bliss: great happiness

The newlyweds seemed full of *bliss*.

blithe

adj blithe: gay, cheerful

She was considered a *blithe* person, ready for anything.

bloat

v bloat: to swell up

His stomach was *bloated* from all the food he ate.

blotch
v blotch: to mark with blotches
   Chicken pox *blotched* the
   child's skin.

blotch
n blotch: a stain
   There was a dark *blotch* on
   the tablecloth.

bludgeon
n bludg-eon: a short club
   She was hit by a *bludgeon* in
   back of the head.

bludgeon
v bludg-eon: to hit, strike heavily
   He was *bludgeoned* into
   unconsciousness.

blunt
adj blunt: dull
   He tried to cut the meat with
   a *blunt* knife.

blunt
v blunt: to make dull, take the
edge off
   She was able to *blunt* his
   anger by speaking calmly.

blurry
adj blur-ry: hazy, unclear
   His eyes were *blurry* from
   the smoke.

blurt
v blurt: to say suddenly
   The child *blurted* out his
   name in the middle of the
   conversation.

bluster
v bluster: to blow stormily
   It was constantly *blustering*
   outside the cabin.

boar
n boar: a male pig or wild hog
   They shot a wild *boar* in the
   jungle.

boast
v boast: to brag, praise oneself
   The neighbor *boasted* that
   he had the fastest car on
   the block.

bogus
adj bo-gus: counterfeit, sham
   He didn't realize that he had
   received a *bogus* dollar bill.

boisterous
adj bois-ter-ous: cheerfully loud
   The crowd grew *boisterous*
   when the acrobat appeared.

bombastic
adj bom-bas-tic: pompous,
high-sounding
   The *bombastic* politician
   sounds like a fool on
   television.

bond
n bond: uniting force, agreement
   The *bond* was strong between
   the two friends.

bond
v bond: to assure payment
   The electrician was *bonded* by
   his company.

boon
n boon: blessing, benefit
   The new subway is a *boon* to
   those in this area.

boor

n boor: rude, clumsy individual

Her dinner companion was a noisy *boor*.

botch

v botch: bungle, spoil

Because they were careless, they *botched* the job.

bough

n bough: tree branch

The apples bent the *bough* to the ground.

boundary

n bound-a-ry: limit, border

The *boundary* was at the edge of the river.

bountiful

adj boun-ti-ful: abundant, generous

The trees were *bountiful* with fruit.

bouquet

n bou-quet: a bunch of flowers

She was surprised at the *bouquet* he brought.

bovine

adj bo-vine: cowlike

Persons with a sluggish disposition are called *bovine*.

boycott

v boy-cott: to refuse to buy or deal with

Due to the high price of grapes, customers *boycotted* the pickers' crops.

brace

n brace: a couple or pair as applied to dogs, ducks

He owned a *brace* of German shepherds.

brash

adj brash: hasty, rash

Don't make *brash* decisions before you think them over.

brawny

adj brawn-y: strong, muscular

They used *brawny* young men to paddle the boat.

brazen

adj bra-zen: without shame

She was *brazen* in her attempt to get the job.

breach

n breach: gap, opening

The water flowed through a *breach* in the dam.

brevity

n brev-i-ty: shortness

The *brevity* of the overture made the rest of the musical easy to listen to.

brigand

n brig-and: robber

She was stopped along the road by a group of *brigands*.

brim

n brim: edge, margin

The coffee cup was filled to the *brim*.

brine

n brine: salt water

They soaked the fish in *brine*.

brisk

adj brisk: quick and lively

The old man took a *brisk* walk.

brittle

adj brit-tle: easily broken

Her bones grew *brittle* as she grew older.

brittle

n brit-tle: a crisp sugar candy

His daughter made him peanut *brittle* for his trip.

brochure

n bro-chure: a pamphlet

Brochures on many topics are available free of charge.

brusque

adj brusque: abrupt, blunt

They were put off by his *brusque* behavior.

buccaneer

n buc-ca-neer: pirate

The *buccaneer* raided all the towns along the coast.

bucolic

adj bu-col-ic: pertaining to a farm, rural

The *bucolic* personality is usually thought of as hearty, simple, and lusty.

buff

v buff: to polish

He wanted to *buff* the car with a rag.

buff

n buff: dull, brownish yellow

The couch was black and the carpet was *buff*.

buffoon

n buf-foon: clown, fool

He acted silly, and they thought he was a *buffoon*.

bulge

n bulge: swelling outward

The *bulge* in the can caused them to discard it.

bulge

v bulge: to swell out

The box began to *bulge* at the seams.

bulky

adj bulk-y: large, ungainly

He wore a *bulky* sweater when he skated.

bullion

n bul-lion: gold or silver in the form of bars

Nations exchange *bullion* to pay their trade balances.

bulwark

n bul-wark: protection, defense

The men hid behind the stone *bulwark* of the fort.

buoyant

adj buoy-ant: floatable

He found his clothing to be *buoyant* in the pool.

burden

n bur-den: heavy load, cargo

The *burden* was too large for the mule to carry.

burden

v bur-den: to load

He *burdened* himself with too many problems.

burly
adj bur-ly: strong, solid
   The lumberjack was old
   but *burly*.

burnish
v bur-nish: to polish by rubbing
   Metal that is *burnished* will
   gleam in the light.

bustle
n bus-tle: excitement, activity
   He liked the *bustle* in the
   stores during Christmas.

butt
n butt: the object of a jest
   The dullard is the *butt* of his
   classmates' tricks.

buttress
v but-tress: strengthen
   The wooden supports *buttress*
   the building.

buttress
n but-tress: a structure built
against a wall to support
   The *buttress* of the church was
   made of stone.

buxom
adj bux-om: plump, jolly
   The *buxom* maid is a stock
   character in many plays.

C

cache
n cache: hiding place
   The *cache* was later found by
   the police.

cache
v cache: to store or hide
   The money was *cached* behind
   the rock.

cacophony
n ca-coph-o-ny: harsh sounds
   He was awakened by the
   cacophony of the chickens.

cadaver
n ca-dav-er: corpse, dead body
   They moved the *cadaver* into
   the other room.

cadence
n ca-dence: rhythm
   The drummer set the *cadence*
   for the rest of the band.

cajole
v ca-jole: to persuade, coax
   I tried to *cajole* him into going
   to the circus.

calamity
n ca-lam-i-ty: great misfortune,
disaster
   The great flood was a
   calamity that caused suffering
   to everyone.

caliber
n cal-i-ber: capacity of mind,
quality
   Men of the highest *caliber* are
   wanted for these positions.

calligraphy
n cal-lig-ra-phy: beautiful
penmanship
   The *calligraphy* of the monks
   is the basis of many printing
   typefaces today.

callow
adj cal-low: young, without experience
>He was a *callow* lad, just up from the country.

calumniate
v ca-lum-ni-ate: to slander
>He was known to *calumniate* anyone who disagreed with him.

camisole
n cam-i-sole: ornamental woman's under-bodice
>*Camisoles* return to style periodically when thin blouses are in fashion.

camouflage
n cam-ou-flage: disguise
>The man wore his *camouflage* well, and no one recognized him.

camouflage
v cam-ou-flage: to conceal by changing appearance
>The wolf was *camouflaged* as a sheep.

candid
adj can-did: frank, sincere
>The young girl was *candid* about her feelings.

candor
n can-dor: honesty
>He spoke to them with complete *candor*.

canine
n ca-nine: dog
>The *canine* bared his teeth as he growled.

canine
adj ca-nine: like a dog
>The dentist removed his *canine* teeth.

canister
n can-is-ter: small container
>He hid his water in a wooden *canister*.

canopy
n can-o-py: a cover, shelter
>The *canopy* protected them from the rain.

cantankerous
adj can-tan-ker-ous: bad natured
>He was a *cantankerous* old man who annoyed everyone.

caress
v ca-ress: to embrace, to hug
>She *caressed* her daughter's back to calm her.

caress
n ca-ress: an affectionate touch, kiss
>His *caress* was enough to stop her tears.

caricature
n car-i-ca-ture: a distorted sketch
>*Caricature* is the weapon of the political cartoonist.

caries
n car-ies: tooth decay
>The dentist told her she had a severe case of *caries*.

carmine
n car-mine: red or purplish-red color
>They painted the room *carmine* and blue.

carnage
n car-nage: destruction of life
The *carnage* of modern warfare is frightful to consider.

carom
v car-om: bounce off
The car was out of control and *caromed* off the wall.

carom
n car-om: a billiard shot
He tried to play a *carom* off the rail.

cartographer
n car-tog-ra-pher: map maker
The ancient *cartographers* did not have scientific measuring devices.

casing
n cas-ing: covering
It was interesting to watch them pack the sausage into the *casings*.

cask
n cask: barrel
The *cask* of wine was taken out of the cellar.

castigate
v cas-ti-gate: to criticize severely, to punish
The judge *castigated* the plaintiff before he fined him for contempt of court.

catalyst
n cat-a-lyst: substance causing change in other substances
After the scientist added a *catalyst* to the test tube, the rock dissolved.

catastrophe
n ca-tas-tro-phe: a calamity, disaster
The recent fire was a *catastrophe* to his family.

catechism
n cat-e-chism: elementary book of religious principles
She read from her *catechism* every morning before work.

categorical
adj cat-e-gor-i-cal: not conditional, absolute, unqualified
Theirs was a *categorical* surrender.

catholic
adj cath-o-lic: universal, widespread
His taste in literature was *catholic*, encompassing all fields.

caucus
n cau-cus: meeting
He attended the late-night *caucus*.

caucus
v cau-cus: to hold a meeting
They tried to *caucus* during the nomination speeches.

caulk
v caulk: to fill a seam with paste
He *caulked* the windows to keep the water from seeping through.

caustic
adj caus-tic: biting, stinging
He had a *caustic* sense of humor.

cauterize

v cau-ter-ize: to burn, especially to prevent infection

The surgeon *cauterized* the wound, removing dead tissue.

cavalcade

n cav-al-cade: procession on horseback

The Queen's *cavalcade* entered the castle before she arrived.

caveat

n ca-ve-at: a warning, a legal notice preventing some action

A *caveat* may be entered to stop the reading of a will.

cavern

n cav-ern: large cave

They hid in the dark *cavern* for two days.

cavity

n cav-i-ty: hole, hollow place

He had a *cavity* in his front tooth.

cease

v cease: to stop

Please *cease* banging on the table.

cede

v cede: surrender, give up

The army *ceded* to the men in the tanks.

celestial

adj ce-les-tial: heavenly

The sounds of the harp were almost *celestial*.

celibate

adj cel-i-bate: unmarried, abstaining from sexual intercourse

He was still *celibate* after all these years.

celibate

n cel-i-bate: an unmarried person

The monk remained a *celibate* throughout his life.

censure

v cen-sure: to blame, condemn as wrong

The judge *censured* the man for his crime.

censure

n cen-sure: formal criticism

He was greatly upset by the *censure*.

chagrin

n cha-grin: disappointment

Much to his *chagrin*, nobody showed up at the party.

chalice

n chal-ice: cup, goblet

The *chalice* was made of gold and studded with gems.

chaos

n cha-os: confusion

The huge hall was filled with *chaos* from all of the soldiers who had entered.

chaperone

n chap-er-one: protector, escort, guide

The *chaperone* accompanied the young lovers.

chaperone
v chap-er-one: to escort
> The man in the tuxedo *chaperoned* the starlet.

char
v char: to burn, scorch
> The flames *charred* the curtains.

charger
n charg-er: horse
> She rode proudly upon her white *charger.*

charlatan
n char-la-tan: a phony, quack
> The doctor was accused of being a *charlatan.*

chasm
n chasm: deep hole
> The supplies slid down the hill into the dark *chasm.*

chassis
n chas-sis: frame or body
> The *chassis* of the car was painted red.

chastise
v chas-tise: punish, beat
> He *chastised* his son for coming home late.

chastity
n chas-ti-ty: purity
> Everyone in the neighborhood knew of her devotion to *chastity.*

chatter
v chat-ter: to talk continually
> The two women always *chatter* on the telephone like birds.

cherish
v cher-ish: hold dear
> She *cherished* her photographs more than her money.

chieftain
n chief-tain: leader
> He was elected *chieftain* of the tribe.

chimes
n chimes: bells
> They could hear the *chimes* ringing all day.

chivalrous
adj chiv-al-rous: courteous, marked by honesty
> His *chivalrous* manner warmed the hearts of all who knew him.

chronic
adj chron-ic: continual, constant
> She had a *chronic* cough that wasn't helped by her smoking.

churlish
adj churl-ish: rude, surly
> He was both *churlish* and abrupt in the way in which he chose to deal with the problem.

churn
v churn: stir, shake, turn around
> The engine continued to *churn* after it was shut off.

churn
n churn: container to make butter or cream
> She removed the fresh butter from the *churn.*

cicatrix
n cic-a-trix: a scar

The doctor found the *cicatrix* behind the patient's ear.

cipher
n ci-pher: a code

They were able to understand the *cipher* by using a computer.

circumlocution
n cir-cum-lo-cu-tion: talking around a subject

The audience became impatient as the speaker's *circumlocution* went on and on.

circumspect
adj cir-cum-spect: careful, cautious

The driver was *circumspect* as he turned his car around.

citadel
n cit-a-del: fortress, safe place

The horses and men lived in the *citadel* at night.

cite
v cite: to quote, to give an example, to refer to or name

She was able to *cite* exactly how the speech was written in the paper.

civil
adj civ-il: polite, courteous

She tried to be *civil* to her teacher.

clairvoyance
n clair-voy-ance: ESP, insight

The woman was respected for her *clairvoyance*.

clamor
n clam-or: loud noise

There was such a *clamor* in the street that they couldn't sleep.

clamor
v clam-or: to make a loud noise

They *clamored* for their breakfast.

clandestine
adj clan-des-tine: concealed, secret

That was their *clandestine* meeting place.

clatter
n clat-ter: confused sounds, noise

The *clatter* came from the back room where the children were playing.

clatter
v clat-ter: to make noise

They *clattered* the dishes until we had to leave.

cleave
v cleave: to divide, split

He tried to *cleave* the diamond in half.

clemency
n clem-en-cy: mercy

President Nixon was shown *clemency* by President Ford.

clique
n clique: group

He hung around with the *clique* from the East Side.

clutter
n clut-ter: a mess, confusion
　His apartment was a *clutter* of clothes, dishes, and magazines.

clutter
v clut-ter: to put into disorder
　She began to *clutter* her bag with her makeup.

coagulate
v co-ag-u-late: to thicken
　Once the blood *coagulates*, bleeding stops.

coalesce
v co-a-lesce: to grow together
　The vines *coalesced* as they climbed up the tree.

coax
v coax: persuade
　Can I *coax* you to buy this suit?

coddle
v cod-dle: to pamper
　She always *coddled* her dog too much.

coerce
v co-erce: to force, compel
　She tried to *coerce* them into joining the committee.

cogent
adj co-gent: convincing
　The lawyer's *cogent* argument easily persuaded the jurors.

cognizant
adj cog-ni-zant: aware of
　I was fully *cognizant* of your actions yesterday.

cohere
v co-here: to connect, stick to
　The story just did not *cohere* with the facts.

coherent
adj co-her-ent: logically connected
　His argument was *coherent* and easy to follow.

cohort
n co-hort: a group of people who have something in common
　In the evening, he went to the movies with his *cohorts*.

collision
n col-li-sion: crash, conflict
　The *collision* of the two trailers blocked the road.

colloquial
adj col-lo-qui-al: informal, familiar
　It was a *colloquial* saying she had heard before.

comatose
adj com-a-tose: unconscious
　The patient was *comatose* when they brought him in.

combustible
adj com-bus-ti-ble: easily burned
　Oil-soaked rags are very *combustible*.

comely
adj come-ly: attractive
　She was a *comely*, young housewife.

commemorate
v com-mem-or-ate: to honor
This parade was to
commemorate Christopher
Columbus.

commence
v com-mence: to begin
The party will *commence* after
dinner.

commerce
n com-merce: business, trade
The main *commerce* of the
town was exporting sardines.

commiserate
v com-mis-er-ate: to console, pity
They came over to *commiserate*
with them after the accident.

commotion
n com-mo-tion: confusion
The news about the king
created a *commotion* in the city.

commute
v com-mute: exchange,
substitute; to travel
His sentence was *commuted*
from life to a full pardon.
He liked *commuting* from the
farm to the city.

compact
adj com-pact: closely or firmly
packed
He drove an American
compact car.

compact
n com-pact: small case
containing mirror, powder, etc.
She took out her *compact* to
put on her makeup.

compact
v com-pact: to pack together
tightly
He tried to *compact* everything
into one box.

compatible
adj com-pat-i-ble: agreeable
They reached a *compatible*
solution for their difficulties.

compel
v com-pel: to force
She tried to *compel* him to
attend the party.

competent
adj com-pe-tent: qualified
They felt she was *competent*
in her typing and gave her
the job.

complacent
adj com-pla-cent: self-satisfied
He was a *complacent* person,
unconcerned about the future.

compliant
adj com-pli-ant: yielding
He was completely *compliant*
with the doctor.

complicity
n com-plic-i-ty: partnership
in crime
They were accused of
complicity in the bank
robbery.

comply
v com-ply: to accede, yield
I *comply* with your wishes
and will stay home.

comportment
n com-port-ment: behavior
  The teacher criticized the *comportment* of her class.

composure
n com-po-sure: calmness
  She tried to regain her *composure* after the incident.

compress
v com-press: to squeeze together
  He was able to *compress* all of the papers into the folder.

compress
n com-press: folded cloth or gauze pad
  She applied a cold *compress* to his injured eye.

compromise
n com-pro-mise: settlement
  The *compromise* made between the tenant and the landlord was decided upon in the afternoon.

compromise
v com-pro-mise: to settle by negotiation
  They *compromised* on the conditions and signed the contract.

compulsory
adj com-pul-so-ry: required
  Mathematics is a *compulsory* subject in high school.

concave
adj con-cave: curved inward
  The dish was *concave* enough to be able to hold water.

concede
v con-cede: to yield, to admit
  The candidate *conceded* his defeat to his opponent.

conceit
n con-ceit: vanity
  The *conceit* she showed made her friends turn away.

conch
n conch: large sea shell
  You can hear the ocean if you hold the *conch* to your ear.

concise
adj con-cise: brief
  The report was clear and *concise*.

concoct
v con-coct: to prepare
  He *concocted* a strange punch from all of the juices.

concord
n con-cord: an agreement
  The union was able to reach a *concord* with management.

concrete
adj con-crete: specific, tangible, real
  It was a *concrete*, well-thought-out idea.

concrete
n con-crete: solid substance
  The stairs were made from poured *concrete*.

condolence
n con-do-lence: sympathy
  She received their *condolences* when her father died.

condone
v con-done: to forgive, approve reluctantly
> I am not able to *condone* what you did the other night.

conducive
adj con-du-cive: favorable to
> The time was *conducive* to introducing the new product.

conduit
n con-duit: passageway, tube
> The *conduit* was filled with metal wiring.

confer
v con-fer: to consult together
> The partners wanted to *confer* before making a decision.

confine
v con-fine: to imprison, restrain
> He was *confined* to his room for two days.

confirm
v con-firm: to prove to be true, verify
> The airline called to *confirm* our flight.

confiscate
v con-fis-cate: to seize
> The illegal cigarettes were *confiscated* by the police.

conflagration
n con-fla-gra-tion: large fire
> The *conflagration* threatened to spread to the other buildings.

congenial
adj con-gen-ial: pleasant, agreeable
> He was a *congenial* host, and everyone liked him.

congest
v con-gest: to overcrowd
> The traffic *congested* the intersection.

conglomeration
n con-glom-er-a-tion: a mixture
> The meal was a *conglomeration* of various leftovers.

congregate
v con-gre-gate: to assemble, gather together
> The crowd began to *congregate* around the statue.

conjecture
n con-jec-ture: guess, opinion
> It was not a fact, only *conjecture*.

conjecture
v con-jec-ture: to guess
> If you wish to *conjecture*, go right ahead.

connive
v con-nive: to cooperate secretly, conspire
> They *connived* to cheat the firm of the extra money.

connoisseur
n con-nois-seur: expert
> He was a *connoisseur* of fine wines.

conscious
adj con-scious: knowing, aware
> He was *conscious* of the woman next to him.

consecrated
v con-se-crat-ed: made sacred
> The field behind the church was *consecrated* by the bishop.

consensus

n con-sen-sus: general agreement

It is the *consensus* of this club to raise the dues.

consequence

n con-se-quence: a result

He is responsible for the *consequences* of his bad manners.

conserve

v con-serve: to preserve, protect

It is important to *conserve* water during the shortage.

console

v con-sole: to comfort

Each time she would cry, the puppy would *console* her.

console

n con-sole: a cabinet, desk, or storage space

The *console* was made of walnut.

conspire

v con-spire: to plot

The men *conspired* to overthrow the government.

constitute

v con-sti-tute: to make up, to form

These three pieces *constitute* the entire collection.

constrict

v con-strict: to compress, squeeze

She felt *constricted* by the small belt.

construe

v con-strue: explain, interpret

From the evidence, he was able to *construe* what actually happened.

consume

v con-sume: use up, eat

The two of them *consumed* all of the cake.

contemplate

v con-tem-plate: to think about

He *contemplated* all day long and then made his move.

contend

v con-tend: to fight, struggle for; to claim

They were going to *contend* for the world championship.

I *contend* that I am right.

contention

n con-ten-tion: belief, claim

It was her *contention* that the painting was worth more.

contingent

adj con-tin-gent: dependent on, associated with

His arrival is *contingent* upon getting through customs quickly.

contingent

n con-tin-gent: a group of people, troops

The entire *contingent* moved its operations down river.

contort

v con-tort: to twist

His face was *contorted* with pain.

contrary
adj con-trary: opposite
His opinion was *contrary* to what his friends believed.

contrive
v con-trive: invent
His excuse seemed totally *contrived*.

controversy
n con-tro-ver-sy: a quarrel, disagreement
He could not resolve the *controversy* between them.

convalesce
v con-va-lesce: to recover strength, regain health
He was able to *convalesce* at home after his illness.

convene
v con-vene: to meet, assemble
The group *convened* in the school yard.

convert
v con-vert: to change
He was able to *convert* the dollars into pesos.

convert
n con-vert: a person who has changed beliefs or religions
She was a *convert* to Christianity.

convey
v con-vey: to carry
I will *convey* your message to your mother.

convivial
adj con-viv-i-al: sociable
It was a small group of *convivial* people.

convoy
n con-voy: small group
There was a *convoy* of ships in the North Atlantic Ocean.

convoy
v con-voy: to escort
The man was able to *convoy* the trucks cross-country.

convulse
v con-vulse: to shake
The child began to *convulse* from the fever.

cope
v cope: to struggle and succeed
She *coped* well after the death of her husband.

copious
adj co-pi-ous: plentiful, abundant
She took *copious* notes during the lecture.

coquette
n co-quette: a flirt
She was a well-known *coquette* in Paris.

cordial
adj cor-dial: friendly, sincere
The children appeared *cordial* to the visitors.

cordial
n cor-dial: alcoholic drink
After dinner, he served *cordials* to his guests.

corpulent
adj cor-pu-lent: fat
His *corpulent* body was sprawled across the chair.

corridor

n cor-ri-dor: long hallway or passage

He stood in the *corridor* outside the senator's office.

corrupt

adj cor-rupt: evil, wicked

He was the most *corrupt* ruler they ever knew.

cosmos

n cos-mos: the universe

The stars twinkled throughout the *cosmos*.

council

n coun-cil: group of people

He was a member of the local safety *council*.

counsel

n coun-sel: advice, lawyer

The *counsel* met with the prisoner in his cell.

counsel

v coun-sel: to give advice

I will *counsel* him with his problem.

course

n course: direction, school subject

He followed the *course* of the road to the next town.

covenant

n cov-e-nant: a contract, agreement

They signed a *covenant* before their wedding.

covert

adj cov-ert: secret

It was a *covert* operation, designed to surprise the enemy.

covet

v co-vet: to desire enviously

He *coveted* all the items and would not share with his sister.

cower

v cow-er: hide, crouch in fear

The cat *cowered* in the corner when the dog walked by.

cowl

n cowl: hood

He pulled a *cowl* around his head for warmth.

coy

adj coy: shy

The child acted *coy* in front of the strangers.

crass

adj crass: gross, stupid

It was a *crass* remark to make to your father.

crave

v crave: to desire, yearn for

He *craved* a piece of chocolate cake.

craven

adj cra-ven: cowardly

His actions labeled him a *craven* individual.

credible

adj cred-i-ble: believable

His story was not entirely *credible*.

cremate
v cre-mate: to burn to ashes
The body was *cremated* and the ashes scattered over the ocean.

crestfallen
adj crest-fall-en: upset, discouraged
They were *crestfallen* because they did not get the house they wanted.

crevice
n cre-vice: crack
The *crevice* was where the spiders lived.

crimson
adj crim-son: dark red
Her face turned *crimson* with embarrassment.

cringe
v cringe: to crouch in fear
The dog *cringed* in the corner.

criterion
n cri-te-ri-on: rule, a standard
His *criterion* for success was much higher than hers.

crochet
v cro-chet: to knit
She *crocheted* the yellow yarn into a sweater.

crony
n cro-ny: friend, pal
He and his old *crony* played cards all day.

croon
v croon: to sing
He *crooned* love songs to her as he paddled the canoe.

crouch
v crouch: to stoop, bend
He *crouched* behind the bush to avoid being seen.

crucial
adj cru-cial: extremely important
The last play was the most *crucial* of the second half.

crucible
n cru-ci-ble: a container
They were able to carry the food in a small *crucible*.

crude
adj crude: raw, unrefined
The *crude* sugar was sent to be refined.

crude
n crude: unrefined petroleum
The *crude* was taken from deep beneath the ground.

crypt
n crypt: tomb, vault
They discovered the gold buried in the ancient *crypt*.

cue
n cue: hint, suggestion
Let me give you a *cue* about the new boss.

cue
v cue: to give a hint to
The actor *cued* the actress but forgot his own lines.

culinary
adj cu-li-nar-y: pertaining to food, cooking
The table was spread with assorted *culinary* delights.

cull

v cull: to select, choose

He tried to *cull* the broken toys from the collection.

culminate

v cul-mi-nate: to result

The argument *culminated* in a fistfight.

cult

n cult: group, religious system

The *cult* carried the message to all the people.

cumbersome

adj cum-ber-some: hard to manage

Its size made the package *cumbersome* for the woman.

cunning

adj cun-ning: skillful, clever

He was a *cunning* hunter.

cunning

n cun-ning: slyness, craftiness

She was known for her *cunning*.

cur

n cur: worthless person or dog

He was a vicious *cur,* and they had to give him away.

curb

v curb: to restrain

The owner was asked to *curb* his dog.

curb

n curb: stone street edge

The *curb* of the street was cracked and broken.

curriculum

n cur-ric-u-lum: a program of studies, courses

The new *curriculum* included several new courses.

curt

adj curt: brief and rude, short

She was *curt* with her friend, which surprised both of them.

curtail

v cur-tail: to shorten, lessen

The trip was *curtailed* due to the man's illness.

custom

n cus-tom: habit, usual action

It was her *custom* to feed the children after school.

custom

adj cus-tom: made to order

He enjoyed wearing *custom* shirts from his tailor.

cyclic

adj cy-clic: periodic

He made *cyclic* appearances on the show.

cyclone

n cy-clone: windstorm

The *cyclone* tore through the house as if it was made of paper.

cynical

adj cyn-i-cal: sneering, sarcastic

He was *cynical* about their ability to finish the project.

D

daft
adj daft: silly, crazy
　　The people in town considered him a little *daft*.

dainty
n dain-ty: something special
　　He picked out the *dainty* from the selected candies.

dainty
adj dain-ty: delicate
　　He refused to sit on the *dainty* seat.

dais
n da-is: platform
　　The chairman stood on the *dais* and waved to the crowd.

dale
n dale: a small valley
　　He trudged over hill and *dale*.

damask
n dam-ask: a fine fabric with a figured weave
　　The crystal bowls were displayed on a fine *damask*.

dank
adj dank: damp, moist
　　The cave was dark and *dank*.

dapper
adj dap-per: neat, trim
　　Despite his age, he always looked *dapper*.

dappled
adj dap-pled: marked with small spots
　　The *dappled* horse won the race.

dastard
n das-tard: complete coward
　　He was a *dastard* and a cheat.

data
n da-ta: information
　　He received the latest *data* on the project.

dauntless
adj daunt-less: fearless, brave
　　The men were *dauntless* in their quest for the gold.

davit
n dav-it: a crane for hoisting boats
　　The *davit* supported the lifeboats.

dawdle
v daw-dle: to waste time, trifle
　　Do not *dawdle* at your tasks.

de facto
adj de fac-to: actual as opposed to legal
　　Although the *de facto* government was not duly elected, it was in power.

deacon
n dea-con: clergyman
　　The *deacon* gave a long, tiresome sermon.

dearth
n dearth: scarcity
　　There was a *dearth* of grain last year in Russia.

debacle
n de-ba-cle: disaster
　　The final battle was a *debacle* for the English.

debase
v de-base: to degrade
She felt *debased* by the criticism.

debate
v de-bate: to discuss
They *debated* about the rules for hours.

debate
n de-bate: a discussion of opposing reasons
The candidates were featured in the *debate* on TV.

debauch
v de-bauch: to corrupt
The temptations they offered could not *debauch* her.

debilitate
v de-bil-i-tate: to weaken
He was *debilitated* from lack of food.

debonair
adj deb-o-nair: courteous
Suave and *debonair*, the gentleman impressed the ladies with his city manners.

debut
n de-but: first appearance
Her *debut* as a violinist was well attended.

decade
n dec-ade: ten-year period
At the end of her sixth *decade*, they had a large party.

decadence
n de-ca-dence: decay
The *decadence* of the neighborhood upset the visitors.

decamp
v de-camp: to depart suddenly
The patrol prepared to *decamp* before daylight.

decant
v de-cant: pour out, pour off
It is important to *decant* the wine well before you serve it.

decanter
n de-cant-er: ornamental wine bottle
They poured port from the *decanter*.

decapitate
v de-cap-i-tate: to behead
During the French Revolution, people were *decapitated*.

deciduous
adj de-cid-u-ous: leaf-shedding
Most trees are *deciduous*, but evergreens retain their foliage throughout the winter.

decipher
v de-ci-pher: to interpret, decode
He was able to *decipher* the enemy's codebook.

declivity
n de-cliv-i-ty: downward slope
The *declivity* offered fine skiing.

décolleté
adj dé-col-le-té: low-necked
The *décolleté* dress attracted much attention from the men.

decompose
v de-com-pose: to decay, rot
The tree began to *decompose* shortly after it died.

decorous
adj dec-o-rous: proper
Decorous conduct is the mark of a gentleman.

decoy
n de-coy: a lure
They used a *decoy* to attract the ducks to the pond.

decoy
v de-coy: to trick, fool
He tried to *decoy* his opponent into running to the left.

decrepit
adj de-crep-it: old, feeble
They finally sold their *decrepit* car.

decry
v de-cry: to condemn, strongly disapprove
He *decried* his enemy's actions.

deduce
v de-duce: to derive by reasoning
From the facts presented, we *deduce* this conclusion.

deduct
v de-duct: to subtract
The bank *deducted* a monthly service charge.

deem
v deem: to have an opinion, think
They did not *deem* him worthy of the honors he received.

deface
v de-face: to spoil, mar
The students *defaced* the wall of the school.

defame
v de-fame: to destroy one's reputation, slander
The politician was *defamed* by the reporter's remarks.

default
v de-fault: to fail to pay
Unfortunately, he *defaulted* on his loan.

defect
v de-fect: to desert
He planned to *defect* from his country.

defect
n de-fect: a flaw
The diamond contained a *defect* and was worthless.

defer
v de-fer: to put off
I'd like to *defer* my opinion until I've heard the arguments.

deficit
n def-i-cit: shortage
The auditor uncovered a *deficit* in their bank balance.

defile

v de-file: to befoul, make profane

A man is not allowed to wear shoes in a mosque, lest he *defile* it.

deflect

v de-flect: to turn away

The steel plate *deflected* the bullet.

defraud

v de-fraud: to cheat

He tried to *defraud* the bank by changing the records.

deft

adj deft: nimble

He tied the knots with *deft* fingers.

defunct

adj de-funct: extinct

That railroad line has been *defunct* for a long time.

degenerate

v de-gen-er-ate: grow worse

Without medical care you will *degenerate* quickly.

degenerate

n de-gen-er-ate: low person, one who has fallen to a lower state

He refused to give a loan to the *degenerate*.

degrade

v de-grade: demote, lower

After the poor performance, his job status was *degraded*.

dehydrated

adj de-hy-drat-ed: without water

The man was *dehydrated* after running in the marathon.

deify

v de-i-fy: to make as a god

They would *deify* Caesar.

deign

v deign: to condescend

He *deigned* to reply to their criticism.

deity

n de-i-ty: god, goddess

In ancient Greece they worshipped many *deities*.

delectable

adj de-lec-ta-ble: delightful

The food is delicious, the girls *delectable*, and the music delirious.

delegate

v del-e-gate: to appoint

He was *delegated* to be the first speaker.

delegate

n del-e-gate: representative

The country's *delegate* spoke at the meeting.

delete

v de-lete: leave out, omit

If you *delete* that word, the sentence will be clearer.

deleterious

adj del-e-te-ri-ous: injurious, harmful

DDT, when taken internally, has a *deleterious* effect on the body.

deliberate
adj de-lib-er-ate: unhurried, intentional

It was a *deliberate* act, intended to anger them.

deliberate
v de-lib-er-ate: to consider carefully

They *deliberated* for two hours before making their decision.

delineate
v de-lin-e-ate: to mark off the boundary of

They asked him to *delineate* the areas where play was permitted.

delude
v de-lude: to trick, mislead

She was *deluded* into believing the job was easy.

deluge
n del-uge: a flood, overflowing

Noah was the only one to escape the *deluge*.

deluge
v del-uge: to flood, to overwhelm

They were *deluged* by the quantity of gifts.

demagogue
n dem-a-gogue: false leader

He was only a *demagogue*, and nobody respected him.

demean
v de-mean: to humble

I don't want to *demean* you, only caution you.

demeanor
n de-mean-or: behavior

His child's calm *demeanor* was appropriate for the wedding.

demented
adj de-mented: crazy

He acted as if he was *demented*, and he was locked up.

demise
n de-mise: death

His early *demise* was truly surprising.

demote
v de-mote: to lower in rank

The soldier was *demoted* for his failure to perform properly.

demur
v de-mur: to hesitate, object

Once he *demurred*, we knew we had the advantage of additional time to prepare.

demure
adj de-mure: serious, sober

The *demure* maiden was an object of their admiration but not their affection.

denizen
n den-i-zen: occupant

The parrot was a *denizen* of the rain forest.

dense
adj dense: thick

The children became lost in the *dense* forest.

depict
v de-pict: show, to portray
His role was to *depict* a Frenchman.

deplete
v de-plete: to empty, exhaust
We do not want to *deplete* our entire oil supply.

deplore
v de-plore: to regret, to grieve for
He *deplored* the soldiers' attack on the village.

deploy
v de-ploy: to position, spread out
The troops were *deployed* on the battlefield.

deport
v de-port: to exile, to send away
He was *deported* to his native country.

depot
n de-pot: station, warehouse
The train was standing in the *depot*.

depraved
adj de-praved: sordid, corrupt
Only a *depraved* mind would think of committing a heinous crime.

deprecate
v dep-re-cate: to detract from
Do not *deprecate* what you cannot understand.

depreciate
v de-pre-ci-ate: to lessen in value
Property will *depreciate* rapidly unless kept in good repair.

deranged
adj de-ranged: insane, disordered
The working of the *deranged* mind baffles even those trained in mental care.

derelict
adj der-e-lict: abandoned
The building was old and *derelict*.

derelict
n der-e-lict: worthless person
The *derelict* stood begging on the corner.

deride
v de-ride: to make fun of, ridicule
The boys *derided* him because he could not ride a horse.

derivation
n der-i-va-tion: origin, root
It is fun to learn the *derivation* of words.

descend
v de-scend: to go down; derive from
He *descended* the stairs slowly.
She is *descended* from a long line of jewelers.

descry
v des-cry: to pry out, discover by eye
In the distance we could *descry* a small cabin.

designate
v des-ig-nate: to indicate, name
I will *designate* you to take charge of the party.

designate
n des-ig-nate: person chosen for a specific task
> He is the *designate* for the new office manager.

desist
v de-sist: to stop
> I wish you would *desist* from constantly calling me.

desolate
adj des-o-late: cheerless, empty, barren
> The area was *desolate* and lonely.

desolate
v des-o-late: to lay waste to
> The fire *desolated* the entire block of houses.

despair
n de-spair: loss of hope
> She was filled with *despair* after her accident.

despair
v de-spair: to lose hope
> He began to *despair* that he would ever see her again.

despise
v de-spise: to dislike intensely
> She *despised* him for his ill manners.

despot
n des-pot: tyrant
> Stalin was one of the worst *despots* in history.

destitute
adj des-ti-tute: poor
> The family was *destitute* after the flood destroyed their home.

destitution
n des-ti-tu-tion: poverty
> They lived in complete *destitution*, without any income.

detain
v de-tain: to hold back
> They were unable to *detain* the train any longer.

deter
v de-ter: to hinder, stop one from doing something
> If you continue to *deter* me from my goal, I will never finish.

detergent
n de-ter-gent: cleanser
> She washed the dishes with a less abrasive *detergent*.

deteriorate
v de-te-ri-o-rate: to grow worse
> The building began to *deteriorate* from lack of upkeep.

determine
v de-ter-mine: to decide
> He was unable to *determine* which job to choose.

detest
v de-test: to hate
> I *detest* having to eat fish.

detonate
v det-o-nate: to cause to explode
>The bomb was *detonated* under the house.

detract
v de-tract: to take away
>His dirty shoes *detracted* from his new tie.

detrimental
adj det-ri-men-tal: harmful
>Artificial supplements may be *detrimental* to your health.

devastate
v dev-as-tate: to ruin, destroy
>The community was *devastated* by the epidemic.

deviate
v de-vi-ate: to turn aside from
>His new attitude caused him to *deviate* from his goal.

device
n de-vice: a plan, a mechanical apparatus
>The new *device* was able to turn on the lights by itself.

devise
v de-vise: to plan, contrive
>She *devised* an escape.

devour
v de-vour: to eat hungrily
>The children began to *devour* the sandwiches immediately.

dew
n dew: moisture
>The *dew* on the morning grass soaked their shoes.

dexterous
adj dex-ter-ous: skillful, expert
>He was extremely *dexterous* at juggling.

diabolic
adj di-a-bol-ic: devilish, fiendish
>The ancients used charms to ward off the influence of *diabolic* creatures.

dialogue
n di-a-logue: conversation
>They continued their *dialogue* on the way to work.

diaphanous
adj di-aph-a-nous: almost transparent, sheer
>Her *diaphanous* negligee revealed the outlines of a beautiful figure.

diction
n dic-tion: style of speech
>His *diction* was easily understood.

dictum
n dic-tum: an authoritative statement
>The professor's *dictum* ended the debate.

didactic
adj di-dac-tic: instructive, intended to teach
>The *didactic* approach may be well suited for a textbook but should be avoided in other books.

diffident
adj dif-fi-dent: reserved, shy, timid

They grew used to his *diffident* behavior.

diffuse
adj dif-fuse: spread; scattered

It was a *diffuse* vapor that covered the city.

diffuse
v dif-fuse: to spread in many directions

He tried to *diffuse* the crowd's anger by telling jokes.

dignity
n dig-ni-ty: worth, nobleness

He sat with *dignity* upon the throne.

digress
v di-gress: to turn aside

I'd like to *digress* a moment in my discussion with you.

dilapidated
adj di-lap-i-dat-ed: rundown; decayed

She lived in a *dilapidated* building across town.

dilate
v di-late: to swell, enlarge

His pupils *dilated* from the drops the doctor used.

dilemma
n di-lem-ma: difficult choices or situations

His *dilemma* was solved by his boss, who made the decision for him.

dilettante
n dil-et-tante: aimless follower of the fine arts

A *dilettante* may be more interested in talking of his artistic pursuits than following them.

diligent
adj dil-i-gent: hard working

He was extremely *diligent* at the job.

dilute
v di-lute: to weaken

He felt it was better to serve *diluted* drinks.

diminish
v di-min-ish: to lessen, reduce

Their supply of food slowly began to *diminish*.

din
n din: noise

She couldn't hear over the *din*.

dingy
adj din-gy: dirty and dark

He felt uncomfortable in the *dingy* hallway.

dirigible
n dir-i-gi-ble: a blimp

The old *dirigibles* were filled with helium.

disarray
n dis-ar-ray: disorder, confusion

Her room was in complete *disarray*.

disaster
n dis-as-ter: terrible tragedy

The airplane crash was one of the worst *disasters* in history.

disavow
v dis-a-vow: to deny
I *disavow* any knowledge of their plot.

disburse
v dis-burse: pay, expend
The checks were *disbursed* at noon.

discard
v dis-card: to cast aside
He planned to *discard* the old sweater.

discard
n dis-card: something thrown aside
Her dress was originally a *discard* from the factory.

discern
v dis-cern: to recognize
I am able to *discern* the truth when I hear it.

disciple
n dis-ci-ple: pupil, follower
He was a *disciple* of the great philosopher.

disclaim
v dis-claim: to renounce, give up claim to
To obtain United States citizenship, one must *disclaim* any title from another nation.

discord
n dis-cord: disagreement
The only *discord* between them was the meeting place.

discourse
v dis-course: to talk
He was able to *discourse* on any subject.

discourse
n dis-course: a speech
After hearing her *discourse* for an hour, I left.

discreet
adj dis-creet: cautious, secretive
The couple was *discreet* about their relationship.

discrete
adj dis-crete: separate, distinct
These were two *discrete* events, totally unrelated.

discretion
n dis-cre-tion: power of decision, individual judgment
The penalty to be imposed is often left to the *discretion* of the judge.

disdain
v dis-dain: to regard as beneath one's dignity
He *disdained* the actions of his peers.

disinfect
v dis-in-fect: to kill germs
The nurse sprayed the room to *disinfect* it.

disingenuous
adj dis-in-gen-u-ous: sophisticated, not innocent
His slip of the tongue indicated that he was not as *disingenuous* as he wished to appear.

disinterested
adj dis-in-ter-est-ed: not involved in, unprejudiced
> A *disinterested* witness is one who has no personal involvement in the outcome of the matter.

disjointed
adj dis-joint-ed: disconnected, dislocated
> The story was so *disjointed* it was unbelievable.

dismal
adj dis-mal: gloomy
> After two weeks of rain, he felt as *dismal* as the weather.

disparage
v dis-par-age: to belittle
> The father continually *disparaged* his son's ideas.

disparity
n dis-par-i-ty: difference
> There was a great *disparity* in their ages.

dispatch
v dis-patch: send off
> They were given their orders and *dispatched* to the coast.

dispatch
n dis-patch: a message; speed
> They received an urgent *dispatch* from the general.

dispel
v dis-pel: to scatter, cast away
> I want to *dispel* your fear about air travel.

disperse
v dis-perse: to scatter, spread out
> Their children were *dispersed* throughout the country.

dispute
v dis-pute: to argue or debate
> They began to *dispute* ownership of the baseball.

dispute
n dis-pute: a debate or quarrel
> Neither of them won the *dispute*.

dissect
v dis-sect: cut apart
> In biology, the students *dissected* a frog.

disseminate
v dis-sem-i-nate: to scatter
> The literature was *disseminated* to the crowd.

dissension
n dis-sen-sion: quarreling
> The *dissension* between them was enough to cause their breakup.

dissertation
n dis-ser-ta-tion: a formal essay
> The *dissertation* is an important requirement for an advanced degree.

dissipate
v dis-si-pate: to scatter, spread, dissolve
> The seeds were *dissipated* throughout the countryside.

dissolute
adj dis-so-lute: immoral
　The *dissolute* young man
　was soon without friends
　or reputation.

dissonant
adj dis-so-nant: harsh sounding
　The music was *dissonant* and
　hard to appreciate.

dissuade
v dis-suade: to advise against,
divert by persuasion
　His friends *dissuaded* him from
　that unwise plan of action.

distend
v dis-tend: to enlarge, expand,
stretch
　The balloon was *distended*
　from too much air, and it
　burst.

distinct
adj dis-tinct: clear; separate
　There was a *distinct* pattern
　of footprints in the mud.
　The husband and wife had
　distinct lives of their own.

distortion
n dis-tor-tion: a twisting out of
shape; misstating of facts
　Polio caused *distortion* of
　the limbs.
　The *distortions* by the
　historians left little of the
　man's true character for
　posterity.

distraught
adj dis-traught: upset, confused
　He was *distraught* about
　losing the game.

diva
n di-va: prima donna, a leading
woman singer in opera
　The *diva* took another bow.

divan
n di-van: couch, sofa
　They sat beside each other on
　the old *divan*.

diverge
v di-verge: to extend in different
directions
　The map showed a main lode
　with thin veins *diverging* in
　all directions.

diverse
adj di-verse: unlike, different
　His furniture collection
　represented *diverse* periods.

divest
v di-vest: to deprive, strip
　After the court martial, he
　was *divested* of his rank and
　decorations.

divulge
v di-vulge: make known
　Don't *divulge* any of the
　information to your brother.

docile
adj doc-ile: easily managed
　Although he looked wild, the
　lion was really *docile*.

doff
v doff: to remove
　He *doffed* his hat to all the
　women.

dogma
n dog-ma: belief, doctrine
   The *dogma* that he followed was based on a strict code of ethics.

dogmatic
adj dog-mat-ic: opinionated
   His *dogmatic* statements were not supported by evidence.

dole
n dole: a free distribution of food or money
   Some people live on the *dole*.

doleful
adj dole-ful: sad, dismal
   His *doleful* expression told the entire story of his misfortune.

domain
n do-main: territory
   The dog's entire *domain* was the backyard.

domestic
adj do-mes-tic: tame, of the home
   She owned a rare *domestic* cat.

domestic
n do-mes-tic: a maid, cook, household worker
   She worked as a *domestic* when she was younger.

domicile
n dom-i-cile: residence, home
   He continued to change his legal *domicile* to avoid creditors.

dominant
adj dom-i-nant: controlling
   She was the *dominant* one in their relationship.

don
v don: to put on
   He wanted to *don* the robe before the ceremony.

dormant
adj dor-mant: inactive, out of use
   The plan was *dormant* for five years until it was revived.

dorsal
adj dor-sal: on the back
   They could see the shark's *dorsal* fin cut through the water.

dossier
n dos-si-er: file on a subject or person
   The French police kept a *dossier* on every person with a criminal record.

dotard
n do-tard: senile person
   The old man is a *dotard*.

doting
adj dot-ing: foolishly fond
   Rhett Butler was a *doting* father.

dour
adj dour: gloomy, sullen
   He was a *dour* person and no fun to be with.

douse
v douse: to drench, soak
   The fireman *doused* the embers to make sure the fire was out.

dowdy
adj dow-dy: shabby
   She wore a *dowdy,* old dress
   to the party.

downy
adj down-y: fluffy
   The quilt was soft and *downy.*

drab
adj drab: dull, monotonous
   The entire room was
   decorated in *drab* colors.

drench
v drench: to soak
   She was *drenched* from the
   sudden rainstorm.

drivel
n driv-el: saliva running from
the mouth
   She wiped away her
   daughter's *drivel* and
   stopped her tears.

drivel
v driv-el: to slobber
   The baby continued to *drivel*
   on his shirt.

droll
adj droll: quaint, amusingly
different
   He had a *droll* sense of
   humor that wasn't always
   appreciated.

dross
n dross: waste matter, scum
   The process of separating the
   valuable metal from the *dross*
   may be too expensive.

drought
n drought: dry weather
   Many crops died during the
   drought from lack of water.

drowsy
adj drow-sy: sleepy
   He grew *drowsy* from all the
   food and drinks.

drudgery
n drudg-er-y: unpleasant work
   I always found that cleaning
   the house was *drudgery.*

dubious
adj du-bi-ous: doubtful
   I am extremely *dubious* about
   your solution.

duct
n duct: tube, pipe
   The engineers designed new
   heating *ducts* for the house.

dupe
v dupe: to deceive, fool
   She was easily *duped* by his
   calm manner.

dupe
n dupe: a person easily tricked
   He was merely a *dupe* in their
   secret plans.

durable
adj dur-able: able to exist, lasting
   The table was covered with a
   durable cloth.

dusky
adj dusk-y: obscure, dim
   The *dusky* light made it hard
   to see the pattern.

dwell

v dwell: to reside

Bears *dwell* in their dens.

dwindle

v dwin-dle: shrink, diminish

As the puddle dried up in the sunlight, it *dwindled* from sight.

 E

earnest

adj ear-nest: serious, grave

It was an *earnest* opinion from someone who cared.

ebb

v ebb: to decline

His strength began to *ebb* as he grew older.

ebb

adj ebb: shallow, low

The boats were stuck in the mud during *ebb* tide.

ebullience

n e-bul-lience: a boiling up, overflow, enthusiasm

The *ebullience of* youth can be wearying to older persons.

eccentric

adj ec-cen-tric: odd, peculiar

His approach to the problem was *eccentric,* but it worked.

eccentric

n ec-cen-tric: a peculiar person,

The wealthy *eccentric* lived in a tent.

eclectic

adj ec-lec-tic: drawing from diverse sources or systems

His *eclectic* record collection included everything from Bach cantatas to punk rock.

eclogue

n ec-logue: pastoral poem

The poet recited her *eclogue* to the audience.

ecology

n e-col-o-gy: science of life's relation to environment

Persons concerned about *ecology* are worried about the pollution of the earth's environment.

ecstasy

n ec-sta-sy: great pleasure

She was in *ecstasy* over her recent promotion.

eddy

n ed-dy: whirlpool

The ship was caught in the *eddy* beneath the bridge.

edible

adj ed-i-ble: fit to be eaten

If the milk has soured, then it is no longer *edible.*

edict

n e-dict: a public notice issued by authority

The *edict* issued by the junta dissolved the government.

edification

n ed-i-fi-ca-tion: instruction

He repeated the material for his son's *edification.*

edifice
n ed-i-face: building
   The stone *edifice* stood taller than the other buildings.

educe
v e-duce: to elicit, draw out
   Can you *educe* any information from her notes?

eerie
adj ee-rie: mysterious
   The *eerie* quality of the house made us feel that it might be haunted.

efficient
adj ef-fi-cient: capable, competent
   She was a very *efficient* office worker.

effigy
n ef-fi-gy: image, statue
   The team burned an *effigy* of their coach.

effrontery
n ef-fron-tery: shameless audacity
   He was surprised at the man's *effrontery* to him.

effusive
adj ef-fu-sive: gushing, demonstrative
   Her *effusive* greeting seemed overdone.

ego
n e-go: self
   He was so absorbed by his own *ego* that he lost all of his friends.

egress
n e-gress: exit
   When you leave, use the *egress* at the rear of the building.

elaborate
adj e-lab-o-rate: detailed, complicated
   The decorations were *elaborate* and festive.

elaborate
v e-lab-o-rate: to work out in detail
   He *elaborated* on how he planned to design the house.

elastic
adj e-las-tic: stretchable
   The *elastic* waistband on the pants made them comfortable to wear.

elastic
n e-las-tic: an elastic band or fabric
   The *elastic* in her hair held her ponytail together.

elate
v e-late: to make happy, joyful
   He was *elated* at the news of his promotion.

elicit
v e-lic-it: draw forth
   I was not able to *elicit* a response from him.

elongate
v e-lon-gate: to stretch
   They *elongated* the cord as far as it could go.

eloquence
n el-o-quence: graceful speech
His *eloquence* was enjoyed by all who listened.

elucidate
v e-lu-ci-date: to explain, clarify
Perhaps if you *elucidate* more, I will understand.

elude
v e-lude: avoid, evade
The man was able to *elude* the posse.

emaciated
adj e-ma-ci-at-ed: thin, lean
He was tall and *emaciated* looking.

emanate
v em-a-nate: to derive from, issue forth
American law *emanates* largely from English common law.

emancipate
v e-man-ci-pate: set free
By opening the cage door, the zookeeper *emancipated* the lions inside.

embargo
n em-bar-go: restriction
The U. S. imposed a grain *embargo* and couldn't ship anything.

embellish
v em-bel-lish: adorn, decorate
The tassels *embellished* the hat.

embezzle
v em-bez-zle: to steal
The man *embezzled* the money from the cash register.

embolism
n em-bo-lism: blood clot
Embolisms, now known to be responsible for many heart attacks, are preventable with certain drugs.

emboss
v em-boss: to decorate, engrave
His case was *embossed* with his initials.

emetic
n e-met-ic: an agent inducing vomiting
An *emetic* is prescribed for most poisons taken by mouth.

eminent
adj em-i-nent: distinguished, evident
The *eminent* speaker approached the podium.

emissary
n em-is-sar-y: agent, representative
He was an *emissary* from another country.

emit
v e-mit: give off, send out
The sound that the horn *emits* can be heard several miles away.

emollient
adj e-mol-lient: soothing
An *emollient* lotion is good for sunburn.

emolument
n e-mol-u-ment: reward for work
> Teachers receive comparatively greater *emoluments* in the Soviet Union than in the United States.

emphatic
adj em-phat-ic: forceful
> Mother was *emphatic* when she told us not to eat the cake.

emporium
n em-po-ri-um: marketplace
> The *emporium* was filled with fresh fruit and vegetables.

emulate
v em-u-late: to vie with, try to equal
> He tried to *emulate* the feats of the older boys.

encounter
v en-coun-ter: to meet
> While driving his jeep, he *encountered* a train.

encroach
v en-croach: trespass
> The man *encroached* upon the stranger's territory.

endeavor
v en-deav-or: to attempt, strive
> He *endeavored* to win the race and was successful.

endeavor
n en-deav-or: an attempt to accomplish something
> It was a very difficult *endeavor*, but he volunteered anyway.

endemic
adj en-dem-ic: peculiar to or prevalent in an area or group
> Malaria is *endemic* in many southern countries.

endure
v en-dure: tolerate, last
> How long could he continue to *endure* the pain?

enervate
v e-ner-vate: weaken
> She was *enervated* by the hot sunshine

engender
v en-gen-der: produce, cause
> Don't *engender* trouble by starting an argument.

engross
v en-gross: occupy fully
> The book *engrossed* her so much that she didn't have time to do any of her chores.

engulf
v en-gulf: to swallow up
> The rising waters *engulfed* the village.

enhance
v en-hance: to add to, to make greater
> Makeup *enhanced* her beauty.

enigma
n e-nig-ma: puzzle
> Her expression was an *enigma* and confused her friends.

enjoin
v en-join: to urge
I *enjoin* you to complete the application.

enmity
n en-mity: hatred
They shared an *enmity* for the director.

ennui
n en-nui: boredom
He was exhausted from the *ennui* he felt.

enormous
adj enor-mous: huge, vast
The *enormous* elephant couldn't fit into the cage.

enthrall
v en-thrall: fascinate
Looking at New York City's skyscrapers *enthralls* tourists.

entice
v en-tice: to tempt
Please don't *entice* me to have any more ice cream.

entomb
v en-tomb: to bury
They found the mummy *entombed* on the other side of the hill.

enumerate
v e-nu-mer-ate: to list; count
She can *enumerate* all of the state flowers.

enunciate
v e-nun-ci-ate: pronounce clearly
She was able to *enunciate* every word even though she was eating.

environment
n en-vi-ron-ment: surroundings
Camping is an enjoyable means of living in an outdoor *environment*.

envoy
n en-voy: messenger
The *envoy* brought the flowers.

eon
n e-on: long period of time
Many *eons* ago, dinosaurs roamed our continent.

epic
n ep-ic: long poem
Tennyson's *epics* are romantic and sad.

epidemic
n ep-i-dem-ic: widespread disease
The measles *epidemic* spread throughout the school.

epigram
n ep-i-gram: a bright or witty thought, tersely expressed
Oscar Wilde is noted for his *epigrams*.

epilogue
n ep-i-logue: concluding section
You'll have to wait until the *epilogue* to discover how the story turns out.

episode
n ep-i-sode: an incident
After the last *episode*, she refused to walk alone.

epistle

n e-pis-tle: letter

The *epistle* was sent by messenger to the pope.

epitaph

n ep-i-taph: tomb inscription

The *epitaph* on his grave states that he lived for fifty years.

epitome

n e-pit-o-me: summary; an ideal example

He was the *epitome* of the well-dressed man.

equanimity

n e-qua-nim-i-ty: calm temper, evenness of mind

Adversity could not disturb his *equanimity*.

equestrian

adj e-ques-tri-an: of horses or riding, on horseback

Polo and fox hunting are both *equestrian* sports.

equilibrium

n e-qui-lib-ri-um: balance

After twirling around and around, the boy tried to regain his *equilibrium*.

equitable

adj eq-ui-ta-ble: just, fair

The opponents came to an *equitable* settlement.

equivocal

adj e-quiv-o-cal: uncertain, ambiguous

The *equivocal* statements left us in doubt as to his real intentions.

eradicate

v e-rad-i-cate: to destroy

Smother the fire to *eradicate* it.

erode

v e-rode: wear away

The ground was *eroded* by the wind and rain.

erratic

adj er-rat-ic: irregular

As the car drove along the beach, it left an *erratic* pattern in the sand.

erratic

n er-rat-ic: an erratic person

People call him an *erratic* because he changes his plans often.

erroneous

adj er-ro-ne-ous: mistaken

His statement was *erroneous* and had nothing to do with the conversation.

erudite

adj er-u-dite: scholarly, learned

He was *erudite* without being stuffy.

erupt

v e-rupt: to break out

The volcano *erupted* streams of lava.

escalate

v es-ca-late: increase

The war *escalated,* and more troops were brought in.

escapade

n es-ca-pade: adventure

When the boys returned from their *escapade,* they were dirty and tired.

eschew

v es-chew: to avoid

I would like to *eschew* that topic, if possible.

esoteric

adj es-o-ter-ic: limited to a few, secret

The *esoteric* rites of the fraternity were held sacred by the members.

espouse

v es-pouse: to marry; to support or embrace, as a cause or idea

They were *espoused* after the party.

He *espoused* the group's doctrine

esteem

v es-teem: to value highly

She was *esteemed* for her ability to deal with difficult situations.

esteem

n es-teem: high regard

The boy had great *esteem* for his father.

estuary

n es-tu-ar-y: part of a river that meets the sea

The ship was caught in the currents of the *estuary* when the tides were going in.

eternal

adj e-ter-nal: everlasting

She wished for *eternal* peace in the world.

ethereal

adj e-the-re-al: delicate, airy, light

She looked *ethereal* as she walked into the room.

ethics

n eth-ics: moral conduct

The judge had the highest *ethics* and was well respected.

ethnic

adj eth-nic: belonging to the customs of a national group

Of all the *ethnic* foods available in this city, Italian pizza is the most popular.

etiquette

n et-i-quette: rules of behavior

It is considered good *etiquette* to say thank you when you receive a present from another person.

eulogy

n eu-lo-gy: praising speech

The *eulogy* delivered at the funeral expressed all of our sentiments.

euphonic

adj eu-pho-nic: pleasant-sounding

Her *euphonic* singing had a soothing effect on the guests.

euphoria

n eu-pho-ri-a: sense of well-being

They went through a period of *euphoria* after winning the lottery.

evacuate
v e-vac-u-ate: to leave, withdraw, to make empty
> The soldiers *evacuated* the town.

evade
v e-vade: avoid
> He *evaded* the police's questioning.

evict
v e-vict: to expel, force out
> The tenants were *evicted* from their apartment.

evince
v e-vince: to make evident, display
> His curt reply *evinced* his short temper.

eviscerate
v e-vis-cer-ate: to disembowel
> Animals must be *eviscerated* before they can be cooked or smoked.

evoke
v e-voke: to bring out
> The photograph *evoked* memories of an earlier time.

evolve
v e-volve: to develop slowly
> These trees have *evolved* from an earlier form of bush.

ewe
n ewe: female sheep
> They gathered the *ewes* and their babies for feeding.

exaggerate
v ex-ag-ger-ate: overstate
> Andrew *exaggerated* the strength and size of his older brother.

exalt
v ex-alt: to glorify, honor
> The king was *exalted* by his subjects.

exasperate
v ex-as-per-ate: to vex, irritate
> Those loud noises are *exasperating* to the man trying to sleep.

excavate
v ex-ca-vate: to dig, make hollow
> The men *excavated* the site to prepare for the new building.

excessive
adj ex-ces-sive: too much
> *Excessive* sun will cause sunburn.

exclaim
v ex-claim: say, speak
> He *exclaimed* that he was very surprised.

excursion
n ex-cur-sion: journey
> The *excursion* lasted a whole day.

execute
v ex-e-cute: to carry out; to kill
> He was unable to *execute* the orders.
> The prisoner was *executed* at dawn.

exert
v ex-ert: to put into action
He physically *exerted* himself as he mowed the lawn.

exhort
v ex-hort: to urge
They continued to *exhort* the troops to move forward.

exhume
v ex-hume: to dig out, disinter
He obtained a court order to *exhume* the body.

exile
n ex-ile: banishment
They had to leave their country for *exile*.

exile
v ex-ile: to banish
The prince was *exiled* from his country because of his bad behavior.

existence
n ex-is-tence: life, being
Some people believe that the *existence* of the world began with a spark.

exodus
n ex-o-dus: departure
Cold weather caused the *exodus* of the birds to warmer climates.

exonerate
v ex-on-er-ate: to free from blame
The man was *exonerated* of the charges.

exorbitant
adj ex-or-bi-tant: excessive
That store charges *exorbitant* prices.

exorcise
v ex-or-cise: to drive out, free from
The men tried to *exorcise* the devil by praying over the child.

exotic
adj ex-ot-ic: foreign, strange
The *exotic* belly dancers performed in the restaurant.

expedite
v ex-pe-dite: to speed up
If you sign this form, it will *expedite* matters.

expel
v ex-pel: to force out
The boy was *expelled* from class.

experiment
n ex-per-i-ment: test, trial
The *experiment* using rats continued in the lab.

experiment
v ex-per-i-ment: to try or test something
He *experimented* with different designs until he was satisfied.

expire
v ex-pire: to end; die
Remember to renew your license before it *expires*.
The patient *expired* at one o'clock.

explicit
adj ex-pli-cit: definite, clear
Be *explicit* in giving directions to your house so that we will have no trouble finding it.

exploit
n ex-ploit: daring deed
The *exploits* of astronauts are applauded by the world.

exploit
v ex-ploit: to promote, publicize
The agency tried to *exploit* the healthy aspects of the product.

expressly
adv ex-press-ly: specifically
I wrote it *expressly* for you.

expurgate
v ex-pur-gate: to remove objectionable matter
The censors *expurgated* the portions of the book they considered obscene.

exquisite
adj ex-qui-site: delicate, lovely
She owned an *exquisite* pearl necklace.

extensive
adj ex-ten-sive: broad, wide
The coverage of the news team was *extensive*.

extinguish
v ex-tin-guish: to put out (like a fire)
The water *extinguished* the fire.

extol
v ex-tol: to praise highly
The teacher *extolled* the pupil's skill.

extract
v ex-tract: pull out
The dentist will have to *extract* that bad tooth.

exult
v ex-ult: to rejoice
The winner *exulted* in his victory.

F

fable
n fa-ble: story
The *fable* about Peter Pan is a favorite with children.

fabricate
v fab-ri-cate: construct
On this hill, they plan to *fabricate* a log house.

facetious
adj fa-ce-tious: joking
I was only being *facetious* and didn't mean what I said.

facsimile
n fac-sim-i-le: a reproduction, copy
That is a *facsimile* of a Picasso painting.

fad
n fad: craze, rage
The mini-skirt *fad* seems to be popular again.

faint
adj faint: feeble, languid, exhausted

The children were *faint* with fatigue and hunger.

fallacy
n fal-la-cy: false or deceiving ideas

His reasoning was filled with *fallacies*.

fallow
adj fal-low: uncultivated; inactive

The farmer's field lay *fallow* for a year.

falter
v fal-ter: to hesitate, stumble

He began to *falter* as he approached the throne.

famine
n fam-ine: starvation

Famine ravaged the countryside and left the people hungry.

fanatic
adj fa-nat-ic: characterized by an extreme viewpoint

Some credos seem to create *fanatic* followers among the discontented.

fantasy
n fan-ta-sy: imagination

Her dreams were full of *fantasy*.

fastidious
adj fas-tid-i-ous: hard to please

He was a *fastidious* person and found fault with almost everything.

fatal
adj fat-al: deadly

The bullet wound was *fatal*.

fathom
n fath-om: a measure of length used chiefly at sea

The water was twenty *fathoms* deep.

fatigue
n fa-tigue: weariness

The *fatigue* continued until he found time to rest.

fawn
n fawn: young deer

A *fawn* is one of the animals in the zoo's nursery.

feasible
adj fea-si-ble: capable, able

That is a *feasible* suggestion, and we will try it.

feeble
adj fee-ble: weak

After her illness, her legs were *feeble*.

feign
v feign: pretend

She tried to *feign* illness to avoid going to the party.

felicity
n fe-lic-i-ty: happiness

Felicity was felt by all when the couple married.

feline
adj fe-line: cat family

Although lions and tigers are different animals, they belong to the same *feline* category.

felonious
adj fe-lo-nious: criminial
>He was charged with a
>*felonious* act.

ferocious
adj fe-ro-cious: cruel, fierce
>He owned a *ferocious* dog.

fetch
v fetch: to bring
>If you throw the ball, the dog
>will *fetch* it.

fetid
adj fet-id: bad smelling
>The meat was *fetid* and had
>to be thrown out.

fetus
n fe-tus: unborn animal in
the womb
>Damage to the *fetus* may be
>caused by any shock to a
>pregnant female.

feud
n feud: quarrel
>The *feud* between the two
>families has gone on for
>many years.

feud
v feud: to carry on a feud
>The boys *feuded* with each
>other over use of the bicycle.

fiasco
n fi-as-co: a ridiculous failure
>The play was a *fiasco* and
>closed the next day.

fickle
adj fick-le: changing
>She is a *fickle* person because
>she is always changing her
>mind.

fictitious
adj fic-ti-tious: imaginary,
assumed
>The story is *fictitious* but
>seems so real.

fidelity
n fi-del-i-ty: loyalty
>You can appreciate his *fidelity*
>but not his stubbornness.

fidget
v fid-get: to be uneasy or restless
>He *fidgeted* in his seat while
>the lecture continued.

fiend
n fiend: evil spirit, demon
>He ate like a *fiend*, as though
>he were possessed.

figurine
n fig-u-rine: statue, sculpture
>The *figurine* stood on a tall
>pedestal.

finagle
v fi-na-gle: to cheat
>The students were caught
>*finagling* on the exam.

finesse
n fi-nesse: skill
>He is considered the best
>mechanic in town because of
>his *finesse* in repairing cars.

finicky
adj fin-ick-y: fussy
>The child's eating habits
>were *finicky*, and he only
>enjoyed soft foods.

finite
adj fi-nite: having a limit, bounded

There was only a *finite* number of men to be considered for the job.

fiscal
adj fis-cal: financial

This is the end of the *fiscal* year.

fission
n fis-sion: splitting

The *fission* of the molecules was something he had been trying to achieve for many years.

flabbergast
v flab-ber-gast: to amaze, to astound

He was *flabbergasted* when he saw how well she danced.

flaccid
adj flac-cid: limp, weak

His hand was *flaccid* and unpleasant to shake.

flagrant
adj fla-grant: outrageous

Be careful that your *flagrant* behavior does not get you into trouble.

flair
n flair: talent

He had a *flair* for dressing nicely.

flamboyant
adj flam-boy-ant: ornate, brilliant

More people will notice you if you wear that *flamboyant* outfit.

flask
n flask: container, bottle

He kept the wine in a silver *flask.*

flaunt
v flaunt: show off

She *flaunted* her new dress at the party.

flaw
n flaw: defect, crack

The *flaw* in the material was hardly evident.

flee
v flee: to run away

They tried to *flee* from the police after the robbery.

fleece
v fleece: to rob; to shear the wool from

The man tried to *fleece* the couple out of their money.

It is necessary to *fleece* sheep in the spring.

flexible
adj flex-i-ble: easily bent, adaptable

The plastic was *flexible* when heated and could be molded into the desired shape.

flimflam
v flim-flam: to cheat, to trick

He was well known for trying to *flimflam* older couples.

flimsy
adj flim-sy: frail, thin

The *flimsy* nightgown revealed her body.

flinch

v flinch: to pull back from

He *flinched* every time the bee flew by him.

flock

n flock: group, crowd

The farmer herded a *flock* of sheep away from the pond.

flog

v flog: whip

The captain had the sailor *flogged* in front of the others.

flotilla

n flo-til-la: fleet of ships

Their boat was in the middle of the *flotilla*.

flotsam

n flot-sam: floating wreckage

The water was covered with *flotsam* from the sunken liner.

flounder

v floun-der: to struggle

The boy was *floundering* in the heavy waves.

flounder

n floun-der: type of flat fish

He enjoyed eating his *flounder* with lemon and butter.

flourish

v flour-ish: to do well

The neighborhood began to *flourish* after the road was built.

flourish

n flour-ish: something done in a showy way

She twirled the baton with a *flourish* to begin the parade.

fluctuate

v fluc-tu-ate: to change, vary

She *fluctuated* in her moods, and we never knew what she would do next.

flue

n flue: chimney pipe

When he lit a fire in the fireplace, smoke rose up out of the *flue*.

flume

n flume: a narrow water channel, often artificial

They diverted the water into a *flume* for sending the logs down the side of the mountain.

flurry

n flur-ry: sudden gust

A *flurry* of leaves blinded him momentarily.

flush

v flush: to blush

She began to *flush* from the heat.

flush

n flush: a rapid going, as of water

The *flush* of water cleaned the tea kettle.

flush

adj flush: well-supplied

He returned from town, *flush* with food and drink.

fluster

v flus-ter: to confuse

The girl was *flustered* by all the attention.

fodder

n fod-der: food for cattle

The truck delivered the pig *fodder* in the morning.

foe

n foe: enemy

They were *foes* on the baseball diamond but friends afterwards.

foible

n foi-ble: weakness

His foible was that he was often shy and private.

foliage

n fo-li-age: leaves

The *foliage* is most colorful during the fall.

fondle

v fon-dle: to caress

She began to *fondle* her daughter's hair.

foray

n for-ay: plundering raid

The bandits made a *foray* into town.

forestall

v fore-stall: to prevent, hold off

You can only *forestall* the battle for a little while.

foretell

v fore-tell: to predict

I can *foretell* the outcome of the game.

forfeit

v for-feit: to give up

He had decided to *forfeit* his comfortable life for the sea.

forfeit

n for-feit: fine, penalty for fault or crime

He was required to pay a *forfeit* when he lost the game.

forlorn

adj for-lorn: neglected, unhappy

The *forlorn* cat sat in the corner, staring at the boy.

format

n for-mat: plan, arrangement

He liked the *format* of the book he was reading.

fortify

v for-ti-fy: strengthen

The sailors *fortified* their position by erecting a wall.

fossil

n fos-sil: remains

The *fossil* of the jaw was found in the tar pit.

fowl

n fowl: a type of bird

He ate a balanced diet of fish, meat, and *fowl*.

foyer

n foy-er: entrance hall

They entered the living room from the *foyer*.

fracas

n fra-cas: brawl, quarrel

They were both bloody from the *fracas*.

fragile

adj frag-ile: easily broken

The *fragile* antique vase sat safely on the shelf.

fragrance
n fra-grance: scent, odor

The sweet *fragrance* of lilacs filled the room.

frail
adj frail: weak

She was tiny and *frail* and frightened of the world.

franchise
n fran-chise: right to vote

Your *franchise* allows you the chance to support your favorite candidate for office.

frantic
adj fran-tic: excited

The squirrel was *frantic* in his search for the acorn.

friction
n fric-tion: irritation caused by rubbing; clash of opinions

The *friction* of the rough cloth on his arm caused an infection.

There was *friction* in the office.

fringe
n fringe: border, trimming, the edge

There was a lace *fringe* on the tablecloth.

He was friends with the radical *fringe*.

frivolous
adj friv-o-lous: silly, foolish

She was completely *frivolous*, with no serious thoughts.

frock
n frock: dress, gown

She wore a simple *frock* made by her mother.

froth
v froth: to foam, bubble

The sick dog began to *froth* at the mouth.

froth
n froth: foam

The *froth* on top of a malted is the best part.

frugal
adj fru-gal: thrifty

The *frugal* couple saved a lot of money.

frustrate
v frus-trate: to thwart

He was *frustrated* in his attempt to get elected.

furnish
v furn-ish: supply, provide

He *furnished* the troops with additional guns.

furtive
adj fur-tive: secret

His *furtive* movements made him a likely suspect.

fuse
v fuse: unite, blend

He was able to *fuse* the ends of the rope together.

futile
adj fu-tile: useless, trivial
   The helicopters returned to
   their base after a *futile*
   search.

G

gadget
n gad-get: device
   This new house is filled with
   interesting *gadgets*.

gainsay
v gain-say: to deny
   It was impossible to *gainsay*
   the truth of the statement the
   man made.

gale
n gale: strong wind
   The *gale* blew down most of
   the palm trees.

gallant
adj gal-lant: stately, grand
   His *gallant* stance showed
   everyone how proud he was.

gape
v gape: open wide
   Her eyes *gaped* like huge
   saucepans as she saw him
   come near.

garb
n garb: clothing
   She wore the latest *garb* to
   the party.

garb
v garb: to dress, clothe
   He was *garbed* in his
   father's suit.

garish
adj gar-ish: flashy
   Everyone noticed her *garish*
   clothes.

garland
n gar-land: a wreath
   They hung a *garland* of
   flowers on the winning horse.

garnish
v gar-nish: to decorate
   They *garnished* the wedding
   cake with chocolate.

garnish
n gar-nish: a decoration
   She used the flower as a
   garnish for the dessert.

garrulous
adj gar-ru-lous: talkative
   The *garrulous* man bored his
   listeners.

gash
n gash: deep cut
   She poured antiseptic on the
   gash to prevent infection.

gash
v gash: to make a long, deep cut
   He *gashed* the bark of the tree
   to mark the path.

gaudy
adj gau-dy: showy and cheap,
flashy
   Her make-up was *gaudy* and
   made her look ridiculous.

gauge
n gauge: a standard measure
   You can determine the *gauge*
   of the tire by measuring it.

gauge
v gauge: to measure the size, amount, etc.
   Gauge your distance from the curb before you park the car.

gaunt
adj gaunt: thin
   Her hands seemed *gaunt* in the tight-fitting gloves.

gauntlet
n gaunt-let: glove
   The hawk rested on the leather *gauntlet* before he took off in flight.

gawky
adj gawk-y: clumsy
   The teenager was *gawky* and knocked down everything.

gazette
n ga-zette: newspaper
   He read the story in the local *gazette*.

generate
v gen-er-ate: produce
   Pianos *generate* beautiful sound if you strike the right keys.

genesis
n gen-e-sis: origin, creation
   A dinner conversation sparked the *genesis* of his idea.

genial
adj gen-ial: pleasant
   She was a *genial* hostess.

genteel
adj gen-teel: polite, well-bred
   People liked her *genteel* manner.

germane
adj ger-mane: relevant
   The topic was *germane* to the discussion.

gist
n gist: main idea
   He got the *gist* of it when he finished the book.

glaucoma
n glau-co-ma: eye disease
   He suffered from *glaucoma* and needed an operation.

glean
v glean: gather
   Glean as much information as you can before you start writing your book.

glee
n glee: great joy, merriment
   He shouted with *glee* when he found the money.

gloss
n gloss: shiny covering
   The floor was buffed to a high *gloss*.

gloss
v gloss: pass over quickly
   He tried to *gloss* over the real reason he had come.

glut
v glut: to fill fully
   He *glutted* himself as he continued to eat and drink.

glutton
n glut-ton: overeater
   He was a *glutton* at the table.

gnash
v gnash: to grind
> The animal *gnashed* his teeth as he ate.

gnome
n gnome: dwarf
> The Grimm Brothers wrote about *gnomes* and elves.

goad
v goad: to urge on
> He was *goaded* by his parents to finish the project.

goblet
n gob-let: drinking glass
> They served the water in crystal *goblets*.

gorge
n gorge: valley
> The *gorge* was flooded with water.

gorge
v gorge: eat greedily
> He *gorged* himself on candy and cookies.

gory
adj gor-y: bloody
> Don't tell me the *gory* details of the murder.

govern
v gov-ern: to rule, control
> He was unable to *govern* his country.

gracious
adj grac-ious: pleasant
> The young, *gracious* girl was escorted to her table.

grapple
v grap-ple: to seize, lay fast hold on
> He *grappled* with the man who had attacked him.

grasp
v grasp: to seize, hold on to
> She *grasped* his hand for safety.

grasp
n grasp: a grip; an understanding
> The man shook hands with a firm *grasp*.
>
> Her *grasp* of the subject was amazing.

gratis
adv gra-tis: free of charge
> The meal was presented *gratis* by the management.

gratuity
n gra-tu-i-ty: tip
> He left a *gratuity* for the chambermaid.

grave
n grave: hole in the ground to bury the dead
> The *grave* was freshly dug and prepared for the deceased.

grave
adj grave: serious
> He made a *grave* error when he stole the car.

grieve
v grieve: to be very sad
> He *grieved* over the loss of his wife.

grim
adj grim: cruel, stern
> His face was *grim* and frightening.

grimace
n grim-ace: ugly, funny smile
> His *grimace* gave a peculiar look to his face.

grimace
v grim-ace: to make grimaces
> She *grimaces* at her reflection in the mirror.

grimy
adj grim-y: very dirty
> The child's *grimy* hands left marks on the furniture.

grind
v grind: to crush
> You can watch them *grind* the coffee beans into powder.

grope
v grope: search blindly
> She *groped* around in the dark, trying to find the light switch.

grotesque
adj gro-tesque: odd, ugly
> Witches are noted for their *grotesque* noses.

grotto
n grot-to: a cave
> Bats lived in the damp *grotto*.

grouse
v grouse: to complain
> There is no use *grousing* over your own mistakes.

grovel
v grov-el: to humble oneself
> The captors forced their prisoners to *grovel* for food.

grudge
n grudge: ill will
> I hold no *grudge* against you.

grudge
v grudge: to give reluctantly
> He *grudged* his son even the privilege of driving the family's car.

grueling
adj gru-el-ing: exhausting
> Two laborers fainted from the *grueling* work.

gruesome
adj grue-some: horrible
> The Halloween mask of the monster was *gruesome*.

gruff
adj gruff: rough
> His *gruff* manner frightened the children.

guffaw
v guf-faw: to laugh loudly
> The man *guffawed* when the child did a flip.

guile
n guile: craftiness, deceit
> Don't practice your *guile* on me.

gullible
adj gul-li-ble: easily cheated
> It is easy to take advantage of *gullible* people.

gush

v gush: pour out

The water *gushed* out of the ground.

gust

n gust: rush of wind

The *gust* blew his hat off his head.

guzzle

v guz-zle: to drink much; to drink frequently

He *guzzled* his liquor like a man dying of thirst.

gyrate

v gy-rate: to rotate

The dancers on the floor *gyrated* to the music.

H

haberdashery

n hab-er-dash-er-y: men's clothing; store that sells men's clothing

His *haberdashery* was the latest style.

hack

v hack: to chop

He was able to *hack* down the branches.

hackneyed

adj hack-neyed: commonplace, ordinary

He used a *hackneyed* expression that everyone knew.

haggle

v hag-gle: to bargain

The old woman *haggled* for an hour about the price.

hail

v hail: to greet

He *hailed* his friend from the other side of the street.

hail

n hail: precipitation in the form of ice lumps

The *hail* began to fall, sounding like cannons firing.

hallucination

n hal-lu-ci-na-tion: false vision

She was awakened by *hallucinations* in the middle of the night.

hamlet

n ham-let: village

He lived in a little *hamlet* alongside the river.

handicap

n hand-i-cap: hindrance; contest with assigned difficulty

She did not consider her blindness a *handicap*.

He played golf with a four-stroke *handicap*.

haphazard

adj hap-haz-ard: random

He was hit by the *haphazard* throw.

hapless

adj hap-less: unlucky

After a *hapless* day hunting, he came home and went to sleep.

harass

v ha-rass: to annoy, worry

The dog began to *harass* the children.

hardy
adj har-dy: strong, capable
  He was a *hardy* fellow, able to lift the logs easily.

harpoon
n har-poon: spear, used in whaling
  The sailor *harpooned* the whale.

harpoon
v har-poon: to strike with a spear or harpoon
  The whale was *harpooned* by the sailor.

harsh
adj harsh: strong, rough
  She couldn't stand the *harsh* winters of Alaska.

hassle
n has-sle: struggle
  It was a *hassle* trying to rent a car.

haste
n haste: quickness
  In his *haste* he tripped over the bush.

haughty
adj haugh-ty: proud, insolent
  Because of his new job, he was *haughty*.

haul
v haul: to transport by wagon, truck, etc.
  They planned to *haul* the dirt to his house.

haven
n ha-ven: safe shelter
  The boat pulled into the *haven* with the others.

havoc
n hav-oc: chaos, ruin
  The runaway bull caused *havoc*.

hazardous
adj haz-ard-ous: dangerous, risky
  Although he was frightened, he volunteered for the *hazardous* mission.

hazy
adj ha-zy: misty, smoky
  The sky was *hazy* from the pollution.

heap
n heap: a pile
  He found a *heap* of dirt in the yard.

heap
v heap: to make into a pile
  She *heaped* the vegetables onto his plate.

hearth
n hearth: a fireplace
  They sat around the open *hearth*, warming their hands.

heathen
n hea-then: nonbeliever
  He considered himself to be a *heathen*, compared to his friends.

heave
v heave: to lift
  They *heaved* the package to the second floor window.

heckle
v heck-le: to annoy, bother
>They began to *heckle* the speaker from the audience.

heinous
adj hei-nous: hateful, offensive
>He committed a *heinous* crime.

hence
adv hence: thus, therefore
>I am tired, *hence* I won't go with you.

heresy
n her-e-sy: unaccepted belief
>His book attacked the group's *heresy*.

hex
n hex: magic spell
>The roof on the barn had a *hex* symbol painted on it.

hiatus
n hi-a-tus: space where something is missing
>After a long *hiatus* in the conversation, he began speaking again.

hibernate
v hi-ber-nate: to sleep
>The bear crawled into its cave to *hibernate* for the winter.

hideous
adj hid-e-ous: extremely ugly
>She wore a *hideous* fright mask to the party.

hieroglyphics
n hi-er-o-glyph-ics: symbolic pictures
>They found the ancient *hieroglyphics* painted on the walls of the cave.

hindrance
n hin-drance: obstacle
>The rock in the road is a *hindrance* to motorists trying to pass by.

hint
n hint: suggestion
>Give me a little *hint* about the present.

hint
v hint: to intimate
>She *hinted* at a new project she might begin.

hoard
v hoard: to save, store away
>He wanted to *hoard* all of the gold for himself.

hoard
n hoard: a stored supply
>We found his private *hoard* of food in the cave.

hoax
n hoax: trick
>He was fooled by the children's *hoax*.

hoax
v hoax: to deceive with a trick
>She was *hoaxed* into believing he would be there.

hobble
v hob-ble: to limp
> After the game, he had to *hobble* home.

hoist
v hoist: to lift up
> He tried to *hoist* the box on his back.

hoist
n hoist: machine for lifting
> The huge *hoist* unloaded the car from the hold of the boat.

holocaust
n ho-lo-caust: destruction by fire
> After the *holocaust,* there were no buildings left standing.

homage
n hom-age: honor, respect
> They paid *homage* to the retired general.

homely
adj home-ly: ugly, plain looking
> She was a pleasant but *homely* child.

homicide
n hom-i-cide: killing
> The police accused the man of *homicide.*

homogeneous
adj ho-mo-ge-ne-ous: similar
> A *homogeneous* group of people came to the lecture.

hone
v hone: to sharpen
> He *honed* his knife on the stone.

horde
n horde: crowd
> The *horde* of bees made us leave the picnic.

hormone
n hor-mone: organic fluid that affects certain cells
> Our bodies respond to changes in *hormone* levels.

hose
n hose: stockings
> Be careful that you don't get a run in your *hose.*

hose
v hose: to water
> If she *hoses* the garden, the flowers will grow faster.

hostile
adj hos-tile: unfriendly
> The neighbors were *hostile* to the new family.

hover
v hov-er: to stay close to
> The bird *hovered* above the water, watching for bugs.

humane
adj hu-mane: merciful, kind
> It was an *humane* act to take in the stray cat.

humbug
n hum-bug: fraud
> His plan was pure *humbug.*

humdrum
adj hum-drum: boring, commonplace
> It was a very *humdrum* job, so he quit.

humid

adj hu-mid: damp

   The air was so *humid* that my clothes were wet.

humiliate

v hu-mil-i-ate: to embarrass

   She was *humiliated* in front of her family.

hurdle

n hur-dle: barrier, obstacle

   The *hurdle* in the road prevented the cars from going any farther.

hurdle

v hur-dle: to jump over, to overcome

   The runner *hurdled* the puddles.

hygienic

adj hy-gi-en-ic: sanitary, healthful

   Keep the sick patients in *hygienic* rooms.

hypocrite

n hyp-o-crite: one who pretends to be something else; liar

   Since you smoke, you are a *hypocrite* to tell me to stop.

hypothetical

adj hy-po-thet-i-cal: assumed

   Their plan to attack the building was only *hypothetical*.

hysterical

adj hys-ter-i-cal: uncontrollable emotion, very excited

   She became *hysterical* after the accident.

ideal

adj i-de-al: standard of perfection

   He found the *ideal* gift for his wife.

ideal

n i-de-al: an idea of perfection

   She was his *ideal* of the perfect woman.

idiom

n id-i-om: expression common to a specific group

   "Bury the hatchet" is a typical *idiom* and means something other than what it says.

idle

adj i-dle: not busy

   He was out of work and *idle* for almost a month.

idle

v i-dle: to move slowly, waste time

   They *idled* their way home from the movies.

ignoble

adj ig-no-ble: low, base

   His *ignoble* gesture embarrassed them.

ignominious

adj ig-no-min-i-ous: disgraceful

   It was an *ignominious* defeat.

illuminate

v il-lu-mi-nate: to light up

   The tree was *illuminated* with a hundred bulbs.

illusory
adj il-lu-so-ry: misleading
   Because your report was
   illusory, I came to the wrong
   conclusion.

imbibe
v im-bibe: to drink
   The man continued to *imbibe*
   too much alcohol.

immense
adj im-mense: huge
   The aircraft carrier was
   immense.

immerse
v im-merse: put into liquid
   He *immersed* his head in the
   water to stop the pain.

imminent
adj im-mi-nent: about to occur
   His arrival is *imminent*.

immobile
adj im-mo-bile: not movable
   The rock was completely
   immobile, so they built
   around it.

immortal
adj im-mor-tal: to live forever,
without death
   Shakespeare's plays are
   immortal.

immune
adj im-mune: protected, safe
   He was *immune* from measles
   because of the injection.

imp
n imp: little devil, troublemaker
   My son is an *imp*, but cute.

impair
v im-pair: to damage
   Too much loud noise may
   impair your hearing.

impale
v im-pale: pierce
   The animal was *impaled* on
   the spear.

impartial
adj im-par-tial: fair
   It was an *impartial* jury that
   made the decision.

impasse
n im-passe: deadlock
   They had reached an *impasse*
   in their negotiations.

impeccable
adj im-pec-ca-ble: flawless,
without fault
   He was an *impeccable* dresser.

impel
v im-pel: to force
   They tried to *impel* him to tell
   the truth.

imperative
adj im-per-a-tive: urgent,
necessary
   It is absolutely *imperative*
   that you call home.

impetus
n im-pe-tus: incentive
   The bonus is enough *impetus*
   to get me to finish the job.

implicate
v im-pli-cate: to involve
   He tried to *implicate* him in
   the robbery.

implore
v im-plore: beg, plead with
> The child *implored* her mother to let her stay up longer.

imply
v im-ply: to suggest
> He tried to *imply* that he was guilty.

inane
adj in-ane: silly
> They played an *inane* game.

inanimate
adj in-an-i-mate: without life
> He enjoyed painting *inanimate* objects rather than people.

incarcerate
v in-car-cer-ate: to imprison
> He was *incarcerated* for five years.

incense
v in-cense: to make angry
> He was *incensed* by his friend's statement.

incense
n in-cense: substance producing fragrant odor when burned
> The children lit the *incense* in the bedroom.

incentive
n in-cen-tive: motive, goal
> I will offer you more money as an *incentive* to finish the project early.

inception
n in-cep-tion: beginning
> At the *inception* of the project, he tried to resign.

incessant
adj in-ces-sant: continuous
> The *incessant* barking of the dog makes me angry.

incident
n in-ci-dent: happening, event
> I remember the *incident* of the missing ring.

incinerate
v in-cin-er-ate: to burn to ashes
> He *incinerated* the secret papers.

incision
n in-ci-sion: cut
> The doctor made an *incision* along his ribs.

incite
v in-cite: to arouse, stir up
> The speaker began to *incite* the crowd to violence.

inclement
adj in-cle-ment: stormy, rough
> During *inclement* weather, be sure to carry an umbrella.

inclination
n in-cli-na-tion: tendency
> His *inclination* was to go home early.

incognito
adv in-cog-ni-to: disguised
> The movie star went to the party *incognito*.

incoherent
adj in-co-her-ent: rambling, confused
> After drinking too much, her speech was *incoherent*.

incredulous
adj in-cred-u-lous: unbelieving, doubting

I am absolutely *incredulous* that you found that job.

increment
n in-cre-ment: gradual increase

He filled the glass in *increments* with different colored liquids.

indefinite
adj in-def-i-nite: not clear

I don't like it when you are *indefinite* about our plans.

indelible
adj in-del-i-ble: that which can not be removed, washed away, blotted out, or effaced

He dripped *indelible* ink on his shirt.

index
n in-dex: a list

He consulted the *index* at the back of the book.

index
v in-dex: to categorize items

He started to *index* his coin collection.

indict
v in-dict: to charge with an offense

The judge *indicted* him for assault.

indigo
n in-di-go: blue dye; a plant that yields blue dye.

The natives harvested the *indigo* for sale to the traders.

induce
v in-duce: to influence

He tried to *induce* the woman to buy his car.

induct
v in-duct: install in office or military position

He was *inducted* into the army when he was eighteen.

inert
adj in-ert: inactive

That machine will remain *inert* until you turn it on.

inevitable
adj in-ev-i-ta-ble: unavoidable

It was *inevitable* that we would meet.

infallible
adj in-fal-li-ble: without fail, reliable

I have an *infallible* system for memorizing names.

infamy
n in-fa-my: disgrace, vile act

Custer's Last Stand will live in *infamy* forever.

infer
v in-fer: conclude

From her tears, he *inferred* that she was worried.

inferior
adj in-fer-i-or: lower in rating

The workmanship in that coat is *inferior* to this one.

infinite
adj in-fi-nite: without limits,
The number of stars seems
infinite.

infirm
adj in-firm: weak, feeble
He was old and *infirm* and
unable to attend the party.

inflate
v in-flate: to puff out, swell
He *inflated* his son's balloon
until it burst.

inflexible
adj in-flex-ible: rigid, firm
The negotiator was *inflexible*
in his demands.

inflict
v in-flict: to give, cause
The soldier *inflicted* a bayonet
thrust on the practice dummy.

influx
n in-flux: flowing in
There was an *influx* of new
people into the neighborhood.

inform
v in-form: instruct, tell
Please *inform* the messenger
where to deliver the package.

infraction
n in-frac-tion: violation
You will be punished even
for minor *infractions* of the
rules.

infringe
v in-fringe: to trespass, intrude
Try not to *infringe* on your
brother's privacy.

infuriate
v in-fu-ri-ate: to anger, enrage
His statements always
infuriate me.

ingenious
adj in-gen-ious: clever
It was the most *ingenious*
solution to the problem.

ingredient
n in-gre-di-ent: part of a mixture
He added another secret
ingredient to the perfume.

inhabit
v in-hab-it: to live in
The gophers *inhabited* those
holes in the desert.

inhale
v in-hale: to breathe
He *inhaled* the aroma of the
cookies.

inherent
adj in-her-ent: essential part of
This book is an *inherent* part
of a reference library.

inhibit
v in-hib-it: to restrict, restrain
I think it's necessary to *inhibit*
your spending.

initiate
v in-i-ti-ate: begin
He was the lawyer who
initiated the defendant's
lawsuit.

injunction
n in-junc-tion: an order
She received an *injunction*
against opening a business
in town.

inkling
n ink-ling: slight suggestion
She had an *inkling* that there would be a party for her.

inn
n inn: a small hotel
We stayed at a lovely, old country *inn*.

innate
adj in-nate: natural
He had an *innate* sense of right and wrong.

innocuous
adj in-noc-u-ous: inoffensive, harmless
It seemed to be an *innocuous* incident that angered him.

innovate
v in-no-vate: to introduce something new
Bureaucracy makes it hard to *innovate*.

innuendo
n in-nu-en-do: indirect suggestion
I'm tired of his *innuendos* about my work habits.

inordinate
adj in-or-di-nate: too much, excessive
He spent an *inordinate* amount of money.

inquest
n in-quest: legal inquiry
There was an *inquest* into the accident.

inquisitive
adj in-quis-i-tive: questioning, curious
My children are all *inquisitive* about most things.

insane
adj in-sane: crazy
He was judged to be *insane* and was sent to a hospital.

insight
n in-sight: understanding, intuition
He had an *insight* into their problem and offered a solution.

insignia
n in-sig-nia: badge, emblem
He wore his captain's *insignia* on his hat.

insinuate
v in-sin-u-ate: to hint at
She tried to *insinuate* that she had gone to the same party.

insipid
adj in-sip-id: tasteless
It looks good but has an *insipid* flavor.

insolent
adj in-so-lent: rude, insulting
He was continually *insolent* to his teacher.

insolvent
adj in-sol-vent: bankrupt
They cannot pay the rent in their *insolvent* state.

install
v in-stall: to establish, put in
I will *install* the sink myself.

instigate
v in-sti-gate: to stir up
> She continued to *instigate* problems in the meeting.

instinct
n in-stinct: a natural tendency
> Birds fly south because of age-old *instincts.*

institute
v in-sti-tute: to start, establish
> He *instituted* a new plan to make the work flow faster.

institute
n in-sti-tute: professional organization or place
> He was elected to be head of the *institute.*

insurgent
adj in-sur-gent: rebel
> The *insurgent* troops came to the island by boat.

intact
adj in-tact: untouched, uninjured
> The train was surprisingly *intact* after the crash.

intangible
adj in-tan-gi-ble: vague
> He continues to make *intangible* demands.

integral
adj in-te-gral: important, necessary
> That cog is *integral* to the operation of the motor.

integrity
n in-teg-ri-ty: honesty
> His *integrity* could not be questioned.

intent
n in-tent: purpose
> It is my *intent* to complete the manuscript by tonight.

intent
adj in-tent: firmly directed, earnest
> His *intent* efforts quickly completed the job.

inter
v in-ter: to bury
> She was *interred* in the local cemetery.

interim
n in-ter-im: intervening time, temporary
> In the *interim* while the film is being shown, let's take a walk.

interject
v in-ter-ject: to insert
> I wish to *interject* my thoughts on that matter.

intermittent
adj in-ter-mit-tent: recurrent
> An *intermittent* siren sounded from the firehouse.

interpret
v in-ter-pret: to translate, explain
> I am able to *interpret* these diagrams so they make sense.

interrogate
v in-ter-ro-gate: to question
> The prisoner was *interrogated* for three hours.

intervene
v in-ter-vene: to come between
 I had to *intervene* to stop the
 fight.

intimate
adj in-ti-mate: familiar, personal
 He is an *intimate* friend
 of mine.

intimate
v in-ti-mate: to suggest, hint at
 She *intimated* that she knew
 the secret already.

intimidate
v in-tim-i-date: to frighten
 He tried to *intimidate* the
 smaller children.

intolerable
adj in-tol-er-able: unbearable
 The heat was *intolerable.*

intoxicate
v in-tox-i-cate: to make drunk
 He was *intoxicated* after two
 drinks.

intrepid
adj in-trep-id: fearless, bold
 The *intrepid* leader of the
 troop marched into the
 combat zone.

intricate
adj in-tri-cate: complicated
 It was a very *intricate*
 mathematics problem.

intrigue
n in-trigue: secret plot
 They were caught up in
 political *intrigue.*

intrigue
v in-trigue: to arouse the
interest of
 He was *intrigued* by her
 invitation to the dance.

invert
v in-vert: reverse, turn upside
down
 He *inverted* the box over
 the frog.

invincible
adj in-vin-ci-ble: unbeatable
 The athlete was *invincible* at
 his own sport.

iota
n i-o-ta: tiny quantity
 I won't give you one *iota* of
 this money.

irate
adj i-rate: angry
 The *irate* customer
 demanded his money back.

ire
n ire: anger
 I think you are unreasonable
 in your *ire.*

irk
v irk: to annoy
 His habits always *irk* me.

irrigate
v ir-ri-gate: supply water
 It is necessary to *irrigate*
 the desert before those trees
 will grow.

irritable
adj ir-ri-ta-ble: touchy
 He was in a very *irritable*
 mood.

isolate
v i-so-late: to place apart, separate
> He *isolated* the sick child from the others.

isthmus
n isth-mus: connecting strip of land
> Thousands of years ago, Alaska and Russia were connected by an *isthmus*.

iterate
v it-er-ate: to repeat
> He continued to *iterate* his story to the jury.

itinerant
adj i-tin-er-ant: traveling
> The *itinerant* salesman came to town again.

J

jab
v jab: to poke
> He continued to *jab* her in the back with his pencil.

jab
n jab: a quick thrust or blow, a punch
> The boxer had a strong left *jab*.

jackal
n jack-al: African wild dog
> The remains of the kill were finished off by the *jackals*.

jaded
v jaded: dulled by excess
> He was *jaded* by too much money.

jaunt
n jaunt: short pleasure trip
> I just came back from a European *jaunt*.

jaunty
adj jaun-ty: happy, carefree
> He walked with a *jaunty* step as he approached his girlfriend.

javelin
n jav-e-lin: spear
> He was the winner of the *javelin* throw.

jealous
adj jeal-ous: envious
> She was *jealous* of her sister's new clothes.

jeer
v jeer: to make fun of, mock
> The clown *jeered* at the crowd.

jeer
n jeer: a jeering remark
> The reporter's *jeer* about the man upset him.

jeopardy
n jeop-ar-dy: danger
> He was in constant *jeopardy* on the mountain climb.

jest
n jest: a joke
> He was not in the mood to be amused by her *jest*.

jest
v jest: to joke, leer, banter
> They continued to *jest* throughout the dinner.

jester

n jest-er: a joker

He was a perpetual *jester*, never serious for a moment.

jettison

v jet-ti-son: to throw overboard

They *jettisoned* the luggage to lighten the load.

jibe

v jibe: to agree with

His story *jibes* with yours.

jinx

n jinx: bad luck

She felt that her knife was a *jinx*, so she threw it away.

jocular

adj joc-u-lar: funny, humorous

He was a *jocular* old man, loved by everyone.

jostle

v jos-tle: to shove, push

She was *jostled* about in the train.

jovial

adj jo-vi-al: merry, jolly

In his *jovial* way, the old man entertained the children.

jowl

n jowl: jaw, cheek

The wolf dug his claws into the rabbit's *jowl*.

jubilant

adj ju-bi-lant: rejoicing, happy

He was *jubilant* after winning the race.

judicious

adj ju-di-cious: wise, well thought out

You made a *judicious* decision.

junction

n junc-tion: place where things join

There was a leak at the *junction* of the two pipes.

junket

n jun-ket: long trip, journey

They just returned from a European *junket*.

junta

n jun-ta: group controlling government

The *junta* was now in charge of everything.

jury

n ju-ry: a committee, appointed group

The *jury* voted him the first prize in the art contest.

justify

v jus-ti-fy: to defend, prove to be right

I am able to *justify* my position on that matter.

jut

v jut: to stick out

That tree *juts* out onto the sidewalk.

jut

n jut: a part that juts

The *jut* in the road is causing traffic to reroute around it.

juvenile
adj ju-ve-nile: young
    It was a *juvenile* story.

juvenile
n ju-ve-nile: a young person
    He was considered a *juvenile*
    by the authorities.

K

keen
adj keen: shrewd
    He had a *keen* mind and
    grasped ideas quickly.

keg
n keg: barrel, small cask
    He brought a beer *keg*
    upstairs from the basement.

kelp
n kelp: seaweed
    In Japan, *kelp* is a basic part
    of the diet.

kettle
n ket-tle: pot
    She put the tea *kettle* on
    the stove.

kin
n kin: family, close relatives
    My closest *kin* live in
    Wisconsin.

kink
n kink: twist, curl
    You will not be able to use
    that wire with the *kink* in it.

kink
v kink: to form or cause to form
    Be careful not to *kink* the
    antenna out of shape.

kleptomania
n klep-to-ma-ni-a: impulse
to steal
    They were concerned about
    their child's *kleptomania*.

knack
n knack: ability, aptitude, skill
    He had a *knack* for getting
    out of trouble.

knapsack
n knap-sack: a backpack
    She threw the *knapsack* across
    her back and marched away.

knave
n knave: dishonest individual
    He was a coward and a *knave*.

knead
v knead: to mix, stir
    It's important to *knead* the
    clay to get out air bubbles.

knell
n knell: ringing of a bell
    The happy *knell* was heard
    throughout the city.

knoll
n knoll: small hill
    It will be safe to let the
    children climb up the *knoll*.

L

labyrinth
n lab-y-rinth: a maze
    They were quickly lost in the
    dark *labyrinth*.

lacerate
v lac-er-ate: tear roughly, mangle
    The clothing was *lacerated* by
    the machine.

lackadaisical
adj lack-a-dai-si-cal: listless
    He was *lackadaisical* about
    finishing the job.

lackey
n lack-ey: a servant
    He was treated like a *lackey*,
    so he quit the job.

laconic
adj la-con-ic: terse, brief
    The *laconic* statement was
    right to the point.

lacquer
n lac-quer: varnish
    He applied the *lacquer* over
    the old surface.

laden
adj lad-en: loaded
    The mules were *laden* with
    supplies for the trip.

lagoon
n la-goon: a shallow pond
    They went swimming in the
    nearby *lagoon*.

lair
n lair: den, resting place
    The animals were safe in
    their *lair*.

lament
v la-ment: to mourn
    I need time to *lament* the loss
    of my mother.

lament
n la-ment: a crying out of grief
    She could hear his sad *lament*
    in the other room.

lampoon
n lam-poon: satire
    The newspaper published a
    lampoon about the party.

lampoon
v lam-poon: to attack in a
lampoon
    The host *lampooned* the guest
    of honor in a witty speech.

lance
n lance: a spear
    The warriors carried *lances* to
    protect themselves.

lance
v lance: to pierce, cut
    The doctor *lanced* the infection.

lanquish
v lan-guish: to weaken
    He continued to *languish* as
    he lay in his bed.

languor
n lan-guor: weakness,
indifference
    Because of his *languor*, no one
    wanted him on the team.

lanky
adj lanky: tall and thin
    The basketball player was
    lanky, and nothing fit him.

lapse
v lapse: to slip
    He *lapsed* into his old speech
    pattern for a moment.

lapse
n lapse: a slight error
    A momentary *lapse* caused
    the accident.

larceny
n lar-ceny: theft
> He committed *larceny* when he stole the car.

lard
n lard: fat
> They saved the bacon *lard* to make candles.

lard
v lard: to insert fat strips into meat before cooking
> The chef *larded* the roast before he put it into the oven.

lariat
n lar-i-at: lasso, rope
> The cowboy threw his *lariat* over the cow's head.

larva
n lar-va: insect egg
> The mosquito left its *larva* on a leaf.

latch
n latch: fastener
> Be sure to hook the *latch* on the door before you leave.

latch
v latch: to fasten with a latch
> *Latch* the windows tightly against the rain.

latent
adj la-tent: hidden
> Psychologists look for *latent* meanings behind what you say.

lather
n lath-er: foam
> He applied the *lather* to his face before shaving.

laud
v laud: to praise
> I must *laud* your recent performance in the play.

laurel
n lau-rel: wreath, praise, award
> He received the *laurels* for winning the race.

lava
n la-va: molten rock
> The *lava* poured from the mouth of the volcano.

lavish
adj lav-ish: abundant
> It was a *lavish* wedding with all of the trimmings.

lavish
v lav-ish: to give or spend abundantly
> He continued to *lavish* gifts upon his girlfriend.

lax
adj lax: loose, without discipline
> His *lax* control annoyed his employees.

lease
n lease: rental contract
> She signed a new *lease* for her apartment.

lease
v lease: to rent
> She was able to *lease* a car for a week.

lecherous
adj lech-er-ous: lewd, lustful
> His *lecherous* remarks made him unwelcome at the party.

lecture

n lec-ture: a speech

They sat through his entire *lecture* without taking notes.

lecture

v lec-ture: to give a speech to

If you continue to *lecture* me, I will leave.

ledge

n ledge: shelf

I put the vase on the upper *ledge.*

ledger

n ledg-er: account book

The *ledger* contained all of their financial records.

leer

n leer: suggestive glance

He stood on the corner with a *leer* on his face.

legible

adj leg-i-ble: easily read

Her handwriting was extremely *legible.*

legion

n le-gion: soldiers, army

The Roman *legion* came down from the hills.

legitimate

adj le-git-i-mate: lawful

He was the *legitimate* grandson of King Edward.

legume

n leg-ume: vegetable

The garden was filled with *legumes* and fruits.

leniency

n le-ni-en-cy: mildness, mercy

Since this was her first offense, her lawyer asked the judge for *leniency.*

leonine

adj le-o-nine: lionlike

His hair was a *leonine* mane, golden and shaggy.

lesion

n le-sion: injury, hurt, sore

He had a *lesion* on his arm that had to be treated.

lethal

adj le-thal: deadly

They gave the wolf a *lethal* dose of poison.

lethargic

adj leth-ar-gic: sluggish

After the operation, he was very *lethargic.*

lever

n lev-er: tool for prying or lifting

He used the *lever* to open the crate.

levitate

v lev-i-tate: to rise and float in air

The magician made her *levitate,* much to the pleasure of the crowd.

levity

n lev-i-ty: frivolity, lack of seriousness

His *levity* was out of place at the funeral.

levy
v lev-y: to impose upon (tax, fine, etc.)

  The government *levied* high taxes on its citizens.

lewd
adj lewd: not decent

  You will not be allowed in the restaurant in that *lewd* attire.

lexicon
n lex-i-con: dictionary

  This *lexicon* will help you understand how to spell words.

liability
n li-a-bil-i-ty: debt, something disadvantageous

  His financial *liabilities* were more than he could pay.

liaison
n li-ai-son: connection, contact between groups

  She was the *liaison* between the White and Red teams.

liberate
v lib-er-ate: to set free

  They were able to *liberate* the prisoners from the enemy troops.

limber
adj lim-ber: flexible

  Exercise kept her *limber*.

limber
v lim-ber: to make loose, flexible

  They began to *limber* up in exercise class.

limerick
n lim-er-ick: short poem, usually five lines

  The children wrote a humorous *limerick* in class.

limp
adj limp: without rigidity

  The *limp* piece of celery sat uneaten on his plate.

limp
v limp: to walk with a lame leg

  He was able to *limp* across the room.

limp
n limp: a halt or lameness in walking

  He walked with a noticeable *limp*.

linger
v lin-ger: to remain, stay on

  He *lingered* long after the game was over.

listless
adj list-less: tired, without energy

  The hot, *listless* people sat around all day.

lithe
adj lithe: supple, easily bent

  The gymnast had a *lithe* body.

litigation
n lit-i-ga-tion: lawsuit

  The *litigation* will be presented in court.

loam
n loam: fertile soil

  He had no trouble growing the flowers because of the *loam*.

loathe

v loathe: to hate

Children seem to *loathe* vegetables.

locust

n lo-cust: migratory grasshopper

The *locusts* descended upon the area, darkening the sky.

lodestone

n lode-stone: magnet

Columbus used a *lodestone* to navigate.

lofty

adj loft-y: high, proud

He had very *lofty* ideals and thought himself better than others.

logic

n log-ic: science of reasoning

He used *logic* to make a wise decision.

loiter

v loi-ter: linger, hang around

The boys were *loitering* on the corner all evening.

loot

n loot: stolen goods, spoils, plunder

They divided the *loot* among the three of them.

loot

v loot: to plunder or steal

They were arrested for *looting* the bank.

lope

v lope: to run

The dog *loped* across the field.

loquacious

adj lo-qua-cious: extremely talkative

Once he had a few drinks, he became *loquacious*.

lubricate

adj lub-ri-cate: make smooth with grease or oil

He *lubricated* the chain to make the bike go faster.

lucid

adj lu-cid: clear

It was a *lucid* explanation, and I understood everything.

lucrative

adj lu-cra-tive: profitable

His scheme proved to be very *lucrative*.

ludicrous

adj lu-di-crous: ridiculous

That's a *ludicrous* statement.

lugubrious

adj lu-gu-bri-ous: sad, dismal

He wore a *lugubrious* look on his face.

lull

v lull: to calm, quiet

Lull the baby to sleep with soft music.

lull

n lull: a short period of calm

The *lull* between the storms did not last long enough to dry the ground.

luminous
adj lu-mi-nous: bright, shining
I can read the sign in the *luminous* reflection of the sunlight.

lunacy
n lu-na-cy: insanity, craziness
That plan was absolute *lunacy*.

lunar
adj lu-nar: related to the moon
Last night we saw the *lunar* eclipse.

lupine
adj lu-pine: like a wolf
His *lupine* movements amazed his audience.

lurch
v lurch: to move suddenly
The train *lurched* forward.

lurch
n lurch: a difficult situation
She left him in the *lurch*, without any reason.

lure
v lure: attract
He used low prices to *lure* people into his store.

lurid
adj lu-rid: sensational, startling
Newspaper headlines announced the *lurid* story.

lurk
v lurk: to stay out of sight
The man *lurked* in the bushes.

luscious
adj lus-cious: delicious
She was overwhelmed by the *luscious* desserts.

lush
adj lush: covered with abundant growth
The *lush* forest housed many different animals and birds.

lush
n lush: a heavy drinker
He was the neighborhood *lush*.

lust
n lust: strong desire, often sexual
He could not control his *lust* for her.

lustrous
adj lus-trous: shining
Your hair is always *lustrous* after a shampoo.

lynx
n lynx: wildcat
The *lynx* was surrounded by the dogs.

lyre
n lyre: harp-like instrument
Classical music sometimes uses a *lyre* to add beautiful tones.

M

macabre
adj ma-ca-bre: gruesome
　The end of the movie was *macabre* and depressing.

maelstrom
n mael-strom: whirlpool
　The boat was caught in the unexpected *maelstrom*.

maestro
n mae-stro: conductor
　The *maestro* strode to the podium and raised his baton.

magistrate
n mag-is-trate: government official, judge
　They appeared before the *magistrate* to ask for more time.

magnanimous
adj mag-nan-i-mous: generous
　She was always *magnanimous* during holiday season.

magnify
v mag-ni-fy: to enlarge
　He tried to *magnify* his position in the firm to her, but she knew the truth.

magnitude
n mag-ni-tude: size
　The *magnitude* of your gift is overwhelming.

maim
v maim: to cripple
　He was almost *maimed* when the pipe fell on him.

maintain
v main-tain: to keep, carry on
　I want to *maintain* control of the company.

maize
n maize: corn
　Maize grew in the field.

maize
adj maize: yellow
　That blouse is a very pretty *maize* color.

majestically
adv ma-jes-ti-cal-ly: with grandeur or nobility
　The trees stood *majestically* along the roads.

maladroit
adj mal-a-droit: clumsy
　His *maladroit* actions always got him into trouble.

malady
n mal-a-dy: illness
　She had a strange *malady*, and they couldn't discover a cure.

malediction
n mal-e-dic-tion: a curse, oath
　He cast a *malediction* upon his own family.

malicious
adj ma-li-cious: show bad feelings, ill will
　It was a *malicious* action, totally uncalled for.

malign
v ma-lign: to slander
　You *maligned* him for no reason.

malignant

adj ma-lig-nant: evil, life-endangering disease

They found a *malignant* tumor when they operated on him.

mall

n mall: promenade, public walk

She met him for lunch at the new shopping *mall*.

mallard

n mal-lard: wild duck

A flock of *mallards* flew overhead.

malleable

adj mal-le-a-ble: adaptable

The artist was able to use gold because it was so *malleable*.

mallet

n mal-let: hammer

He used a wooden *mallet* to tap the shelf into place.

mammoth

adj mam-moth: huge, gigantic

A *mammoth* wave overturned the boats.

mammoth

n mam-moth: extinct elephant with long tusks

They found the remains of a *mammoth* in the tar pits.

manacle

n man-a-cle: handcuff

The *manacles* bit into his wrists.

manacle

v man-a-cle: to put on handcuffs

The policeman *manacled* the prisoner's hands behind his back.

mandate

n man-date: command, an order

She was given a *mandate* to change the entire office staff.

mandible

n man-di-ble: jaw

The doctor had to operate on her lower *mandible*.

mangle

v man-gle: to cut or tear roughly

The book was *mangled* by the broken machine.

mania

n ma-ni-a: insanity, extreme enthusiasm

He had a *mania* for French wines.

manipulate

v ma-nip-u-late: to operate skillfully

He was able to *manipulate* the pliers with ease.

manor

n man-or: estate

He was the lord of the *manor*.

mansion

n man-sion: regal residence

They lived in a *mansion*, surrounded by trees and streams.

manual
adj man-u-al: accomplished
by hand
  He enjoyed *manual* labor.

manual
n man-u-al: a book of
instructions
  He fixed the car, following
  the *manual* carefully.

manure
n ma-nure: fertilizer
  The lawn was covered with
  manure.

mar
v mar: to spoil, damage
  The wet glass *marred* the oak
  tabletop.

maraud
v ma-raud: to raid, plunder
  The jackals began to *maraud*
  through the hunter's camp.

margin
n mar-gin: the border, edge
  She wrote in the *margin* of
  her notebook.

marina
n ma-ri-na: dock, wharf
  He brought his boat into the
  marina for refueling.

marinate
v mar-i-nate: to soak
  The meat was *marinated* in
  the sauce to make it tender.

marionette
n mar-i-o-nette: puppet
  The *marionette* danced on its
  strings.

maroon
v ma-roon: to leave abandoned
  He was *marooned* on the
  island for a week.

maroon
adj ma-roon: dark brownish red
  He wore a *maroon* formal
  jacket.

marsh
n marsh: swamp
  He caught frogs in the *marsh*.

marsupial
n mar-su-pi-al: a mammal with
an external pouch
  Marsupials can be seen
  running free in Australia.

marsupial
adj mar-su-pi-al: having
characteristics of marsupials
  This building housed all the
  marsupial animals.

martial
adj mar-tial: military
  They were inspired by the
  martial music.

masonry
n ma-son-ry: brickwork
  He admired the *masonry*
  around the border of the
  house.

masquerade
v mas-quer-ade: to disguise,
dress up, pretend
  He tried to *masquerade* as a
  doctor.

masquerade

n mas-quer-ade: a costume party

She went to the *masquerade* dressed as a chef.

massacre

n mas-sa-cre: wholesale killing, without mercy

Custer's Last Stand is an infamous *massacre*.

massacre

v mas-sa-cre: slaughter

The buffalo were *massacred* by the hunters.

massive

adj mas-sive: bulky, large

It was a *massive* box, big enough for an elephant.

masticate

v mas-ti-cate: to chew

Please *masticate* the food thoroughly before swallowing.

matador

n mat-a-dor: bullfighter

The *matador* entered the ring to wild cheers.

maternal

adj ma-ter-nal: motherly

She showed her *maternal* feelings for the kitten.

mature

adj mature: fully grown

The apples were not yet *mature, so* we couldn't pick them.

mature

v ma-ture: to reach full development

She began to *mature* before her older brother.

mausoleum

n mau-so-le-um: tomb

They found the *mausoleum* of the ancient Egyptian king.

maxim

n max-im: proverb

My favorite *maxim* is "Do unto others."

meager

adj mea-ger: scanty

They ate a *meager* meal of cereal and water.

meander

v me-an-der: to wander without purpose

They *meandered* slowly through the department store.

meddle

v med-dle: interfere

Why do you *meddle* in everyone's business?

mediocre

adj me-di-o-cre: average, ordinary

Although he is not the quickest worker, his work is certainly not *mediocre*.

meditate

v med-i-tate: to think, contemplate

She wished to *meditate* on the problem for a while.

medium
adj me-di-um: middle, moderate
   He liked his steak done
   medium rare.

meek
adj meek: mild-mannered,
patient
   He was much too *meek* to
   become a salesman.

megaphone
n meg-a-phone: funnel-shaped
horn for amplification
   The cheerleaders shouted
   to the crowd through their
   megaphones.

melancholy
n mel-an-choly: depression,
gloom
   He had sunk into a deep
   melancholy, and only his
   daughter could bring him
   out of it.

melee
n me-lee: a wild, confused fight
   The passersby were drawn
   into the *melee* without
   warning.

mellow
adj mel-low: soft, calm
   He was in a *mellow* mood.

melodius
adj mel-o-di-us: sweet sounding
   My daughter has a *melodius*
   singing voice.

memento
n me-men-to: reminder, usually
an object
   He bought a drawing of the
   village as a *memento* of his visit.

menace
n men-ace: danger, threat
   Wild animals can be a *menace*
   to the neighborhood.

menace
v men-ace: to threaten
   Those dark clouds are
   menacing the picnickers.

mend
v mend: to repair, fix
   She was not able to *mend* the
   torn dress herself.

mendacious
adj men-da-cious: lying, untrue
   It is a *mendacious* story.

mendicant
n men-di-cant: beggar
   The ragged *mendicant* came
   to our back door.

menial
adj me-ni-al: degrading, low
   He felt he was working in a
   menial job.

mentor
n men-tor: teacher
   He was my *mentor* in
   business.

mercenary
n mer-ce-nary: hired soldier
   The *mercenary* went to fight
   in Africa.

mercenary
adj mer-ce-nary: done for
money only
   She was extremely *mercenary*
   and cared nothing for the
   people, only the money.

merchandise
n mer-chan-dise: goods for sale
   Let's see what *merchandise* that store supplies.

merchandise
v mer-chan-dise: to buy or sell
   Merchandise your pictures at the art fair.

merge
v merge: to combine
   Two roads *merged* at the top of the hill.

merit
v mer-it: to deserve
   I don't think he *merits* a raise in pay.

merit
n mer-it: worth, value
   I can better judge the *merit* of that film after seeing it again.

mesa
n me-sa: plateau
   In New Mexico, the highway runs between the *mesas*.

metamorphosis
n met-a-mor-pho-sis: change of form
   The *metamorphosis* of a caterpillar into a butterfly is interesting to watch.

metropolis
n me-trop-o-lis: large city
   New York is a major *metropolis* in the East.

microbe
n mi-crobe: bacteria
   They traced the illness to an airborne *microbe*.

midget
adj midg-et: miniature
   He raced *midget* cars around the track.

migrate
v mi-grate: to wander, travel
   Every year the birds *migrate* south.

militant
adj mil-i-tant: aggressive, fighting
   A *militant* group of citizens gathered outside.

millennium
n mil-len-ni-um: one thousand years
   After the first *millennium*, life on earth began to develop.

mimic
v mim-ic: to ape, imitate
   She was able to *mimic* everything her mother did.

miniature
adj min-i-a-ture: small, tiny
   It was a *miniature* music box set into a watch.

miniature
n min-i-a-ture: small painting or portrait
   He was renowned for his *miniatures* of noblemen.

minimal
adj min-i-mal: least possible
   Finish the work with *minimal* effort.

minion
n min-ion: servant
   He was surrounded by his *minions*.

minstrel
n min-strel: poet or musician

The *minstrel* strolled through the garden.

mirage
n mi-rage: an illusion

In the desert, the heat causes you to see *mirages* of waterholes.

mire
n mire: soft, deep mud

The car was stuck in the *mire* in the meadow.

mire
v mire: to cause to get stuck

The wheels were *mired* in the mud.

mirth
n mirth: laughter, fun

He could hear the shouts of *mirth* coming from the room.

misanthrope
n mis-an-thrope: hater of mankind

The town *misanthrope* lived alone on top of the hill.

mischievous
adj mis-chie-vous: naughty

The kids were *mischievous* but rarely were caught.

misdemeanor
n mis-de-mean-or: small crime

Because his offense was considered a *misdemeanor,* the judge let him go with just a warning.

miser
n mi-ser: one who hoards money

He was a *miser,* and none of his children liked him.

mitigate
v mit-i-gate: to lessen, soften

He tried to *mitigate* the blows from his father.

mobile
adj mo-bile: able to be moved

They rented a *mobile* home for the summer.

mobile
n mo-bile: sculptor's movable construction

Alexander Calder created famous *mobiles;* many of them hang in museums.

mock
v mock: to laugh at, make fun of

He could only *mock* her appearance.

mock
adj mock: false, imitation

The vegetarians serve *mock* hamburgers, actually made from vegetables.

modest
adj mod-est: shy, bashful

She was extremely *modest* and didn't speak to many people.

modify
v mod-i-fy: to change

I want to *modify* your computer to make it faster.

mogul
n mo-gul: important executive
　He was the image of the
　cigar-smoking movie *mogul*.

molar
n mo-lar: a tooth
　The dentist removed a loose
　molar from the boy's mouth.

molest
v mo-lest: to annoy, bother
　The man *molested* his
　co-workers.

mollify
v mol-li-fy: to appease, soften
　I tried to *mollify* him, but he
　was still angry.

molt
v molt: to shed feathers
　Birds *molt* at the end of the
　cold season.

momentous
adj mo-men-tous: very
important
　The promotion was a
　momentous occasion for her.

monarch
n mon-arch: ruler
　He was the supreme *monarch*
　of all the countries.

mongrel
n mon-grel: an animal or plant
of mixed breed
　The dog was cute, but he was
　only a *mongrel*.

monopoly
n mo-nop-o-ly: total control
　Their family had the local
　monopoly on vegetables.

monstrous
adj mon-strous: enormous
　The balloon was *monstrous*
　and held twenty people.

moratorium
n mor-a-to-ri-um: legal delay
　The crowd called for a
　moratorium in the arms race.

morbid
adj mor-bid: unhealthy, diseased
　He had a *morbid* fear of
　insects.

mores
n mo-res: customs, rules
　It's important to follow the
　local *mores* in order to fit in.

morose
adj mo-rose: gloomy
　After dinner, John grew
　morose and refused to talk.

morsel
n mor-sel: small piece, fragment
　There was only a *morsel* of
　food left on her plate.

mortician
n mor-ti-cian: undertaker
　The *mortician* was able to
　preserve the corpse for the
　police.

mortified
v mor-ti-fied: ashamed,
embarrassed
　I am *mortified* by my error.

motto
n mot-to: slogan
　"The buck stops here" was
　President Truman's *motto*.

mucilage
n mu-ci-lage: glue
  The teacher attached the
  poster with *mucilage*.

muddle
v mud-dle: to confuse, mix up,
struggle with
  He continued to *muddle*
  through the test.

muddle
n mud-dle: a mess, confusion
  They were caught in the
  middle of the *muddle*.

muffle
v muf-fle: to cover up; wrap
warmly
  He was able to *muffle* the
  sounds by closing the door.

multitude
n mul-ti-tude: crowd
  His speech was attended by
  a *multitude* of friends.

mum
adj mum: silent, without speech
  I will keep *mum* on the subject
  of your brother.

mum
n mum: a chrysanthemum
  He brought her a bouquet
  of *mums*.

mundane
adj mun-dane: worldly, common
  Although he was a
  philosopher; his ideas
  were very *mundane*.

murky
adj murk-y: dark, cloudy,
gloomy
  The cave was damp and
  murky, and we couldn't see.

murmur
v mur-mur: to speak quietly
  He tried to *murmur* in her ear
  during the party.

murmur
n mur-mur: a low, continuous
sound
  The *murmur* of voices spread
  quickly through the room.

muster
v mus-ter: to gather together
  He tried to *muster* all of the
  horses.

muster
n mus-ter: an assembling
  He called the men to *muster*
  in order to conduct an
  inspection.

mute
adj mute: quiet, silent
  The *mute* man learned sign
  language.

mute
v mute: to soften
  She tried to *mute* the noise
  with a pillow.

mutiny
n mu-ti-ny: rebellion
  The captain of the ship was
  overthrown by a *mutiny* of
  his sailors.

mutiny
v mu-ti-ny: to revolt
　　The unhappy workers decided to *mutiny* against the boss.

myopic
adj my-op-ic: near-sighted
　　She was extremely *myopic* and unable to see the screen.

myriad
adj myr-i-ad: countless
　　He went through *myriad* nights without sleep.

myth
n myth: legend, tale
　　I think that story is only a *myth* and not to be believed.

N

nadir
n na-dir: lowest point
　　When he lost his job, he had reached the *nadir* of his career.

nag
v nag: to irritate, annoy
　　Her mother *nagged* her to clean up her room.

nag
n nag: the act of nagging; an inferior horse
　　Don't be such a *nag*.
　　The old *nag* finished last.

narrate
v nar-rate: to tell, relate
　　She *narrated* the incident as she remembered it.

narrative
adj nar-ra-tive: telling a story
　　His *narrative* speech delighted the audience.

narrative
n nar-ra-tive: story form
　　Present your experience in a *narrative*.

nasal
adj na-sal: pertaining to the nose
　　This *nasal* medicine may help clear up your breathing.

natal
adj na-tal: birth
　　Come view the newborn infants in the *natal* department of the hospital.

naught
n naught: nothing
　　Her efforts were for *naught* because no one appreciated her work.

nausea
n nau-se-a: seasickness
　　A constant feeling of *nausea* spoiled her fun on the cruise.

nebulous
adj neb-u-lous: cloudy, hazy, vague
　　It was a *nebulous* gesture and meant very little to anybody.

needy
adj need-y: poor
　　The church is accepting donations for the *needy* survivors of the flood.

nefarious
adj ne-far-i-ous: very wicked
Many people dislike him because of his *nefarious* reputation.

neglectful
adj ne-glect-ful: careless
Because of his *neglectful* use of the radio, it was ruined.

negligent
adj neg-li-gent: careless
They won't entrust their boat to you if you treat it in a *negligent* manner.

negotiate
v ne-go-ti-ate: arrange terms
They *negotiated* the contract between the teams.

neigh
v neigh: to utter the characteristic cry of a horse
The horses *neighed* to their master from the barn.

nestle
v nes-tle: settle
The cat *nestled* in the blanket.

neurotic
n neu-rot-ic: emotionally unstable
Too many accidents have made her *neurotic* about driving.

neutral
adj neu-tral: impartial, fair
The judge listened to the appeals with a *neutral* mind.

neutral
n neu-tral: an impartial person or nation
A *neutral* will decide which of us is right.

nicety
n ni-ce-ty: accuracy
He is a reliable accountant because of his *nicety* with figures.

niche
n niche: a recess in a wall; a small, special market segment
The cat hid in a *niche*.

nigh
adv nigh: almost
The report is *nigh* finished.

nil
n nil: nothing
All their efforts were for *nil*.

nimble
adj nim-ble: active; agile
It took the efforts of two teachers to keep up with the *nimble* children.

nocturnal
adj noc-tur-nal: of the night
His *nocturnal* wanderings through the woods go undetected by his neighbors.

nomad
n no-mad: wanderer
The *nomad* was seen in every state.

nominate
v nom-i-nate: to designate
She will surely be *nominated* for the chairperson's position.

nonchalant
adj non-cha-lant: unconcerned
> We assumed you did not like the movie because of your *nonchalant* manner.

norm
n norm: standard
> The *norm* in our neighborhood is for everyone to display a flag on July fourth.

nostalgia
n nos-tal-gia: homesickness
> Her *nostalgia* for her family was strengthened after seeing their photographs.

notarize
v no-ta-rize: certify
> You must certify the sale of your house by having the papers *notarized*.

notorious
adj no-to-ri-ous: well known
> Jesse James was a *notorious* bandit out west.

nourish
v nour-ish: to make grow
> *Nourish* the flowers now so that they will bloom in the spring.

novel
adj nov-el: new
> Only the professor thinks of such *novel* ideas.

novel
n nov-el: a relatively long fictional prose narrative
> After receiving praise for his poems, the writer started work on a *novel*.

novice
n no-vice: beginner
> Although she is a *novice*, she swims very well.

nuisance
n nui-sance: annoyance
> All that traffic noise is a *nuisance* while I am trying to study.

nullify
v nul-li-fy: to make void, to cancel
> They *nullified* their vacation plans after the travel rates went up again.

numbness
n numb-ness: loss of feeling
> That bandage was wrapped so tightly that it left a *numbness* in his arm.

numismatics
n nu-mis-mat-ics: study of coins
> *Numismatics* is an interesting and profitable hobby.

O

obdurate
adj ob-du-rate: stubborn
> They won't be able to settle anything if they both stay as *obdurate* as they've been.

obese
adj o-bese: very fat
> If you keep eating that way, you will soon be *obese*.

obituary
n o-bit-u-ar-y: notice of death
   The *obituary* in the newspaper announced the demise of the editor.

objective
n ob-jec-tive: aim, goal
   The painter's *objective* is to see his art on display in the museum.

oblige
v o-blige: compel, force
   She was *obliged* to attend the meeting.

oblique
adj ob-lique: slanting
   Don't place any heavy objects against the *oblique* side of that building.

obliterate
v ob-lit-er-ate: to destroy, blot out
   The tornado *obliterated* the downtown district.

obnoxious
adj ob-nox-ious: disagreeable
   Nobody wanted to be around the *obnoxious* man.

obscene
adj ob-scene: indecent, impure
   Such *obscene* language is not allowed here.

obscure
adj ob-scure: not clear, dim
   Your statements seem too *obscure* this early in the morning.

obscure
v ob-scure: to conceal
   The fog *obscured* our view of the gardens.

obsess
v ob-sess: fill the mind, haunt
   She is *obsessed* by constant thoughts of food.

obsolete
adj ob-so-lete: no longer in use
   He had difficulty finding parts for his *obsolete* lawnmower.

obstacle
n ob-sta-cle: hindrance
   Please remove that *obstacle* from our path so that we may continue.

obstinate
adj ob-sti-nate: stubborn
   She refused to budge from her *obstinate* opinion.

obstreperous
adj ob-strep-er-ous: noisy, boisterous
   That class is particularly *obstreperous*.

obstruction
n ob-struc-tion: obstacle
   An *obstruction* in the plans will delay completion of the project.

obtuse
adj ob-tuse: blunt, not sharp
   He did not understand because of his *obtuse* wit.

occult
adj oc-cult: mysterious, magical
His *occult* attitude made us suspicious.

ocular
adj oc-u-lar: of the eye
Keep those tools away from the *ocular* region.

odious
adj o-di-ous: very displeasing
An *odious* sound emitted from the cellar.

odor
n o-dor: scent, smell
The *odor* of food cooking filled the building.

offal
n of-fal: garbage, refuse
Place any *offal* in the containers around the corner.

offensive
adj of-fen-sive: on the attack
His *offensive* behavior annoyed the guests.

offensive
n of-fen-sive: attitude, position, or operation of attack
It was a famous military *offensive*.

ogre
n o-gre: monster
The child was afraid an *ogre* would appear in her room in the night.

olfactory
adj ol-fac-to-ry: of smell
An animal's *olfactory* senses are more developed than a human's.

ominous
adj om-i-nous: acting as an omen
The sudden cold weather created an *ominous* sign of winter ahead.

omniscient
adj om-nis-cient: all-knowing
His *omniscient* gaze made the children fear that he was aware of what they had done.

omnivorous
adj om-niv-o-rous: eating both animal and vegetable matter
We are *omnivorous* animals.

onerous
adj on-er-ous: burdensome
Everyone avoids those kinds of *onerous* tasks.

onset
n on-set: attack
An *onset* of poison ivy covered his body after he fell in the bushes.

onus
n o-nus: responsibility
The *onus* is on the caretaker to keep the land in good condition.

ooze
v ooze: slow flow
Ketchup *oozed* out of the crack in the bottle.

opaque
adj o-paque: not transparent
They painted the walls in a
dark, *opaque* color.

opiate
n o-pi-ate: narcotic
An *opiate* was given to the
patient to dull his pain.

opponent
n op-po-nent: adversary
The officer and his *opponent*
argued their views.

oppress
v op-press: govern harshly
He *oppressed* his nation with
his rigid rules.

optical
adj op-ti-cal: of the eyes, visual
His *optical* senses were
strengthened when his
hearing weakened.

optimal
adj op-ti-mal: most favorable
They will decide which is the
optimal course of action.

option
n op-tion: choice
Their only *option* is to eat at
a restaurant tonight.

opulent
adj op-u-lent: wealthy
They lived in an *opulent*
neighborhood.

oracle
n or-a-cle: prophet, priest
People crowded round the
oracle to hear his sermon.

oral
adj o-ral: spoken
An *oral* review of your book
will be heard tonight.

oration
n o-ra-tion: long speech
The tired guests tried in vain
to stay awake throughout the
oration.

orb
n orb: sphere, globe
They traveled around the *orb*
of the planet.

ordain
v or-dain: to order, appoint
The committees *ordained*
him as secretary of the
organization.

ordinance
n or-di-nance: rule, decree
The *ordinance* forbids
swimming in the fountain.

orgy
n or-gy: wild, drunken revel
Many people celebrate the
arrival of the new year in an
orgy of partying.

oriel
n o-ri-el: bay window
Their new house offers a
lovely *oriel* overlooking
the hill.

orifice
n or-i-fice: mouth, opening
The odd creature had several
orifices.

origin
n or-i-gin: source, root
  The *origin* of their family goes back to England.

orthodox
adj or-tho-dox: customary
  It is *orthodox* to leave your keys at the front desk.

orthopedist
n or-tho-pe-dist: bone doctor
  If you think you broke your finger, have it checked by an *orthopedist*.

oscillate
v os-cil-late: to vary, swing
  Her singing *oscillated* up and down the scales.

osprey
n os-prey: sea hawk
  From the boat's deck, we took pictures of the *osprey*.

ostensibly
adv os-ten-si-bly: apparently
  They have *ostensibly* decided to go ahead with your plans.

ostentatious
adj os-ten-ta-tious: showy, vulgar
  She paraded by in her new coat in such an *ostentatious* manner that she offended many people.

ostracize
v os-tra-cize: to banish
  The leader of the tribe *ostracized* the offender.

outlandish
adj out-land-ish: ridiculous
  His suggestions were *outlandish*.

outpost
n out-post: guard
  Station an *outpost* at the entrance to the museum.

outrageous
adj out-ra-geous: shocking
  Such an *outrageous* display of bad manners will not be tolerated here.

outstrip
v out-strip: go beyond, excel
  His invention *outstripped* all expectations.

oval
adj o-val: egg-shaped
  An *oval* table would best suit this room.

overcast
adj o-ver-cast: cloudy, gloomy
  The *overcast* sky caused a break in the heat wave.

overseer
n o-ver-seer: supervisor, foreman
  He was appointed *overseer* of the family trust.

overwhelm
v o-ver-whelm: overpower, crush
  All this homework *overwhelms* me.

overwhelming
adj o-ver-whelm-ing: above normal size

His *overwhelming* size scared the tiny children.

ovum
n o-vum: egg

They examined the *ovum* under the microscope.

P

pachyderm
n pach-y-derm: elephant, hippo

The *pachyderm* is the most popular attraction at the zoo.

pacific
adj pa-cif-ic: peaceful, calm

Only a slight breeze blew in from the *pacific* water.

packet
n pack-et: small parcel

I'm sure that *packet* will fit into my bag.

pact
n pact: agreement

They signed a *pact* to keep peace between their nations.

pageant
n pag-eant: procession

The *pageant* started at one end of town and ended at the other.

pagoda
n pa-go-da: tower, temple

My favorite place to lunch in the park is near the *pagoda* in the gardens.

palatable
adj pal-at-a-ble: agreeable

I did not find his suggestion *palatable,* and I refused to go along with it.

palate
n pal-ate: roof of the mouth

He made clicking noises with his tongue on his *palate.*

pallid
adj pal-lid: pale, lacking color

His face was *pallid* from fear.

palomino
n pal-o-mi-no: cream-colored horse

Her favorite animal on the farm is the *palomino.*

palpitate
v pal-pi-tate: tremble

His heart began to *palpitate* in anticipation of her arrival.

paltry
adj pal-try: almost worthless

That *paltry* amount will not feed the whole family.

pamper
v pam-per: to indulge too much

They *pamper* their baby by allowing him anything he wants.

panacea
n pan-a-ce-a: remedy, cure-all

The *panacea* for your cold is to get lots of sleep and drink lots of liquids.

panda
n pan-da: black and white bear
   One of the favorite attractions at the zoo is the *panda.*

pandemonium
n pan-de-mo-ni-um: tumult
   Pandemonium resulted when the snake escaped from the cage into the crowd.

pang
n pang: sharp pain
   All that running caused a *pang* in his side.

panorama
n pan-o-ra-ma: wide view
   The windows offered a *panorama* of the city.

paragon
n par-a-gon: model of excellence, especially a person
   The child thought her mother was a *paragon* of virtue.

paramount
adj par-a-mount: highest in power or importance
   It is *paramount* that this report be finished today.

paranoia
n par-a-noi-a: mental disorder, fear of persecution
   She is hoping that the therapy will cure her *paranoia.*

paraphernalia
n par-a-pher-na-lia: equipment
   Be sure to lock up all your *paraphernalia* at the end of each day.

parasite
n par-a-site: hanger-on
   Too many *parasites* clustered around the actor's door.

parcel
n par-cel: package
   Please send that *parcel* to him in time for the holidays.

parcel
v par-cel: to divide into portions
   So many people wanted to taste the pie that I had to *parcel* it out into many pieces.

parch
v parch: dry with heat
   She *parched* the meat in the oven.

pare
v pare: to cut, shave
   Pare the potatoes into medium-size pieces.

pariah
n pa-ri-ah: outcast
   He was considered a *pariah* by the rest of that group.

parka
n par-ka: jacket
   Better wear your *parka* and boots when you go out in that blizzard.

parody
n par-o-dy: imitation
   The actress presented a brilliant *parody* of the character.

parole
n pa-role: release of a prisoner before sentence expires

His *parole* from jail came unexpectedly.

parole
v pa-role: to release on parole

Because of overcrowded cells, guards *paroled* several prisoners.

parry
v par-ry: evade

I need your answer, so don't *parry* the question.

parsimonious
adj par-si-mo-ni-ous: stingy

She is so *parsimonious* that she doesn't leave tips.

partisan
n par-ti-san: supporter

His successful campaigning is bringing many *partisans* over to his side.

partition
n par-ti-tion: division

The *partition* of the country made them enemies.

pastel
adj pas-tel: pale shade of a color

Redo the bedroom in *pastel* colors.

pastel
n pas-tel: a crayon of ground coloring

Use the *pastel* on this sheet.

paternal
adj pa-ter-nal: fatherly

He treated the boys on his team with a *paternal* attitude.

pathetic
adj pa-thet-ic: pitiful

It was such a *pathetic* sight that she burst into tears.

patience
n pa-tience: tolerance

Try to keep your *patience* around the crowds.

patron
n pa-tron: supporter

The performing arts organizations seek *patrons* to back their productions.

pattern
n pat-tern: arrangement

The *pattern* created by the fallen leaves was interesting.

paucity
n pau-ci-ty: scarcity; lack

A *paucity* of food is creating a panic in the camp.

paunch
n paunch: stomach

Tuck your shirt in so that it covers your *paunch*.

pauper
n pau-per: very poor person

The *pauper* continued to wear the same ragged coat every day.

peal
v peal: sound loudly

The church bells *pealed* from the loft.

peal

n peal: the loud ringing of a bell or bells

It seems so *peculiar* to walk
The *peal* filled the village
with pleasant sounds.

peasant

n peas-ant: farmer

The *peasants* harvested their
fall crops together.

peculiar

adj pe-cul-iar: strange, odd

It seems so *peculiar* to walk
barefoot after wearing shoes
all year.

pedagogue

n ped-a-gogue: teacher

Listen to the lessons of the
pedagogue.

peddle

v ped-dle: travel about and sell

They *peddled* their ceramics
during the summer months.

pedestrian

n pe-des-tri-an: walker

The *pedestrians* waited on the
corner for the light to change.

pedigree

n ped-i-gree: ancestry

Her *pedigree* dates back to the
first settlers in this country.

peerless

adj peer-less: matchless

They are the first-place team
because their team members
are *peerless*.

peevish

adj pee-vish: irritable

He was very *peevish* when
he found out he had failed
the test.

penance

n pen-ance: punishment

His *penance* for behaving
badly was to go without
supper.

penitentiary

n pen-i-ten-tia-ry: prison

Criminals are locked up in
the *penitentiary* until their
sentence is over.

pensive

adj pen-sive: thoughtful,
musing

She sat quietly in a *pensive*
mood.

penurious

adj pe-nu-ri-ous: stingy

Although he is extremely
rich, he is quite *penurious*
with his money.

perch

v perch: to roost, sit high

The pigeons *perched* on the
telephone wire.

perch

n perch: a horizontal pole; small
spiny-finned fish

That telephone pole serves as
a popular *perch* for birds.
The boy caught three *perch*.

perdition
n per-di-tion: utter loss; hell
The town's *perdition* was caused by the flood.
The man's soul was bound for *perdition*.

perennial
adj per-en-ni-al: unceasing
His *perennial* playing is getting on her nerves.

perfunctory
adj per-func-to-ry: mechanical, without enthusiasm
Her dull eyes and *perfunctory* smile did not encourage him.

perigee
n per-i-gee: closest point in orbit
The rocket was visible as it approached its *perigee*.

peril
n per-il: danger
The *peril* in entering the wilderness alone is that there is no one to protect you.

peril
v per-il: to expose to harm or injury
He *periled* himself by climbing the mountain.

perimeter
n pe-rim-e-ter: boundary
They erected a fence around the *perimeter* of their land.

perish
v per-ish: to be destroyed
The man *perished* in the earthquake.

perjure
v per-jure: to swear falsely
He *perjured* himself by blaming his friends.

perpendicular
adj per-pen-dic-u-lar: at right angles
The *perpendicular* arrangement was pleasing to the eye.

perpendicular
n per-pen-dic-u-lar: a line at right angles to another line
A *perpendicular* is formed in the corner.

perpetrate
v per-pe-trate: to commit, do
The crime was *perpetrated* by that person standing against the wall.

perpetual
adj per-pet-u-al: eternal
The cemetery is responsible for the *perpetual* care of the gravesite.

perplex
v per-plex: puzzle, confuse
The footsteps outside her door *perplexed* her.

persecute
v per-se-cute: treat badly
He *persecuted* his younger sister until his parents made him stop.

persevere
v per-se-vere: to persist
You will have to *persevere* with your project if you wish to be finished tonight.

persist
v per-sist: to continue
  Please *persist* with what you
  were doing until the bell rings.

perspiration
n per-spi-ra-tion: sweat
  The *perspiration* shook off his
  body as he ran.

pert
adj pert: jaunty, lively, vivacious
  The *pert* young lady became
  a cheerleader.

perturb
v per-turb: disturb
  Try to be quiet so that you
  don't *perturb* the readers.

peruse
v pe-ruse: read thoroughly
  Peruse the map before you
  attempt to drive this road.

pessimism
n pes-si-mism: gloomy outlook
  He always faces Monday
  mornings with *pessimism*.

pester
v pes-ter: to annoy
  The dog is *pestering* his owner
  for dinner.

pestilence
n pes-ti-lence: disease, epidemic
  A *pestilence* struck down the
  vacationers.

petrify
v pet-ri-fy: turn to stone; terrify
  The ancient bones *petrified*
  over a period of several
  hundred years.
  The howling sound *petrified* her.

petty
adj pet-ty: small; small-minded
  Such a *petty* amount of money
  will not buy much.

philander
v phi-lan-der: to flirt
  The coy young girl *philandered*
  with the boys.

philanthropy
n phi-lan-thro-py: love of
mankind
  He was recognized for his
  philanthropy.

philharmonic
adj phil-har-mon-ic: loving music
or harmony
  The *philharmonic* group
  supported the orchestra.

philharmonic
n phil-har-mon-ic: a society that
sponsors a symphony orchestra
  The *philharmonic* will present
  two concerts this weekend.

phobic
adj pho-bic: morbidly fearful
  Ever since her near drowning
  as a child, she is *phobic* about
  swimming.

phonetics
n pho-net-ics: science of sound
  Phonetics is his specialty.

phrenetic
adj phre-net-ic: frenzied, fanatic
  The dogs ran around the
  house at a *phrenetic* pace.

pier
n pier: dock, wharf
They always sit at the end of the *pier* to fish.

pigment
n pig-ment: coloring matter
Use more *pigment* in that picture to make it more noticeable.

pilfer
v pil-fer: to steal
He was so hungry that he *pilfered* eggs from the farmer's hen house.

pilgrim
n pil-grim: wanderer
Pilgrims landed on the coast and set out to find the nearest village.

pillage
v pil-lage: to rob, plunder
Pirates *pillaged* the ship after overtaking it.

pillage
n pil-lage: loot
When the police broke in to the house, they discovered the stolen *pillage*.

pinnacle
n pin-na-cle: highest point
His goats climb to the *pinnacle* of that mountain.

pious
adj pi-ous: devout, religious
She spoke about her experiences in a *pious* manner.

piquant
adj pi-quant: stimulating, especially to the palate
Her *piquant* sauce enlivened the otherwise dull meal.

pitch
n pitch: tar
The maintenance crew poured fresh *pitch* onto the road.

pitch
v pitch: to throw
He *pitched* the ball over the wall.

pitch
n pitch: act or manner of pitching
Her *pitch* was too high.

pithy
adj pith-y: substantial, significant
Her *pithy* comments were always appreciated by her students.

pittance
n pit-tance: small amount
Although your fee is only a *pittance*, it is sufficient to pay the bills.

placate
v pla-cate: to soothe, satisfy
Such sweet music should *placate* his foul mood.

placid
adj pla-cid: calm, quiet
A *placid* breeze greeted them when they opened the door.

plagiarize
v pla-gia-rize: to copy from another
> He was accused of *plagiarizing* to write his term paper.

plague
n plague: disease, epidemic
> An undefined *plague* struck the town, leaving all the residents ill.

plague
v plague: to afflict with a plague; to vex, torment
> Cholera *plagued* the villagers.
> His gout *plagued* him every time it rained.

plaintive
adj plain-tive: sad; mournful
> *Plaintive* cries were heard at the funeral.

plaudit
n plau-dit: praise
> The *plaudits* he heard from his fans were well deserved.

plausible
adj plau-si-ble: reasonable
> Your conclusions are *plausible* to us.

plea
n plea: request, appeal
> Her *plea* was granted by the king.

pliable
adj pli-a-ble: easily bent, flexible
> He used *pliable* wire to get into the sewer grating.

plod
v plod: walk heavily, trudge
> The vendor *plodded* on, loaded down by his merchandise.

plume
n plume: large feather
> Her hat featured a purple *plume.*

plume
v plume: to adorn with plumes
> *Plume* the costume at the last moment.

plunder
v plun-der: rob
> Criminals *plundered* the warehouse for merchandise.

plunder
n plun-der: something taken by force or theft
> They were discovered hiding out with the *plunder* from the warehouse robbery.

poach
v poach: trespass
> He fenced in his land so that hunters would not *poach* on it.

poach
v poach: to cook
> *Poach* the eggs on the stove's back burner.

podiatrist
n po-di-a-trist: foot doctor
> You'd better have a *podiatrist* examine your toe injury.

podium
n po-di-um: platform
> The spotlight shone on the *podium.*

poise
n poise: composure, balance
Her *poise* was upset when the kids ran through the house.

pollute
v pol-lute: to make dirty, defile
Those gas fumes will *pollute* the air.

pompous
adj pom-pous: acting proudly
The *pompous* professor strutted around his classroom.

ponder
v pon-der: to consider
They *pondered* which way to turn at the fork in the road.

porous
adj po-rous: full of tiny holes
This *porous* boat will not float.

porridge
n por-ridge: oatmeal; mush
The *porridge* was getting cold.

portent
n por-tent: warning; omen
The ringing of the alarm bell sounded a *portent* of invaders.

portfolio
n port-fo-li-o: briefcase
His *portfolio* presented a report of the company's activities in the past year.

portly
adj port-ly: stout, corpulent
She will never be able to stuff her *portly* figure into that tiny outfit.

portray
v por-tray: to describe
He *portrayed* the woman he met at the party in his novel.

possess
v pos-sess: to control, own
Germany *possessed* France and Poland during World War II.
He wanted to *possess* the complete set of books.

postdate
v post-date: future date
Postdate that letter for next week.

posterior
adj pos-te-ri-or: back, rear
The *posterior* view of the house is more appealing than the front.

posterior
n pos-te-ri-or: the buttocks
She could not sit on her *posterior* for a while after receiving the shot.

posthumous
adj post-hu-mous: after death
His widow received the *posthumous* prize.

posture
n pos-ture: position of the body
Your *posture* will improve if you don't slouch in that chair.

potable
adj po-ta-ble: fit for drinking
Keep that milk in the refrigerator so that it will be *potable* tomorrow.

potable
n po-ta-ble: something drinkable
Potables will be available after the meal.

potent
adj po-tent: powerful
A *potent* fuel in the engine caused the diesel to travel faster.

potion
n po-tion: drink
The hostess prepared a special *potion* for her guest of honor.

poultry
n poul-try: fowl, chickens
That market offers a wide selection of *poultry*.

prank
n prank: playful trick
He is continually pulling *pranks* on his brothers.

prattle
v prat-tle: talk foolishly
Don't *prattle* on while I am trying to read.

preamble
n pre-am-ble: introduction, preface
The *preamble* to the book was very informative.

precede
v pre-cede: go before
A short introduction *preceded* his dance.

precept
n pre-cept: rule of action
Follow the *precepts* that the law states.

precinct
n pre-cinct: district
Each salesperson was assigned to a different *precinct*.

precious
adj pre-cious: valuable
I suggest you store your *precious* jewelry in a safe place.

precipice
n pre-ci-pice: steep cliff
They tried, but it was impossible to climb the *precipice*.

precise
adj pre-cise: exact, accurate
We need a *precise* count of the number of people who attend.

preclude
v pre-clude: prevent
You can *preclude* accidents by being careful.

prejudice
n prej-u-dice: unfair opinion, bias
His *prejudice* interfered with his judgment.

prejudice
v prej-u-dice: to injure or harm (not physically)
She *prejudiced* her chances of getting elected by making that statement.

premonition
n pre-mo-ni-tion: forewarning
She had a *premonition* that it would snow today.

prerogative
n pre-rog-a-tive: right, privilege
It is his *prerogative* to spend his allowance as he wishes.

presage

n pre-sage: omen

As a *presage* of success, they celebrated.

preserve

v pre-serve: to save

They tried to *preserve* the whale that had washed up on shore.

preserve

n pre-serve: place where game are maintained

They took their children to the *preserve* to see the animals.

presume

v pre-sume: suppose

Don't *presume* you know everything about the incident.

pretext

n pre-text: excuse, pretense

His *pretext* for staying home was that he was sick.

prevail

v pre-vail: to win

You'll be in first place if you *prevail* in the race.

prevaricate

v pre-var-i-cate: lie

When one is sworn in on the witness stand, he is not allowed to *prevaricate*.

prim

adj prim: proper, formal

He insists that his children are *prim* and proper.

primitive

adj prim-i-tive: simple

We prefer *primitive* ideas to complicated ones.

primitive

n prim-i-tive: a primitive person or thing

He is the last *primitive* alive from that tribe.

principal

adj prin-ci-pal: main, chief

The *principal* reason for this meeting is to select a new chairperson.

principal

n prin-ci-pal: a governing officer, as of a school

Every Friday afternoon, the *principal* meets with all of the teachers.

principle

n prin-ci-ple: ideal, belief

It is her *principle* that anyone can learn to play the piano.

prior

adj pri-or: earlier, before

His *prior* speech was more didactic than this one.

probe

v probe: investigate, search

The inspector *probed* the apartment for signs of the struggle.

probe

n probe: a surgical instrument for exploring a wound

Doctors applied a *probe* to the man's chest to inspect the damage.

proboscis
n pro-bos-cis: long snout
The *proboscis* on an anteater is particularly lengthy.

procure
v pro-cure: obtain
She *procured* the letter from her uncle.

prodigal
adj prod-i-gal: wasteful
The *prodigal* youth returned from his trip broke and tired.

prodigal
n prod-i-gal: spendthrift
You're too much of a *prodigal* with your allowance.

prodigious
adj pro-di-gious: great, huge
The *prodigious* size of the building prevented them from seeing around it.

prodigy
n prod-i-gy: marvel, a wonder
He is considered to be a *prodigy* with computers.

profanity
n pro-fan-i-ty: swearing
Refrain from using *profanity* around other people.

proficient
adj pro-fi-cient: skilled, advanced
She is such a *proficient* typist that everyone prefers to hire her.

profound
adj pro-found: deeply felt
The *profound* message of the play was successfully conveyed to the audience.

profuse
adj pro-fuse: abundant, lavish
A *profuse* spread of food covered the table.

progeny
n prog-e-ny: children, offspring
Their *progeny* are away at school most of the year.

prognosis
n prog-no-sis: forecast
The weatherman's *prognosis* is for rain tomorrow.

prohibit
v pro-hib-it: forbid, prevent
His father *prohibited* him from riding his bicycle in the park.

prolong
v pro-long: to extend
This book is so good, I wish I could *prolong* the action.

prominent
adj prom-i-nent: well known
Many fans came to see the *prominent* dancer perform.

promote
v pro-mote: to raise, advance
She was *promoted* to the first ranks.

propel
v pro-pel: to drive forward
An internal combustion engine *propels* the truck.

prosperous
adj pros-per-ous: successful
His careful investments
made him *prosperous.*

prostrate
v pros-trate: lay down flat
He *prostrated* himself in front
of the altar.

prostrate
adj pros-trate: lying face
downward
She could not recognize him
in that *prostrate* position.

protoplasm
n pro-to-plasm: matter
Scientists are questioning
that strange *protoplasm* found
in his body.

provoke
v pro-voke: to make angry, vex
She *provoked* him with her
constant chatter.

proximity
n prox-im-i-ty: nearness
The mouse quivered in fear
from the *proximity* of the cat.

proxy
n prox-y: agent, substitute
A *proxy* for the company
presented their case.

prudent
adj pru-dent: wise, sensible
Her *prudent* decision solved
the problem.

pseudo
adj pseu-do: false, sham
He was a *pseudo* artist and
merely played at painting.

puerile
adj pu-er-ile: childish
His *puerile* actions surprised
his co-workers.

pugilist
n pu-gi-list: boxer, fighter
A boxing match will be held
today to determine the best
pugilist here.

pulsate
v pul-sate: throb, vibrate
Her head began to *pulsate*
from the effects of the
medicine.

puma
n pu-ma: wildcat
Several residents in the
country reported seeing a
puma in the hills.

pummel
v pum-mel: to beat with a fist
She *pummeled* the wall when
she heard the bad news.

pummeling
n pum-mel-ing: a beating with
a fist
He received such a *pummeling*
from the gang that he was
hospitalized.

punctual
adj punc-tu-al: prompt
The show starts exactly at
eight, so please be *punctual.*

pungent
adj pun-gent: stinging, sharp
The ointment left a *pungent*
sensation on his skin.

puny
adj pu-ny: weak, small
   The abandoned kittens were *puny* from lack of care.

purge
v purge: to cleanse
   Purge your mind of such wicked thoughts.

purge
n purge: act of cleaning out
   Administrators felt a *purge* was in order.

pursue
v pur-sue: chase, follow
   He would not *pursue* her any longer.

purvey
v pur-vey: to supply, provide
   The neighbors *purveyed* food and clothing for the new tenants.

pusillanimous
adj pu-sil-lan-i-mous: cowardly
   His *pusillanimous* actions did not scare off his attackers.

putrid
adj pu-trid: rotten, foul
   A *putrid* odor escaped from the basement.

pygmy
n pyg-my: dwarf
   The *pygmy* made up for his lack of size with his might.

python
n py-thon: snake (boa)
   She was relieved to see that the *python* was kept in a sealed cage.

Q

quack
n quack: false doctor, pretender
   Victims of the *quack* voiced their indignation to the authorities.

quack
v quack: to utter the cry of a duck
   Ducks *quacked* as they paddled around the pond.

quack
adj quack: fraudulent
   A *quack* certificate was discovered in the papers.

quadruped
n quad-ru-ped: a four-footed animal, having four feet
   These tracks indicate they were made by a *quadruped*.

quagmire
n quag-mire: soft, muddy ground
   The pigs rolled around in the *quagmire*.

quaint
adj quaint: amusing, pleasing
   What a *quaint* little dog that is.

quake
v quake: shake, tremble
   The poundings of the construction crew caused the ground to *quake*.

qualified
v qual-i-fied: competent
   If they consider you *qualified*, chances are good that you will get the job.

qualms
n qualms: doubts
> I have *qualms* about understanding all that is written here.

quantity
n quan-ti-ty: amount
> Tell the clerk the *quantity* you will need so that he can have adequate supplies available.

quarantine
n quar-an-tine: period of detention and isolation
> A *quarantine* was set up for those children with measles.

quarrel
v quar-rel: dispute, fight
> They *quarreled* about who would use the car tonight.

quarrel
n quar-rel: a cause for dispute
> A *quarrel* erupted between the two shoppers when they both grabbed the same merchandise.

quarry
n quar-ry: stone mine
> Each year that *quarry* is dug deeper and deeper.

quartz
n quartz: a hard mineral
> While hiking up the mountain, they found several pieces of *quartz*.

quaver
v qua-ver: to shake, tremble
> The earthquake caused the ground to *quaver* for several minutes.

queasy
adj quea-sy: easily upset
> Her *queasy* stomach makes traveling unpleasant for her.

quench
v quench: to put an end to
> He *quenched* his thirst by drinking lots of water.

querulous
adj quer-u-lous: complaining
> *Querulous* residents told the building owner to make the repairs immediately.

query
n que-ry: question
> Her *query* had an obvious answer.

query
v que-ry: to question
> The police *queried* the suspect about the robbery.

quest
n quest: hunt; search
> A team of twenty men set out on the *quest*.

quill
n quill: stiff feather
> She found several *quills* by the duck pond.

quip
n quip: witty saying
> He replied to her question with a *quip*.

quirk
n quirk: peculiar way of acting
> He is remembered for his *quirks*.

R

rabble

n rab-ble: disorderly crowd

A *rabble* is gathering where the protestors are marching.

rabies

n ra-bies: a disease of many mammals

The dog received his annual *rabies* shot.

radical

adj rad-i-cal: extreme

Most voters do not support him because of his *radical* views.

rafter

n raf-ter: slanting beam

The cabin's roof is supported by several *rafters*.

rage

n rage: violent anger

His *rage* scared off anyone from approaching him.

rage

v rage: to show violent anger

She *raged* at the motorist who backed into her car.

raid

n raid: attack

The troops staged a *raid* on the enemy camp.

raid

v raid: to make a raid on, to take part in a raid

She *raided* the storage closet for extra supplies.

rally

v ral-ly: to bring together

Members of the family *rallied* for a reunion at the campsite.

rally

n ral-ly: a gathering

They met at a massive *rally* after twenty years.

ramble

v ram-ble: to wander about

On this pleasant day, several people *rambled* through the park.

rambunctious

adj ram-bunc-tious: unruly, wild

Not many people can handle her *rambunctious* behavior.

rampage

n ram-page: state of excitement or rage, wild behavior

The untamed dogs went on a *rampage* throughout the countryside.

rancid

adj ranc-id: stale, spoiled

The meat became *rancid* after lying in the refrigerator for a week.

rancor

n ran-cor: hatred

His *rancor* showed through his attempts to be civil to his neighbors.

random

adj ran-dom: by chance

Take a *random* poll of the population to find out if your idea is good.

ransack
v ran-sack: to search, rob
  Somebody broke into their house and *ransacked* it.

rant
v rant: speak wildly
  He *ranted* about his episodes in the city.

rapier
n ra-pier: sword
  His costume was not complete until he added his *rapier*.

rapport
n rap-port: harmony, agreement
  An instant *rapport* developed between the new neighbors and the old tenants.

rarefy
v rar-e-fy: to make thinner or less dense; to refine, as an argument
  The scientist *rarefied* the substance in his lab.

rash
adj rash: careless, hasty
  It is better to take your time deciding than to make a *rash* answer.

rash
n rash: an eruption on the body
  When she had the measles, it showed up as a *rash* on her face and arms.

rasp
n rasp: harsh, grating sound
  A *rasp* escaped from her throat as she endured the fifth day of her cold.

rasp
n rasp: a type of file
  Hand me the *rasp* so that I can finish this job.

ratify
v rat-i-fy: approve, confirm
  Two-thirds of the population have to *ratify* the decision before it is considered accepted.

ration
n ra-tion: fixed allowance
  If you continue that *ration* of food daily, you will surely gain weight.

ration
v ra-tion: to furnish with rations, to hand out
  You will have to *ration* the remaining supplies carefully.

rational
adj ra-tio-nal: sensible
  Study the situation clearly so that you present a *rational* conclusion.

ravage
v rav-age: to damage greatly
  The tornado *ravaged* the land.

ravage
n rav-age: ruin, destruction
  The *ravage* brought on the town by the storm was beyond repair.

rave
v rave: to talk wildly or incoherently
  In his excitement, he *raved* about the accident he witnessed.

rave
n rave: a very enthusiastic commendation
> She endorsed her candidate with a *rave*.

ravenous
adj rav-e-nous: very hungry, greedy
> I am *ravenous* for that steak.

ravishing
adj rav-ish-ing: delightful
> Your friend is a very *ravishing* man.

raze
v raze: to tear down, destroy
> The construction crew had to *raze* the old building before laying the foundation for the new one.

realm
n realm: kingdom
> The queen's *realm* consists of this entire continent.

reap
v reap: to cut, gather
> At the end of the summer season, farmers *reap* the crop.

rebate
n re-bate: partial refund
> When he cancelled his travel plans, the travel agency sent him a *rebate*.

rebate
v re-bate: to give back part of payment
> When you return the remainder of the machine, the office will *rebate* the amount stated.

rebuke
v re-buke: scold, reprove
> He *rebuked* his daughter for running out into the street.

recalcitrant
adj re-cal-ci-trant: disobedient
> Some people send their *recalcitrant* dogs to school to be trained.

recapitulate
v re-ca-pit-u-late: repeat
> Please *recapitulate* the instructions you gave this morning.

receptacle
n re-cep-ta-cle: container
> You will find a *receptacle* for your leftovers in the corner.

recipient
n re-cip-i-ent: receiver
> The *recipient* of the package was delighted.

reciprocal
adj re-cip-ro-cal: in return
> A *reciprocal* agreement will allow both sides to be satisfied.

reciprocal
n re-cip-ro-cal: mathematical inverse
> The *reciprocal* of ½ is 2.

reckless
adj reck-less: rash; careless
> His *reckless* behavior will get him into trouble.

reckon
v reck-on: to count, compute, to estimate

Reckon the figures and enter the result on the bill.

recline
v re-cline: lean back

If your back is aching, *recline* against this pole.

recluse
n re-cluse: hermit

He has become a *recluse* since his family moved away.

recoil
v re-coil: to shrink back

She *recoiled* from the fire.

recoil
n re-coil: a drawing away from

They were offended by his *recoil* from their pet.

recollect
v rec-ol-lect: remember

Try to *recollect* everything that happened to you a year ago today.

recompense
n re-com-pense: reward, payback

His *recompense* for good behavior was a trip to the park.

recompense
v re-com-pense: to repay or reward

They *recompensed* him for his generosity.

reconcile
v re-con-cile: to settle

She *reconciled* their disagreement, and they shook hands.

recuperate
v re-cu-per-ate: to recover

She is still *recuperating* from the measles.

recurrence
n re-cur-rence: repetition

This dream is a *recurrence* of the one I had a week ago.

redeem
v re-deem: buy back

You can *redeem* your boat for the same price you sold it to me.

redundant
adj re-dun-dant: not needed; extra

Your essay is filled with *redundant* statements.

reek
n reek: unpleasant smell

A *reek* escaped from the trash can when the lid was lifted.

reek
v reek: to emit a strong offensive smell

That spoiled food *reeks*.

referendum
n ref-er-en-dum: voting

We will decide tomorrow at the *referendum* if that law should be reinstated.

reflexive
adj re-flex-ive: nonvoluntary action

His *reflexive* shout when he won the prize caused everyone to look at him in surprise.

refract
v re-fract: to bend a ray of light

The window *refracted* the sunlight.

refuge
n ref-uge: shelter, safety

It was raining so hard that we ran to the trees for *refuge*.

refurbish
v re-fur-bish: polish, clean, restore

Refurbish the floor to ensure a fine finish.

regal
adj re-gal: royal, kingly

His status requires that he act in a *regal* manner.

regale
v re-gale: entertain

He always *regales* us with his witty remarks.

regatta
n re-gat-ta: boat race

A *regatta* will be held on Lake Erie on Saturday.

regulate
v reg-u-late: to control

Regulate the amount of candy that you give to the children.

regurgitate
v re-gur-gi-tate: to throw up

Many types of animals *regurgitate* their food.

rehabilitate
v re-ha-bil-i-tate: restore

They tried to *rehabilitate* the old house to its former, elegant style.

rehash
v re-hash: deal with again

We have already *rehashed* that problem, so let's go on to another one.

rehash
n re-hash: a reworking, a new form

The newspaper presented a *rehash* of what we heard on television last night.

rehearse
v re-hearse: practice

The actors *rehearsed* the scene again.

reimburse
v re-im-burse: to pay back

She *reimbursed* her parents for their loan to her during her school years.

reincarnation
n re-in-car-na-tion: rebirth

He believes a *reincarnation* of his soul in a new body will occur after he dies.

reiterate
v re-it-er-ate: to repeat

The speaker *reiterated* the same passage to assure comprehension by the crowd.

rejuvenate
v re-ju-ve-nate: to make young again
> A good diet and daily exercise will *rejuvenate* you.

relentless
adj re-lent-less: unyielding
> This *relentless* ache in my back is bothering me.

reliable
adj re-li-a-ble: trustworthy
> The bank requires that all its employees be *reliable*.

relic
n rel-ic: survival from the past, item of interest because of age
> They brought back several *relics* found on their archaeological expedition.

relinquish
v re-lin-quish: to abandon, give up
> She *relinquished* her right to the estate.

relish
n re-lish: an appetizing condiment
> The casserole was topped with a delicious *relish*.

relish
v rel-ish: to take pleasure in
> He *relished* playing with his young daughter.

remiss
adj re-miss: careless
> She was *remiss* in her treatment of the book.

remit
v re-mit: to send money
> Please *remit* the amount you owe on your bill immediately.

remnant
n rem-nant: small remainder
> Please ask the waiter to wrap the *remnant* of this steak so that I can take it home.

remonstrance
n re-mon-strance: protest
> The parents' *remonstrance* against the teacher's treatment was overwhelming.

remorse
n re-morse: regret, sorrow
> It is with *remorse* that I decline your invitation.

remote
adj re-mote: distant, far away
> A *remote* rumbling could be heard from the other side of the forest.

remunerate
v re-mu-ner-ate: pay
> The finance department will *remunerate* you for your work.

renaissance
n re-nais-sance: revival
> A *renaissance* of the movie brought old fans and new ones.

rendezvous
n ren-dez-vous: meeting
> She wore her favorite dress for their *rendezvous*.

renegade

n ren-e-gade: deserter, traitor

A *renegade* from the troops was reported in this area.

renounce

v re-nounce: give up

With sadness, the dieter *renounced* all fattening foods.

renovate

v ren-o-vate: renew, restore

They are attempting to *renovate* the antique car to its former glory.

repartee

n re-par-tee: witty reply

You never fail to think up delightful *repartee* to whatever anyone says.

repeal

v re-peal: to withdraw, take back

She reconsidered selling her car and *repealed* her offer.

repel

v re-pel: force back, to cause dislike

I am *repelled* by that decaying odor.

repent

v re-pent: regret

After playing a trick on his friend, he *repented* his behavior.

repine

v re-pine: to be discontented

The child *repined* for days at the loss of his puppy.

replete

adj re-plete: filled

The menu was *replete* with dozens of desserts.

replica

n rep-li-ca: copy, reproduction

A *replica* of that masterpiece is for sale.

repose

n re-pose: rest, sleep

Look how peaceful she looks in her *repose*.

repose

v re-pose: to lie at rest

You may *repose* on this sofa.

repress

v re-press: to keep down

Try to *repress* the little boy's excitement in this room.

reprieve

n re-prieve: temporary delay

They requested a *reprieve* from the insurance company until they could make their monthly payment.

reproach

v re-proach: to blame

She *reproached* him for the broken glass even though it was not his fault.

reprove

v re-prove: scold, blame

The teacher *reproved* her students for their noisy actions.

repugnant
adj re-pug-nant: distasteful
That meat left a *repugnant* taste in my mouth.

rescind
v re-scind: to repeal, cancel
His orders were *rescinded* this morning, so he did not have to leave.

reservoir
n res-er-voir: storehouse
A *reservoir* of merchandise is available if they run out of goods in the shop.

residence
n res-i-dence: home, abode
My *residence* is a large house in the country.

residue
n res-i-due: remainder
The *residue* of the shipwreck was washed up on shore.

resilience
n re-sil-i-ence: the ability to spring back or recover from adversity
The child showed *resilience* after being inflicted with abuse.

resolute
adj res-o-lute: determined, firm
A *resolute* look came over her face as she struggled on.

respiration
n res-pi-ra-tion: breathing
The old man's illness slowed his *respiration*.

response
n re-sponse: answer
His *response* to our inquiry was unexpected.

restive
adj res-tive: restless, uneasy
The animals are becoming *restive* from the sounds of thunder.

restrain
v re-strain: hold back
It is hard to *restrain* her fans from following her.

résumé
n re-sum-e: summary
He included a *résumé* at the end of his letter.

resume
v re-sume: to begin again, go on
They *resumed* the game where they left off last week.

resurgent
adj re-sur-gent: rising again
The *resurgent* tide reaches as far as that buoy every day.

retaliate
v re-tal-i-ate: to pay back a wrong
He *retaliated* by playing a trick on them.

retard
v re-tard: to make slow, delay
The heavy load in his car *retarded* his travels.

reticent
adj ret-i-cent: reserved, silent
We assumed she was shy because of her *reticent* behavior.

retinue
n ret-i-nue: followers, attendants
The *retinue* proceeded along the church aisle behind the bride and groom.

retort
n re-tort: quick, sharp answer
She replied with a *retort* to his question.

retract
v re-tract: to take back
I wish I could *retract* the unfair statement I made to him.

retrogress
v ret-ro-gress: move backward
Living conditions have *retrogressed* since the flood.

revenge
v re-venge: do harm in return
I will *revenge* my friend's murder.

revenge
n re-venge: desire to take vengeance
He will surely seek *revenge* because of what you did to him.

revenue
n rev-e-nue: income
Be sure to record all your *revenue* from the past year on the budget sheet.

reverberate
v re-ver-ber-ate: to reflect, echo
The sound of thunder *reverberated* through the canyon.

reverence
n rev-er-ence: respect
They were taught to treat their elders with *reverence*.

reverie
n rev-er-ie: dreamy thoughts
She wastes too much time in *reverie* when she should be working.

revile
v re-vile: to abuse, malign
The child *reviled* his friend because he was envious.

revise
v re-vise: to change, amend
Each year, they *revise* the schedule.

revoke
v re-voke: to cancel
His pass was *revoked* because he failed inspection.

ribald
adj rib-ald: offensive, indecent
Her *ribald* behavior kept her off the team.

ridicule
v rid-i-cule: make fun of, mock
She ran home crying after the other children *ridiculed* her clothes.

ridicule
n rid-i-cule: the act of making one the object of laughter

Their *ridicule* of her made her ashamed of her actions.

riffraff
n riff-raff: worthless people

They fenced in their property to keep *riffraff* off their land.

rift
n rift: an opening caused by splitting

Water is leaking out of the *rift* in the pool.

righteous
adj righ-teous: virtuous, blameless

The child adopted a *righteous* attitude about his low test mark.

rigid
adj rig-id: firm, stiff

Soldiers stand in a *rigid* position for inspection.

rigor
n rig-or: strictness

His *rigor* prevented them from enjoying the class.

rite
n rite: ceremony

Each June, there is a *rite* for all the graduates.

rivet
v riv-et: to fasten firmly

Rivet yourself to the seat before takeoff.

rivet
n riv-et: metal bolt

The plane has approximately eight hundred *rivets* in its body.

roam
v roam: wander

Close the pen so that the cows cannot *roam* around the field.

robust
adj ro-bust: strong, healthy

All that exercise and sensible dieting has transformed him into a *robust* figure of a man.

rodent
n ro-dent: gnawing animal

He suggested that we clean the apartment before moving in so that it would be free of *rodents*.

roe
n roe: fish eggs; small nimble, European deer

Some restaurants serve *roe* as a gourmet specialty.

He shot the graceful, nimble *roe*.

rogue
n rogue: rascal

He is such a *rogue*, but everyone likes him.

roster
n ros-ter: list

He kept a *roster* of the names of all the attendees.

rote

n rote: repetition by memory

The actor presented the speech by *rote*.

rubbish

n rub-bish: trash, litter, debris

Following the party, there was plenty of *rubbish* to be cleaned up.

ruddy

adj rud-dy: healthy red color

A *ruddy* complexion shone on her face following her exercising.

rudimentary

adj ru-di-men-ta-ry: elementary

She needs to complete her *rudimentary* education before entering college.

rueful

adj rue-ful: sorrowful, regretful

She approached the store owner with the broken dish in hand and a *rueful* expression on her face.

ruffian

n ruf-fi-an: cruel person

He is truly a *ruffian* to pick on those boys like that.

ruffle

n ruf-fle: pleated, gathered folds in material

He smoothed out the *ruffle* in the bedspread.

ruffle

v ruf-fle: to disturb the smoothness of

She *ruffled* the water when she dropped the oar in the lake.

rummage

v rum-mage: to search

They were *rummaging* through the attic in search of the old photographs.

rumor

n ru-mor: general talk not based on definite knowledge

The *rumor* going around the office is that she will be promoted soon.

rupture

v rup-ture: to break

The balloon *ruptured* into several pieces when it struck the pin.

rupture

n rup-ture: a breaking apart

The *rupture* in the tire made the car swerve off the road.

rural

adj ru-ral: of the country

I prefer the tranquility of a *rural* environment to the noise of the city.

ruse

n ruse: scheme, trick

They concocted an elaborate *ruse* to keep her out of the house until evening.

rustic

adj rus-tic: countryish, rural

Their home reflects the *rustic* surroundings of the town.

rustic

n rus-tic: a country person

Why don't you ask a *rustic* for directions to the forest?

S

saber
n sa-ber: sword
He faced his enemies with a *saber*.

saccharine
adj sac-cha-rine: cloyingly sweet
Although she did not like him, she was extremely *saccharine* in her manner.

saccharine
n sac-cha-rine: synthetic sweetener
He used *saccharine* in his coffee instead of sugar.

sacrifice
n sac-ri-fice: offering
They presented a *sacrifice* on the altar.

saga
n sa-ga: story of heroic deeds
They loved the *sagas* that the old man told to them every time they visited him.

sagacious
adj sa-ga-cious: shrewd, wise
His *sagacious* advice has helped us solve many dilemmas.

sage
adj sage: wise
The elders of this tribe render all *sage* decisions.

sage
n sage: a very wise man; seasoning
People travel from great distances to seek advice from the *sage*.
She added *sage* to the sauce.

salient
adj sa-li-ent: prominent, striking
His *salient* figure elicits trust from the people.

saline
adj sa-line: salty
There was a *saline* taste in the water.

salon
n sa-lon: large room
Guests will be most comfortable in the *salon*.

salubrious
adj sa-lu-bri-ous: healthy
Part of her good mood is due to her *salubrious* state of mind and body.

salvage
v sal-vage: to rescue
They *salvaged* all the remaining intact furniture from the ruins.

salvage
n sal-vage: a, rescued ship, crew, and cargo
They pulled the *salvage* of the boat onto shore.

salvation
n sal-va-tion: saving
The minister tried to bring about a *salvation* of the gang.

salve
n salve: ointment

Apply a *salve* to that wound right away.

salve
v salve: to apply salve to

Salve the infection with this medicine.

sanatorium
n san-a-to-ri-um: health resort

Following her long illness, she went off to a *sanatorium* to recover her strength.

sanctify
v sanc-ti-fy: to make holy

His baptism was *sanctified* at the altar.

sanctuary
n sanc-tu-ary: refuge, safe place

They ran to the barn for *sanctuary* from the strong wind.

sane
adj sane: rational

We would prefer that you took your time and presented us with a *sane* decision.

sanguine
adj san-guine: cheerful and hopeful

A *sanguine* expression appeared on his face as he saw his mother go to the candy dish.

sanitary
adj san-i-tar-y: free from filth

You must keep the patients in *sanitary* conditions.

sapience
n sa-pi-ence: wisdom

We value his words of *sapience* because of his years of experience in that field.

sapling
n sap-ling: young tree

They planted a *sapling* in the front yard in the hope that it would sprout leaves in the spring.

sardonic
adj sar-don-ic: scornful

A *sardonic* expression appeared on her face when she saw him talking to the new girl in class.

satchel
n satch-el: handbag

She always takes her *satchel* whenever she goes out.

satellite
n sat-el-lite: orbiting sphere

The *satellite* beamed valuable information down to earth.

satiate
v sa-ti-ate: satisfy fully

She *satiated* her hunger only when she had consumed the entire casserole.

satirize
v sat-i-rize: to criticize, ridicule

She *satirized* his attempts to learn to ride the bike.

saturate
v sat-u-rate: to soak thoroughly

Saturate the material with the dye if you want an even color.

saturnalia
n sat-ur-na-li-a: wild merrymaking
Their victory was followed by a *saturnalia*, in which some damage was done to their house.

saucy
adj sau-cy: rude
He answered her inquiry in a *saucy* tone.

savage
adj sav-age: wild, rugged
This barren land is considered *savage* country.

savage
n sav-age: member of a primitive human society
Savages protected their tribe from intruders.

savannah
n sa-van-nah: treeless plain
Miles and miles of *savannah* spread out before them.

savor
n sa-vor: taste or smell, flavor
The *savor* of meat made her hungry.

savor
v sa-vor: to enjoy the taste, smell, or characteristic of
He *savored* the smell of roast beef.

scaffold
n scaf-fold: platform, stage
The artist stood on a *scaffold* to paint the mural on the wall.

scalawag
n scal-a-wag: rascal; scamp
Her pet dog is such a lovable *scalawag*.

scald
v scald: to burn
The oven *scalded* her hand when she got too close to the flame.

scald
n scald: a burn caused by scalding
She applied ointment to the *scald* on her hand.

scallion
n scal-lion: type of onion
He added some *scallions* to the stew for the final touch.

scallop
n scal-lop: kind of shellfish, mollusk
For dinner tonight they will be serving *scallops* with vegetables.

scamper
v scam-per: run quickly
After breaking the window, the boys *scampered* away out of sight.

scan
v scan: to look closely, examine
She *scanned* the papers for errors.

scandal
n scan-dal: shameful action
Their fight had created a *scandal* in the town.

scant
adj scant: not enough
>There won't be any extra desserts tonight since we only have a *scant* supply.

scarce
adj scarce: rare, hard to get
>Those types of pictures are very *scarce* and, thus, are valuable.

scarlet
adj scar-let: bright red
>We could spot her several blocks away in that *scarlet* jacket.

scathing
adj scath-ing: severe
>She gave him a *scathing* look when he questioned her.

scent
n scent: smell
>Her perfume left a pleasant *scent* in the room long after she had left.

scheme
v scheme: to plan, plot
>They *schemed* to give him a surprise party.

scheme
n scheme: a systematic plan for obtaining some object
>They established a *scheme* to put them in first place.

schism
n schism: a split, breakup
>After the *schism,* each partner started a new business.

schooner
n schoon-er: sailing vessel
>They traveled to Europe in a *schooner.*

sciatica
n sci-at-i-ca: painful condition of the hip
>His pain was diagnosed as *sciatica.*

scintilla
n scin-til-la: very small amount
>There was not one *scintilla* of food left in the closet.

scintillate
v scin-til-late: to sparkle, flash
>The diamonds *scintillated* in the bright light.

scoff
v scoff: to make fun of, mock
>They *scoffed* at his attempts to repair the engine.

scoff
n scoff: a mock or jeer
>Even though he failed in his efforts, he did not deserve the *scoff* he received from his friends.

scorch
v scorch: to burn
>He *scorched* his hand when he picked up the hot dish without a protecting mitt.

scorn
n scorn: contempt
>His *scorn* was not easily disguised.

scour
v scour: to clean; search thoroughly
> They *scoured* the attic.
> She *scoured* the closet for her old dress.

scourge
v scourge: to punish
> The warden *scourged* the prisoners for their crimes.

scow
n scow: flat boat
> They glided across the lake in a *scow*.

scrawl
n scrawl: careless handwriting
> His *scrawl* is indecipherable.

scrawl
v scrawl: to write or draw hastily
> She *scrawled* the message on the first piece of paper she found so that she wouldn't forget it.

scrawny
adj scraw-ny: skinny
> Lack of food reduced him to a *scrawny* figure of a man.

scribe
n scribe: writer
> The *scribe* took down every word spoken at the meeting.

scrimp
v scrimp: use sparingly
> Until payday, we'll have to *scrimp* on groceries.

scruff
n scruff: back of the neck
> Be sure to wash the *scruff* of your neck.

scruple
n scru-ple: inability to act because of conscience
> His *scruples* would not let him support the candidate.

scrutinize
v scru-ti-nize: to inspect, examine
> She carefully *scrutinized* his homework for errors but found none.

scurry
v scur-ry: to run quickly, hurry
> The field mouse *scurried* away from the cat.

scurry
n scur-ry: a scampering
> The *scurry* of little feet was heard in the nursery.

secede
v se-cede: to withdraw
> The South wanted to *secede* from the Union.

sect
n sect: a group with particular beliefs
> A *sect* from the school meets here each Monday night to discuss upcoming events.

secular
adj sec-u-lar: worldly, not religious
> He is noted for his *secular* views about mankind.

secure
adj se-cure: safe, protected
A *secure* shed was constructed
to protect their equipment.

sedate
adj se-date: calm, quiet
They met a *sedate* group of
businessmen.

seduce
v se-duce: to lead astray, beguile
He *seduced* the puppy away
from her mother.

sedulous
adj sed-u-lous: hard working
He completed the job in his
customary *sedulous* manner.

seek
v seek: to search for
Seek and you will find.

seep
v seep: to ooze; leak slowly
Water *seeped* from the bottom
of the plant onto the carpet.

seethe
v seethe: to be disturbed
The man *seethed* over his lost
briefcase.

segment
n seg-ment: part, section
A *segment* of this book will
cover the events of the party.

segment
v seg-ment: to divide into
segments
He *segmented* the audience
into two groups.

segregate
v seg-re-gate: to set apart,
separate
The slow-learning children
were *segregated* from their
classmates.

seismology
n seis-mol-o-gy: earthquake
study
He understood the danger
because of his knowledge of
seismology.

seize
v seize: to clutch, grab
She *seized* the nearest branch
as she fell from the tree.

semantics
n se-man-tics: the science of the
meaning of words
A study of English *semantics*
will indicate similarities with
other languages.

semblance
n sem-blance: outward
appearance
He displayed a *semblance*
of calm although he was
actually quite frightened.

sentiment
n sen-ti-ment: tender feeling
His *sentiment* for his child
is touching.

sentinel
n sen-ti-nel: guard, sentry
Post a *sentinel* at the front
and back doors during the
display of the valuable
collection.

sepia

n se-pi-a: dark brown ink

Use *sepia* to dye your sofa that color.

sepia

adj se-pi-a: dark brown

I suggest you use that *sepia* shade for your curtains.

sepulcher

n sep-ul-cher: tomb, grave

Following her funeral, she was buried in the family *sepulcher.*

sequel

n se-quel: continuation

A *sequel* to the book will be published soon.

sequence

n se-quence: order of succession

Be sure to read the manuals in the proper *sequence.*

sequester

v se-ques-ter: to remove into isolation

Officials *sequestered* the prisoner from the courtroom.

sequoia

n se-quoi-a: tall tree

The *sequoia* blocked their view of the mountain range.

serene

adj se-rene: calm, peaceful

A *serene* expression came over his face when he realized that everything was all right.

serf

n serf: slave

The landowner treated his *serf* as if he was one of the family.

serpent

n ser-pent: snake

She screamed when she saw the *serpent* in the garden.

sever

v sev-er: to cut, break off; divide

The knife quickly *severed* the fruit into tiny pieces.

severe

adj se-vere: strict, stern, harsh

He is following a *severe* diet and exercise plan to lose twenty pounds in time for the holidays.

shaft

n shaft: spear, pole

They left for the hunt with *shafts* at their side.

shaft

v shaft: to fit with a shaft

They *shafted* the roof to support it against the wind.

shallow

adj shal-low: not deep

She let the kids wade in the *shallow* pool.

shallow

n shal-low: a shoal

Signs were posted to keep boats out of the *shallow.*

sham
n sham: pretense, fraud
  His injury was an absolute *sham.*

sham
adj sham: not real, false
  He gave a *sham* portrayal of the character's actions.

sham
v sham: to pretend, feign
  He *shammed* an illness to get out of taking the exam.

shanty
n shan-ty: cabin
  He lives in poverty in a *shanty* near the dump.

shatter
v shat-ter: to break into pieces
  The glass *shattered* all over the kitchen when she dropped it.

sheath
n sheath: case for a knife
  Store the knife in its *sheath* after each use so that it will stay in good condition.

sheen
n sheen: brightness, luster
  He polished the fire engine to such a *sheen* that it looked new.

sheer
adj sheer: very thin, airy
  Light showed through the *sheer* material.

sheer
adv sheer: completely, utterly
  The knife cut *sheer* through the bone.

sheik
n sheik: Arab chief or leader
  The *sheik* invited the foreign dignitaries into his quarters.

shiftless
adj shift-less: lazy
  He was fired from his job because of his *shiftless* activities.

shirk
v shirk: to avoid work
  He was fired because he *shirked* his job too often.

shirk
n shirk: one who shirks
  He probably won't get the job because of his reputation as a *shirk.*

shiver
v shiv-er: to shake
  The cold air made her *shiver* in her light clothes.

shoddy
adj shod-dy: inferior
  Their incompetent paint job gave the house a *shoddy* appearance.

shred
n shred: fragment
  A *shred* of glass remained on the floor.

shred
v shred: to tear or cut into shreds
  Shred this paper into small pieces.

shrewd
adj shrewd: clever, astute
> He was *shrewd* in the way he handled the situation.

shrill
adj shrill: piercing sound
> A *shrill* alarm went off when they tried to break into the house.

shrill
v shrill: to make a high-pitched sound
> Alarm bells *shrilled* as the intruders ran away.

shrivel
v shriv-el: to dry up, to shrink
> The flowers and plants began to *shrivel* during the drought.

shrub
n shrub: bush
> She planted the *shrub* in the garden.

shudder
v shud-der: to tremble
> They *shuddered* in their light sweaters when the weather suddenly turned cold.

shun
v shun: to avoid
> He *shuns* anyone who wants his advice.

shy
adj shy: bashful
> Her *shy* child did not say a word to the adults.

shy
v shy: to move suddenly as if startled
> Watch the passengers *shy* away when you place that grotesque object on the seat.

siege
n siege: attack
> A *siege* started when the enemy troops encountered each other.

siesta
n si-es-ta: nap, rest
> If you are planning to be out late tonight, take a *siesta* this afternoon.

sieve
n sieve: strainer
> Remove all the water from the pasta by draining it in the *sieve.*

sift
v sift: to separate
> *Sift* the pebbles out of the sand.

significant
adj sig-nif-i-cant: important
> You will find a *significant* clue in this book.

silhouette
n sil-hou-ette: outlined portrait
> He had the artist draw a *silhouette* of his daughter to give to his wife for her birthday.

silhouette
v sil-hou-ette: to show against a bright background
> He was *silhouetted* behind the flimsy curtain.

simian
adj sim-i-an: apelike
> He can climb trees with *simian* agility.

simmer
v sim-mer: to boil gently
> When the eggs have boiled, let them *simmer* for a while.

simpleton
n sim-ple-ton: silly person
> She is such a *simpleton* that no one takes her seriously.

simulate
v sim-u-late: to feign, pretend
> He *simulated* the actions of a lame person so that he could be excused from doing the exercises.

sincere
adj sin-cere: honest, genuine
> They trust her because of her *sincere* attitude.

sinecure
n si-ne-cure: job requiring little work
> If you are looking for a *sinecure* here, you've come to the wrong place.

singe
n singe: slight burn
> A *singe* appeared on the blouse where the iron had stayed too long.

singe
v singe: to burn superficially or slightly
> She *singed* her neck when the curling iron came too close to her skin.

sinister
adj sin-is-ter: evil, threatening
> He faced them at the door of his house with a *sinister* expression on his face.

sinuous
adj sin-u-ous: with many curves
> The *sinuous* road was hazardous at night.

sire
n sire: male ancestor
> Her *sire* left the house and property to her.

sire
v sire: to beget
> They *sired* seven children.

skeptical
adj skep-ti-cal: doubting
> Their *skeptical* expressions lead me to believe that they don't approve of my ideas.

skew
v skew: to twist, slant, distort
> He *skewed* the data to suit his purpose.

skew
n skew: swerve
> The *skew* of the wheels sent the truck racing off the road.

skillet

n skil-let: frying pan

I have all the kitchen utensils I need except a *skillet* large enough to fry potatoes.

skim

v skim: remove from the top

Be careful to *skim* the grease off the top of the soup before reheating it.

skimpy

adj skimp-y: scanty, not enough

You'll need to wear more than that *skimpy* outfit in this cold weather.

skirmish

n skir-mish: conflict, argument

The sale of the property created a *skirmish* between family members.

skittish

adj skit-tish: easily frightened

Don't take that *skittish* child into the haunted house.

slack

adj slack: loose, not firm; slow, sluggish

The rope hung *slack* over the wall.

They usually start their jobs on Monday mornings in a *slack* manner.

slander

n slan-der: false and harmful remark

Avoid *slander* when talking about them.

slander

v slan-der: to make a damaging statement about

His remarks *slandered* their reputation.

slapdash

adj slap-dash: hasty and careless

His *slapdash* cleaning of the warehouse hardly improved the mess at all.

slapdash

n slap-dash: carelessness

Her *slapdash* left the room looking untidy.

slash

v slash: to cut, gash

He *slashed* his toe while mowing the lawn.

slash

n slash: a gash

An ugly *slash* appeared on her arm where the back door had hit her.

slay

v slay: to kill with violence

Someone has been *slaying* the sheep.

sleazy

adj sleaz-y: flimsy

That *sleazy* dress is not appropriate for such a formal affair.

sleek

adj sleek: soft and glossy

The car has such a *sleek* surface.

sleet
n sleet: frozen rain
Bundle up warmly and take an umbrella to protect you from the *sleet*.

sleet
v sleet: to shower in the form of sleet
Instead of snowing, it *sleeted* all day.

sleuth
n sleuth: detective
They hired a *sleuth* to uncover the reason for her actions.

slime
n slime: mud, filth
She fell into the *slime* and ruined her dress.

slipshod
adj slip-shod: careless, untidy
She cleaned her room in such a *slipshod* manner that it wasn't any neater after she finished.

slither
v slith-er: to slide
The kids *slithered* down the vine into the water.

sliver
n sliv-er: splinter
A *sliver* of wood was stuck in her hand.

sliver
v sliv-er: to cut or split into slivers
He *slivered* the meat into several slices.

slouch
v slouch: to droop, bend downward
She *slouched* in her seat although she had been warned to sit up properly.

slovenly
adj slov-en-ly: untidy, sloppy
Although he owns several nice suits, he prefers to dress in a *slovenly* way.

sluggish
adj slug-gish: slow moving
His *sluggish* walking suggests that he received too little sleep last night.

slump
v slump: to drop, fall, decline
The doll *slumped* down on the floor of the closet.

slump
n slump: a sudden fall
A *slump* of activity in the office left employees with nothing to do.

slur
v slur: to pronounce indistinctly, slide over
He *slurred* his speech so badly that we could not understand what he was saying.

slur
n slur: a line connecting notes
The correct way to write that music is with a *slur* between the first and second notes.

smite

v smite: to hit hard, strike

If you *smite* him one more time, I will tell the officers to take him away from you.

smother

v smoth-er: to deprive of air

Open a window before we *smother* in here.

smudge

v smudge: to smear, streak with dirt

The child *smudged* his outfit with mud.

smudge

n smudge: a dirty spot

All the scrubbing in the world would not remove the *smudge* from his shirt.

snag

n snag: hidden obstacle, a sharp point or projection

A *snag* in the thread prevented him from sewing any further.

snag

v snag: to damage on a snag

She *snagged* her nylons against the nail protruding from the fence.

snarl

n snarl: growl

The dog emitted a menacing *snarl* when the stranger approached.

snarl

v snarl: tangle, or cause to be tangled

The dog twisted around so many times that she became *snarled* in her leash.

snicker

n snick-er: giggle, laugh

A *snicker* escaped her lips even while her mother was scolding her.

snub

v snub: to treat coldly

She was bewildered when some of her new classmates *snubbed* her.

snub

adj snub: short, turned up

Their baby is so cute with her large eyes and *snub* nose.

snug

adj snug: comfortable, sheltered

He preferred to stay in his *snug* bed rather than face the cold morning air.

soar

v soar: to fly high, rise

The birds *soared* above the farm.

sob

v sob: to cry

The kids *sobbed* when their friends went away for the holidays.

sob

n sob: the act or sound of crying

They heard a *sob* from the child when she realized that she was alone in the room.

sober

adj so-ber: not drunk; serious

Don't let him drive the car until he is *sober* again.

The professor had a *sober* expression on his face.

sober

v so-ber: to make or become sober

A cold shower *sobered* her up enough in the morning to report to work on time.

sociable

adj so-cia-ble: friendly

His *sociable* manner has made him very popular here.

sodden

adj sod-den: soaked

They packed up their *sodden* belongings after the rainstorm.

soggy

adj sog-gy: heavy with moisture

Although the air was warm, the grass was still too *soggy* to walk across.

solace

n sol-ace: comfort, relief

He sought *solace* from his mother when he hurt his foot.

solace

v sol-ace: to comfort, to console

She *solaced* her son when he ran in crying.

solar

adj so-lar: of the sun

Their house is warmed naturally with *solar* heat.

sole

adj sole: one and only, exclusive

He was the *sole* guest who showed for the dinner.

solemn

adj sol-emn: serious, grave

This is going to be a *solemn* affair.

solicit

v so-lic-it: to beg, ask for

She *solicited* her parents for the money to pay for her car.

solicitude

n so-lic-i-tude: state of anxiety, concern

The teacher had great *solicitude* for the welfare of her students.

soliloquy

n so-lil-o-quy: monologue

He delivered a witty *soliloquy* to the delighted audience.

somber

adj som-ber: gloomy, dark

A *somber* look appeared on his face when he read the bad news.

sonnet

n son-net: fourteen-line poem

Their assignment was to write a *sonnet* and read it to the class.

sonorous
adj so-no-rous: rich, resonant sound
His *sonorous* voice was the cause of his success.

soothe
v soothe: calm down, comfort
Her soft, quiet voice *soothed* his fears.

soothsayer
n sooth-say-er: predictor
The *soothsayer* told him that he would be sent on a voyage next year.

sorcerer
n sor-cer-er: magician
Children and adults alike were fascinated by the tricks performed by the *sorcerer.*

sordid
adj sor-did: dirty, filthy
I can't understand how he can continue to live in such *sordid* conditions.

souse
v souse: to wet thoroughly
She *soused* the garden vegetables in vinegar.

souse
n souse: a drenching, soaking
A *souse* of water and epsom salts will reduce the swelling in his foot.

souvenir
n sou-ve-nir: keepsake
She kept the program as a *souvenir* of the performance she had just seen.

sovereign
n sov-er-eign: ruler, monarch
As *sovereign* of the tiny country, he governs his countrymen with wisdom.

sovereign
adj sov-er-eign: above all others, chief, supreme
Her *sovereign* position in the office grants her the power of final approval over all decisions.

sow
n sow: female pig
The *sow* escaped her pen and roamed in the garden behind the house.

sow
v sow: to plant seed
They cleared the land so that they could *sow* in time for a summer garden of fresh vegetables.

spacious
adj spa-cious: vast, roomy
They were not used to living in such *spacious* quarters.

spade
n spade: shovel
Use a *spade* to dig up that plant.

spade
v spade: to dig with a spade
Carefully *spade* the flowers out of this row.

span

n span: distance between two points; a period of time

The bridge covers a span of twenty feet.

There is a *span* of twenty years from the time this house was built until it was renovated.

span

v span: to measure, especially by the span of the hand

They *spanned* the distance between the walls.

sparse

adj sparse: scanty, meager

Unfortunately, there is only a *sparse* selection of canned foods left in the cupboard.

specific

adj spe-cif-ic: definite, precise

His *specific* instructions were to turn right at the corner.

specific

n spe-cif-ic: a particular case

The *specifics* stated that we should not enter that house.

spectacles

n spec-ta-cles: eyeglasses

They wore *spectacles* to protect their eyes from the sunlight.

spectator

n spec-ta-tor: viewer

Several *spectators* told the police what had happened.

specter

n spec-ter: ghost

A *specter* appeared at the top of the stairs of the old house.

spigot

n spig-ot: valve, faucet

He hooked up a *spigot* to the outside wall so that they could draw water for the garden.

spinster

n spin-ster: old maid

The *spinster* lives alone in her large house.

spiritual

adj spir-it-u-al: sacred, religious

A *spiritual* ceremony is held here every Sunday night.

spiritual

n spir-it-u-al: a religious folksong of American Black origin

His favorite type of music is *spirituals*.

splice

v splice: to join together

Splice that remaining tape on to this new roll.

splice

n splice: a joint made by splicing

This is the *splice* at which he merged the ropes.

spontaneous

adj spon-ta-ne-ous: not planned

The *spontaneous* concert drew a large crowd.

sprawl

v sprawl: to spread out

The cats *sprawled* on the rug in front of the warm fireplace.

sprawl
n sprawl: a sprawling movement or position
> He meant to dive into the pool head first, but he hit the water in a *sprawl*.

spree
n spree: a binge
> They went on a shopping *spree*.

sprig
n sprig: twig, small branch
> A *sprig* from a maple tree floated in the pool.

sprightly
adj spright-ly: lively, gay
> A *sprightly* group of elderly men and women danced for hours.

sprint
v sprint: to run fast
> She *sprinted* to the finish line in record-breaking time.

sprint
n sprint: fast run
> Seeing that he was losing time, he broke into a *sprint*.

sprite
n sprite: elf, fairy
> It is rumored that a *sprite* lives in the forest.

sprout
v sprout: to grow
> The seeds you planted last fall are *sprouting* now.

sprout
n sprout: a young growth on a plant
> The arrival of spring brought about several new green *sprouts* on the tree.

spry
adj spry: active, lively
> Her *spry* motions surprised the guard, who thought she was asleep.

spurious
adj spu-ri-ous: false
> The student's *spurious* excuse did not fool his teacher.

spurn
v spurn: to refuse with disdain
> He *spurned* her invitation for dinner because he thought she was unworthy of his attention.

spurt
v spurt: to gush, squirt
> When she shook the bottle, the cap flew off and water *spurted* all over the floor.

spurt
n spurt: a brief, sudden effort
> All I need is one more *spurt* of energy to get this job done.

squalid
adj squal-id: filthy
> When he moved out, he left the apartment in *squalid* condition.

squall
n squall: violent windstorm

A *squall* hit the resort town and ruined the weekend for the tourists.

squander
v squan-der: to waste

She *squandered* her wealth on useless projects.

squash
v squash: to crush

The fallen tree *squashed* the garden.

squash
n squash: a game played with rackets; a fleshy fruit

Their favorite evening activity is to play *squash*.

The *squash* is a relative of the pumpkin.

squat
v squat: to crouch

They *squatted* behind the furniture so that they could surprise him when he arrived.

squat
adj squat: short and heavy or thick

The *squat* dog ambled slowly down the path.

squat
n squat: the position of squatting

She bent in a *squat* while doing her gardening.

squelch
v squelch: to crush

The trash compacter *squelched* the leftovers into tiny piles.

squelch
n squelch: a crushing retort

He replied to her rude question with a *squelch*.

stabilize
v sta-bi-lize: to make firm, steady

Stabilize the sign by bracing it against this pole.

staff
n staff: stick, pole, rod; personnel

She leaned on the *staff* as she hobbled down the road.

The boss was kind to his *staff*.

stag
n stag: male deer

The *stag* bent to drink from the brook.

stag
adv stag: unaccompanied by a date

The invitation requests that you attend *stag*.

stagnant
adj stag-nant: not moving

The odor remained in the *stagnant* air for several hours.

stale
adj stale: not fresh

The bread that was left out overnight is now *stale*.

stale
v stale: to become dry or flat

That cereal will *stale* if you don't cover it.

stallion

n stal-lion: male horse

That horse is the finest *stallion* at the race.

stalwart

adj stal-wart: strong, brave

He defended his family with a *stalwart* stance.

stamina

n stam-i-na: endurance

He built up his *stamina* for the race by jogging every morning.

stammer

v stam-mer: to stutter

She was so frightened that she *stammered* out her account of what had happened.

stammer

n stam-mer: a stutter

Even though she speaks with a *stammer*, she sings without a trace of difficulty.

stampede

n stam-pede: sudden scattering

The loud, unexpected noise sent the flock into a *stampede*.

stampede

v stam-pede: to move in a stampede

The herd of buffalo *stampeded* across the prairie.

stanchion

n stan-chion: bar, post

The horses were tethered to the *stanchion*.

startle

v star-tle: to surprise, frighten

He was *startled* to see several of his friends waiting for him in his house.

stationary

adj sta-tion-ary: still, not moving

He stood in a *stationary* position for several minutes.

stationery

n sta-tion-ery: paper

Write your letter on the company's *stationery*.

stature

n stat-ure: height of people or animals; status achieved

His *stature* was imposing.

Her creativity improved her *stature* within the company.

status

n sta-tus: condition, rank

Her *status* in the office improved when she completed the job in a short time.

steed

n steed: horse

That animal is the finest *steed* in the county.

steep

adj steep: sharp slope

The *steep* path prevented them from climbing any farther with all their gear.

stench

n stench: bad smell, stink

Those fumes left a *stench* in the air.

sterile
adj ster-ile: germ free, barren
The newborn infants were kept in a *sterile* room.

stern
adj stern: severe, strict
A *stern* expression appeared on her face when she disciplined her children.

stem
n stern: rear end of a boat
Be sure that you balance the weight in the boat by having someone sit in the *stern* as well as in the bow.

stevedore
n ste-ve-dore: unloader of ships
Stevedores waited near the dock for the ship to arrive with its cargo.

stifle
v sti-fle: to suppress, smother
She *stifled* her desire to show the child the way since she knew it was better if he tried it alone.

stigma
n stig-ma: stain, disgrace
His behavior left a *stigma* on his family's good name.

stilted
adj stilt-ed: formal, dignified
She spoke to the crowd in a *stilted* manner.

stimulate
v stim-u-late: to stir up, rouse
The clowns will appear first to *stimulate* the audience to laughter.

stingy
adj stin-gy: not generous
She was *stingy* with her portions of the dessert.

stipend
n sti-pend: salary or allowance
She pays her rent out of her monthly *stipend*.

stocky
adj stock-y: solid, sturdy
All that excess food has given him a *stocky* build.

stoic
adj sto-ic: indifferent to or unmoved by emotions
His *stoic* reaction to the bad news amazed his family.

stoke
v stoke: to stir up
Stoke the fire with this prong to get it burning again.

stout
adj stout: fat and large
She was so *stout* that she could not fit into the chair.

stow
v stow: to pack
Stow the summer gear away for the winter months.

straggle
v strag-gle: to wander, stray
The chickens *straggled* across the yard after she left the hen house open.

strenuous
adj stren-u-ous: very active
The *strenuous* workout left them huffing and puffing.

stress

n stress: pressure, strain

The *stress* of doing two jobs at one time was too great for them to handle.

stress

v stress: to put pressure on

You will *stress* the sofa too much if you continue to jump around on it.

strew

v strew: to scatter, sprinkle

The falling leaves were *strewn* across the park.

strident

adj stri-dent: harsh sounding

She had a *strident* voice that annoyed everyone.

strife

n strife: quarrel, fight

Their *strife* was over the use of the equipment.

strive

v strive: to try hard

They *strive* to climb the mountain every year.

stroll

n stroll: leisurely walk

They enjoy a *stroll* through the woods each evening after dinner.

stroll

v stroll: to walk about leisurely

Many people *stroll* along the beach instead of swimming.

structure

n struc-ture: building, arrangement

The city plans to build several more *structures* on the waterfront next year.

stucco

n stuc-co: plaster

They covered the wall with *stucco*.

stun

v stun: to daze, bewilder

The surprise arrival of her parents *stunned* her.

stupefy

v stu-pe-fy: to astound, stun

His amazing feats of daring *stupefied* the audience.

stupor

n stu-por: dazed condition

A *stupor* came over him as he stared out of the window.

sturdy

adj stur-dy: robust, strong, firm

His *sturdy* build made him very popular with the women.

stymie

v sty-mie: to block completely

The accident at the corner *stymied* traffic in all directions.

suave

adj suave: gracious, polite

They were impressed with his *suave* manners.

subdue

v sub-due: to overcome; conquer

She *subdued* her fears and faced the crowd.

sublime
adj sub-lime: noble, majestic
They were impressed by his *sublime* mannerisms and assumed that he was the head of the house.

subpoena
n sub-poe-na: writ summoning a witness
They issued a *subpoena* to the man who saw the accident.

subsequent
adj sub-se-quent: following, later
Any *subsequent* reports should be filed behind this one.

subside
v sub-side: to decrease, abate
The storm *subsided* during the night and the sun was shining by morning.

subtle
adj sub-tle: delicate, elusive
The *subtle* aroma of his cologne remained in the room after he had left.

subvert
v sub-vert: to ruin, overthrow
He will *subvert* all their careful planning by his actions.

succinct
adj suc-cinct: concise, brief
She wrote a *succinct* report of the long meeting.

succulent
adj suc-cu-lent: juicy
The *succulent* steak made her mouth water in hunger.

succumb
v suc-cumb: yield, give in to
She *succumbed* to his persistent request to go out with him.

suffice
v suf-fice: to be enough, satisfy a need
This first draft will *suffice* for now, but please have the final draft completed by Friday.

suffrage
n suffrage: voting
Woman's *suffrage* is increasing each year.

sulk
v sulk: be sullen, aloof
She *sulked* in her room after her father told her that she could not buy the coat.

sullen
adj sul-len: gloomy, dismal
A *sullen* sky spoiled their plans for a picnic today.

sultry
adj sul-try: hot and moist
The *sultry* weather prevented anyone from wanting to play sports outdoors.

summit
n sum-mit: the top, acme
They reached the *summit* of the hill and then started the long decline.

sumptuous
adj sump-tu-ous: magnificent
They always serve a *sumptuous* Thanksgiving dinner.

sundry
adj sun-dry: various, several
Sundry items were for sale at the store.

superfluous
adj su-per-flu-ous: more than needed
Put any *superfluous* materials into the storage closet.

superlative
adj su-per-la-tive: supreme
The *superlative* compliment you can give him is friendship.

supersede
v su-per-sede: to replace with someone or something better
The assistant *superseded* the boss, who was fired for cause.

supine
adj su-pine: lying flat
The cat stretched out in a *supine* position on the sofa.

supplant
v sup-plant: to displace, set aside
The computer *supplanted* the work previously done by three people.

supple
adj sup-ple: bending easily
The old man could not keep up with the *supple* youth in the race to complete the job.

supplement
n sup-ple-ment: addition
A *supplement* to the newspaper will be included in this week's edition.

supplement
v sup-ple-ment: to fill the deficiencies of, add to
You should *supplement* your diet with vitamin pills.

suppress
v sup-press: to stop, put an end to
He *suppressed* his desire to eat another piece of candy and drank some water instead.

supreme
adj su-preme: utmost, highest
He received the *supreme* honor for his bravery.

surfeit
n sur-feit: an excess of food or drink
A *surfeit* of Halloween candy made them sick.

surfeit
v sur-feit: to overindulge in food or drink
They *surfeited* themselves with snacks.

surge
v surge: to rise, advance
Waves *surged* on the rugged coastline, sending a fine mist into the air.

surge
n surge: a large billow, increase in current, sudden advancement
A *surge* of people moved toward the stage.

surmise
n sur-mise: guess
His *surmise* is that they will arrive around noon.

surmise
v sur-mise: to guess
　She *surmised* that there was a sweater in the box.

surname
n sur-name: family name
　She prefers to use her *surname* rather than her husband's last name.

surpass
v sur-pass: to exceed
　He *surpassed* her efforts and set a new record.

surplus
n sur-plus: excess, extra
　The *surplus* of equipment was sent back to the office.

surrogate
n sur-ro-gate: substitute
　A *surrogate* will be appointed until a new judge can be elected.

surveillance
n sur-veil-lance: close watch
　A *surveillance* was set up during the month that the paintings were on display at the museum.

survey
v sur-vey: to inspect, examine
　They *surveyed* the damage left in the cellar by the flood.

survey
n sur-vey: a general study, as by sampling opinion
　A *survey* of the residents proved that they were in favor of having a shopping mall nearby.

survive
v sur-vive: to outlive, remain alive
　The ninety-year-old woman had *survived* her brothers and sisters.

suspend
v sus-pend: to hang from above; stop for a while
　The decorations were *suspended* from the ceiling beams.
　The boy's television privileges were *suspended*.

sustain
v sus-tain: to support, maintain
　Her friends *sustained* her throughout the ordeal.

swagger
v swag-ger: to sway, strut
　After winning the award, he *swaggered* from the auditorium.

swagger
n swag-ger: swaggering walk or manner
　He walked down the aisle in a *swagger*.

swarm
n swarm: crowd
　A *swarm* of bees buzzed over their heads.

swarm
v swarm: to fly off in a swarm, to move
　The mosquitoes *swarmed* over the unprotected tourists.

swelter

v swel-ter: to suffer from heat

She *sweltered* in the sunlight.

swelter

n swel-ter: oppressive heat

Nobody wants to participate until this *swelter* is over.

swerve

v swerve: to turn aside

The vehicles *swerved* to the right to avoid the obstacle in the road.

swerve

n swerve: a turning aside

A sudden *swerve* of the wheels sent the truck careening off the road into the ditch.

swine

n swine: pigs, hogs

They raise *swine* as well as cattle on this farm.

swirl

v swirl: to twist, whirl

The flag *swirled* in the wind.

swoon

v swoon: to faint

He frightened her so much that she *swooned*.

swoon

n swoon: a faint

She collapsed onto the floor in a *swoon*.

sycamore

n syc-a-more: shade tree

Their favorite meeting place is under the giant *sycamore* in the center of the park.

sylvan

adj syl-van: woodsy

The *sylvan* view from their back window is lovely.

symmetry

n sym-me-try: balanced arrangement

He wants *symmetry* in this room, so move that chair up to the same level as this one.

sympathy

n sym-pa-thy: sharing of sorrow

They all felt *sympathy* for her loss.

symposium

n sym-po-si-um: meeting for discussion of a subject

They held a *symposium* on the subject of security.

synthetic

adj syn-thet-ic: artificial

The *synthetic* fur coat looks just as attractive as the real one.

T

tabloid

n tab-loid: newspaper

He reads the daily *tabloid* at breakfast.

taboo

n ta-boo: forbidden, banned

Those words are *taboo* here.

taboo

adj ta-boo: prohibited or restricted

Politics is a *taboo* subject at our meetings.

taboo
v ta-boo: to prohibit
The officials *tabooed* swimming in the pond.

tabulate
v tab-u-late: to list, arrange
Tabulate the contributions into separate categories according to quality.

tacit
adj tac-it: silent, unspoken
They nodded their heads in *tacit* agreement from opposite ends of the room.

tactile
adj tac-tile: via sense of touch
The plant is so sensitive to *tactile* encounters that it is placed safely out of reach.

tadpole
n tad-pole: young frog
The boys went searching for a *tadpole* to add to their collection in the pond.

taint
v taint: to affect with something unpleasant, spoil
His reputation was *tainted* by nasty rumors.

taint
n taint: a trace of contamination, corruption
The *taint* of their ideas spoiled the event.

talisman
n tal-is-man: magic charm
She is so superstitious that she always carries a *talisman* with her.

tangent
n tan-gent: a curve, line, or surface touching another line without intersecting; a digression
Their conversation went off on a *tangent*.

tangible
adj tan-gi-ble: definite; real
The criminal left *tangible* evidence of his crime.

tankard
n tank-ard: drinking mug
They served his beer in a *tankard*.

tantamount
adj tan-ta-mount: equivalent to
His statement was *tantamount* to a confession.

taper
v ta-per: to gradually decrease
The rain *tapered* off to a fine mist and then stopped completely.

taper
n ta-per: a slender candle
She lit the *taper* on the table for dinner.

tardy
adj tar-dy: late
I missed the lecture because I was *tardy* in arriving.

tariff
n tar-iff: tax
　A *tariff* will be applied to your merchandise.

tarnish
v tar-nish: to dull the luster of
　Scraping the furniture across the floor *tarnished* its surface.

tarnish
n tar-nish: dullness, less coloration, stain
　Constant abuse to the floor left a *tarnish* on it that could not be removed.

tarry
v tar-ry: to remain, to delay
　They *tarried* in the theater long after the show had ended.

tart
n tart: pastry
　For breakfast, she prefers hot chocolate and a cinnamon *tart*.

tart
adj tart: sharp, sour
　The soured milk left a *tart* taste in the casserole.

tattered
adj tat-tered: torn and ragged
　It is time to replace that *tattered* rug.

taunt
v taunt: to mock, jeer, ridicule
　The children *taunted* the newcomer because he wore a pointed hat.

taunt
n taunt: scornful or jeering remark
　She answered his impertinent question with a *taunt*.

taut
adj taut: tight
　He fastened the boat to the pier with a *taut* rope.

tawdry
adj taw-dry: showy, cheap
　She wore a *tawdry* outfit to the theater.

tease
v tease: to annoy, vex; to raise a nap
　The boy *teased* his sister unceasingly.
　She *teased* the blue velvet with her hand.

tease
n tease: a teasing or being teased; a person who teases
　No one takes him seriously because he is such a *tease*.

tedious
adj te-di-ous: monotonous
　The *tedious* task of counting all those receipts seemed endless.

teem
v teem: to be full of
　The train station *teemed* with people rushing to catch their trains.

temerity

n te-mer-i-ty: boldness, rashness

She faced her parents with *temerity*, and made her announcement.

tempest

n tem-pest: storm, disturbance

Warnings of a *tempest* blowing in from sea sent the tourists running for cover.

tenacious

adj te-na-cious: fierce, stubborn

A *tenacious* wind gripped the boat and turned it over.

tendency

n ten-den-cy: trend, inclination

Her *tendency* is to have a hot cup of tea each evening after dinner.

tenement

n ten-e-ment: dwelling

Their *tenement* is on the corner.

tense

adj tense: nervous, stretched tight

There was a *tense* mood throughout the room.

tense

v tense: to make or become tense

He *tensed* his muscles in an attempt to feel warmer in the snow.

tense

n tense: any form of a verb that shows time of action

The *tense* for that word should be in the future.

tepid

adj tep-id: lukewarm

He prefers to shower in *tepid* water.

terrestrial

adj ter-res-tri-al: earthly

Some areas of the moon appear *terrestrial*.

terse

adj terse: brief

She yelled out a *terse* reply as she ran by.

thaw

v thaw: to melt, become warmer

The snow *thawed* in the warm air.

thaw

n thaw: a warm spell to permit melting

Ships cannot pass through this channel until after the spring *thaw*.

theme

n theme: topic, subject

The *theme* of his paper is realism.

theorem

n the-o-rem: an idea that can be demonstrated by reasoning

She presented an argument to prove her *theorem*.

therapy

n ther-a-py: treatment of diseases

This institution provides excellent *therapy* to all its patients.

thermal

adj ther-mal: relating to heat

Cover the baby with a *thermal* blanket.

thrall

n thrall: one who is physically, morally, or intellectually enslaved

She is in *thrall* to her father's philosophy.

thrash

v thrash: to beat

Thrash the rug with this broom to get that dirt out.

threshold

n thresh-old: doorway

They request that we leave our boots at the *threshold* before entering the room.

thrift

n thrift: careful management of resources

Their *thrift* resulted in a considerable amount of money at the end of the year.

thrive

v thrive: to grow, prosper

The flowers *thrived* in the sunny garden.

throb

v throb: to tremble, quiver

His heart *throbbed* with excitement.

throb

n throb: a strong beat or pulsation

The *throb* of pain in her head continued throughout the evening.

throng

n throng: crowd, multitude

A *throng* of thousands lined the streets to view the passing cavalcade.

throng

v throng: to crowd into

They *thronged* into the only bus to come along in an hour.

thud

n thud: dull sound, thump

The sign landed with a *thud* on the ground.

thwart

v thwart: block, defeat

He *thwarted* her attempts to reach the finish line first.

tidbit

n tid-bit: morsel of food

She will get sick if she continues to consume only *tidbits*.

tidings

n ti-dings: information

They drive into town once a week to hear all the neighborhood *tidings*.

tier

n tier: row

A *tier* of seats has been reserved for your group.

tiff

n tiff: a little quarrel

They seldom fight, but sometimes they have a *tiff*.

till

v till: to cultivate; plow

He *tilled* the land for the new crops.

till

n till: a drawer for keeping money

Get his allowance out of the *till*.

timid

adj tim-id: shy

The *timid* child hid behind his mother when the guests arrived.

timorous

adj tim-or-ous: fearful

He spoke to his grandfather in a *timorous* voice.

tirade

n ti-rade: long scolding speech

Their father delivered a *tirade* to his delinquent children.

titanic

adj ti-tan-ic: gigantic, vast

Some people think of the city as a *titanic* hunk of concrete and steel.

toga

n to-ga: robe, garment

She covered her swimsuit with a warm *toga*.

toil

v toil: to work, labor

He *toiled* hour after hour in the garage until the engine was fixed.

token

n to-ken: sign, keepsake

Their embraces are a *token* of their love for each other.

token

adj to-ken: symbolic, minimal

His *token* gesture didn't convince her that he cared.

tolerate

v tol-er-ate: endure; allow

She was not able to *tolerate* his screams.

They refused to *tolerate* discrimination.

toll

n toll: tax, fee

You'll have to pay a *toll* before crossing the bridge.

toll

v toll: to ring or sound

The church bells *tolled* at noon.

toll

n toll: the sound of a bell or alarm ringing

The *toll* of Christmas bells came out of the church.

tomb

n tomb: grave, mausoleum

All their ancestors are buried in the *tomb*.

tomfoolery

n tom-fool-er-y: nonsense

She was becoming annoyed at his persistent *tomfoolery*.

topple

v top-ple: to fall, overturn

The statue *toppled* onto the sidewalk from the strong wind.

toreador
n tor-e-a-dor: bullfighter
> The *toreador* challenged the bulls.

torment
v tor-ment: to cause great physical or mental pain
> The continuous pounding in her head *tormented* her.

torment
n tor-ment: a great physical or mental pain
> Her *torment* is the result of failing the entrance exam.

tornado
n tor-na-do: whirlwind
> A *tornado* swept over the fair, leaving a path of debris behind.

torpid
adj tor-pid: dull, inactive
> A *torpid* mood seemed to come over everyone.

torrent
n tor-rent: violent rush of water
> The split in the dam sent a *torrent* of water racing down the mountain.

torrid
adj tor-rid: very hot from the sun; passionate
> She burned her feet on the *torrid* sand.
> He wrote a *torrid* poem to his lover.

tortoise
n tor-toise: sea turtle
> At the aquarium you will see a *tortoise* basking in the sun or swimming.

totter
v tot-ter: to shake, be unsteady
> The heavy object *tottered* on the flimsy stand.

toxic
adj tox-ic: poisonous
> *Toxic* fumes escaped from the laboratory.

trachea
n tra-che-a: windpipe
> Some food was caught in his *trachea*.

tract
n tract: area of land or water
> The *tract* extended for several miles in each direction from the farm.

tractable
adj trac-ta-ble: easily managed
> The drugged dart made the lion more *tractable*.

trait
n trait: characteristic
> One of his most admirable *traits* is his perseverance.

trample
v tram-ple: to crush
> The child *trampled* the candy into the rug.

trample
n tram-ple: the sound of trampling
> A *trample* of hoofs was heard on the pavement.

trance

n trance: dazed condition

All that loud noise and ceaseless activity has left him in a *trance*.

tranquil

adj tran-quil: calm, peaceful

After the crowds left, a *tranquil* silence was all that remained.

transaction

n trans-ac-tion: the conducting of business

They entered into a *transaction* with the landlord to rent the apartment.

transcript

n tran-script: copy, reproduction

She asked him for a *transcript* of his book.

transform

v trans-form: to change, switch

Her Halloween costume *transformed* her into a witch.

transgress

v trans-gress: to break a law

Samson *transgressed* the laws of his people.

transient

adj tran-sient: not staying long

They will be here for a *transient* visit only.

transient

n tran-sient: one who is transient

The boarding house on the corner caters to *transients*.

transition

n tran-si-tion: a moving from one thing or place to another

The *transition* in leadership will begin next week.

transmit

v trans-mit: to pass along

They *transmitted* the message from one person to another until it reached the other end.

transpire

v tran-spire: to take place

Many events *transpired* over the weekend.

transport

v trans-port: to carry

The moving van *transported* their furniture from their old house to their new residence.

transport

n trans-port: in transportation

A *transport* of merchandise should arrive tomorrow.

transverse

adj trans-verse: across

That route is *transverse* to the main road.

trauma

n trau-ma: physical or mental injury

He suffered a major *trauma* when his child died.

travail

n tra-vail: difficult mental or physical labor

Years of *travail* were required before he became the head of the company.

travesty
n trav-es-ty: an absurd or grotesque imitation
> That painting is a *travesty* of the real masterpiece.

treacherous
adj treach-er-ous: disloyal
> He lost all his friends following his *treacherous* actions.

tread
v tread: to walk, step, trample
> They *tread* softly outside the baby's room.

tread
n tread: the mark of a foot or tire; a step
> The tire *treads* led them to the car.

treason
n trea-son: betrayal
> His act of *treason* was greeted with shocked disbelief.

trek
n trek: journey, trip
> They planned a *trek* across Canada that would last three months.

trek
v trek: to travel or migrate arduously
> The pioneers will *trek* across barren land before reaching their destination in the spring.

trench
n trench: long narrow ditch
> Move the debris out of the road and into the *trench*.

trench
v trench: to dig a ditch
> A crew *trenched* alongside the new highway.

trenchant
adj tren-chant: sharp, effective
> His *trenchant* comments offended the hostess.

trepidation
n trep-i-da-tion: fear, apprehension
> She approached the closed door with *trepidation*.

triad
n tri-ad: group of three
> They were divided into *triads* for the experiment.

tribulation
n trib-u-la-tion: great trouble
> The settlers faced many *tribulations* during the early days of America.

tribunal
n tri-bu-nal: court
> The *tribunal* will meet tomorrow to decide what to do about the issue.

trident
n tri-dent: three-pronged spear
> He fishes with a *trident*.

trifle
n tri-fle: small amount
> A *trifle* of ice cream remains in the freezer for you.

tripod

n tri-pod: three-legged stand

Place the camera on the *tripod*.

trite

adj trite: worn out by use

Avoid relying on *trite* expressions when you write your book.

trivial

adj triv-i-al: unimportant

That information is *trivial* and should be omitted.

truant

n tru-ant: one who avoids duty

The *truants* play in the park rather than show up for class.

truce

n truce: temporary peace

The conflict was partly settled and the troops declared a *truce*.

truculent

adj truc-u-lent: fierce, cruel

Her *truculent* treatment of the dog was unnecessary.

trudge

v trudge: to walk heavily

He *trudged* up five flights of stairs with his laundry.

truncate

v trun-cate: to cut off

The phone conversation was *truncated* when the telephone wire snapped.

truncheon

n trun-cheon: policeman's club

They used their *truncheons* to disperse the crowd.

truss

v truss: to bind, fasten

The leash was *trussed* to the fence so that the dog could not run too far.

truss

n truss: a bundle or pack

The peasant threw his *truss* on his back and laboriously made his way down the path.

tryst

n tryst: appointment, meeting, usually between lovers

They arranged a *tryst* for next Sunday.

tumble

v tum-ble: to fall

The rocks *tumbled* down the mountainside.

tumble

n tum-ble: a fall, disorder

She is in the hospital with a broken leg because of the *tumble* she took from the building.

tunic

n tu-nic: garment

He designed and sewed the *tunic* she is wearing.

turbine

n tur-bine: engine

The *turbine* for the airplane is built in this warehouse.

turbulent

adj tur-bu-lent: unruly, violent, disorderly

The *turbulent* sea tossed the tiny boat onto the rocks.

tureen

n tu-reen: deep dish

Serve the soup in the *tureen*.

turf

n turf: grass, sod, peat

They were warned to stay off the *turf* in the back yard.

turf

v turf: to cover with turf

Their yard took such a beating from the storm that they plan to *turf* it again.

turgid

adj tur-gid: swollen

The *turgid* condition of her ankle led us to believe that she had strained it.

turmoil

n tur-moil: commotion

Her unexpected arrival created a *turmoil* at the office.

tusk

n tusk: projecting tooth

The wild boar used its *tusk* as a weapon.

tutelage

n tu-te-lage: action as teacher or guardian

He developed into a fine actor under his father's *tutelage*.

tutor

n tu-tor: private teacher

She was having such difficulty with her math that she sought extra help from a *tutor*.

twig

n twig: small branch

A *twig* from the tree broke off and landed in the water.

twine

n twine: strong string or thread

Tie the package with *twine* after taping it securely on all corners.

twine

v twine: to twist together, weave

She *twined* the flowers into a necklace and placed it around her neck.

twinge

n twinge: sudden, sharp pain

He felt a *twinge* when the hot iron touched his arm.

twirl

v twirl: to revolve, spin

She *twirled* the baton with dazzling speed.

twirl

n twirl: a spinning

A *twirl* of wind scattered the newspaper in all directions.

tycoon

n ty-coon: important businessman

This restaurant caters to clerks and *tycoons* alike.

tyke

n tyke: mischievous child

The little *tyke* annoyed everyone at the table.

typhoon
n ty-phoon: storm, tempest
People were forbidden to go near the ocean until the *typhoon* was over.

typical
adj typ-i-cal: representative
We were not surprised when he gave us his *typical* reply.

tyrant
n ty-rant: cruel ruler, despot
The citizens rebelled against the treatment they were receiving from the *tyrant*.

tyro
n ty-ro: beginner, novice
He is a *tyro* at business, but he already shows a knack for it.

ultimate
adj ul-ti-mate: final, utmost, maximum
Please let us know your *ultimate* decision by tomorrow.

umbrage
n um-brage: resentment
She took *umbrage* at his unpleasant attitude.

uncanny
adj un-can-ny: strange and mysterious
He has this *uncanny* way of knowing what I am going to say before I say it.

undaunted
adj un-daunt-ed: not frightened
He entered the haunted house in an *undaunted* manner.

undulate
v un-du-late: to move in waves
The field of grain *undulated* in the wind.

unerring
adj un-er-ring: exactly right
His *unerring* answer was amazing since he was only guessing.

ungainly
adj un-gain-ly: clumsy, awkward
The colt was still *ungainly* compared to his mother.

uniform
adj u-ni-form: regular, same
He performs his job with *uniform* ease after all these years.

uniform
v u-ni-form: to supply with a uniform
They *uniformed* all their employees in protective gear.

uniform
n u-ni-form: distinctive clothes of a particular group
The *uniform* worn by all their students consists of a white blouse and black slacks.

unify
v u-ni-fy: to unite
The two teams *unified* their efforts and completed the task in half the time.

unique
adj u-nique: one of a kind
She is envied by her friends for her *unique* job.

unison

n u-ni-son: agreement

Approval was heard in *unison* from every member of the board of directors.

unity

n uni-ty: oneness

A *unity* was felt among the gathered friends.

unkempt

adj un-kempt: untidy

His room always appears in an *unkempt* condition.

unpalatable

adj un-pal-at-a-ble: distasteful

They refused to eat the *unpalatable* seafood.

unravel

v un-rav-el: to take or come apart

The sweater *unraveled* when the yarn got caught on the wire.

upbraid

v up-braid: to reproach, condemn

He *upbraided* his son for his poor grades.

uproarious

adj up-roar-i-ous: noisy and disorderly

His *uproarious* conduct at the meeting resulted in his being banned from any future gatherings.

upshot

n up-shot: result

The *upshot* of the meeting is that you will be named to the committee.

urbane

adj ur-bane: smoothly polite, polished

He is an *urbane* gentleman and admired by many people.

urchin

n ur-chin: poor, ragged child

Although he appears to be an *urchin*, he is actually quite well off.

urge

v urge: to solicit, entreat, impel

She *urged* her parents to buy the luggage for their trip.

urge

n urge: an urging, an impulse

I have an *urge* to eat Chinese food.

urn

n urn: vase

They place the bouquet of flowers in the *urn*.

usher

v ush-er: to escort in, conduct

He *ushered* his mother into the church.

usher

n ush-er: an official doorkeeper

Her arrival was announced by the *usher*.

usurp

v u-surp: to take possession of

His power was *usurped* by the new commander.

utensil

n u-ten-sil: implement

She stocked her kitchen with new *utensils*.

utmost
n ut-most: greatest possible
The *utmost* we can do is to try our best.

utmost
adj ut-most: most extreme
She danced with the *utmost* energy for the audition.

utter
adj ut-ter: complete, total
She had such a headache that her family left her in *utter* silence

utter
v ut-ter: to speak
He *uttered* the words she wanted to hear.

vaccinate
v vac-ci-nate: to inoculate
The school board insists that all students be *vaccinated* for measles before school starts.

vacillate
v va-cil-late: to waver
The members continued to *vacillate* before the vote.

vacuum
n vac-u-um: empty space, void
A *vacuum* was left where the house used to be.

vacuum
v vac-u-um: to clean with a vacuum cleaner
The floor needs to be *vacuumed* after the meeting.

vagabond
adj vag-a-bond: wanderer, vagrant
A *vagabond* camped out in the field last night before resuming his travels south.

vagrant
n va-grant: wanderer
The *vagrant* slept in the hallway at night.

vagrant
adj va-grant: following no fixed course, random
They traveled south in a *vagrant* style.

vague
adj vague: not clear
Your answer is too *vague* for them to understand.

vain
adj vain: unsuccessful; conceited
They made a *vain* attempt to lift the heavy suitcase.
The *vain* woman looked at herself in the mirror repeatedly.

valedictory
adj val-e-dic-to-ry: pertaining to a farewell address
The graduates listened to a particularly interesting *valedictory* speech.

valiant
adj val-iant: courageous
Her *valiant* actions will be rewarded.

valid
adj val-id: true, sound
We need *valid* proof of your story.

valise
n va-lise: luggage
  He packed his *valise* for a weekend trip to the country.

valor
n val-or: bravery, courage
  He approached his foes with such *valor* that they backed away.

vanish
v van-ish: to disappear
  All the cookies she had baked last night had *vanished* by morning.

vanity
n van-i-ty: pride
  Her *vanity* was hurt when he insulted her appearance.

vapor
n va-por: mist, fog
  The *vapor* was so dense that he could not see far enough ahead to drive without lights.

variable
adj var-i-a-ble: changeable
  Their vacation plans are *variable* at this stage.

variation
n var-i-a-tion: change
  After months of following the same schedule, they looked forward to a *variation* in plans.

vassal
n vas-sal: servant, slave
  He was the king's *vassal*.

vast
adj vast: immense
  The *vast* size of the arena was more than they expected.

vault
v vault: to leap, jump
  The horse *vaulted* over the bushes.

vault
n vault: cellar, safe place; vaulting, an arched roof
  The money was hidden in the *vault*.
  The tourists gazed in awe at the cloister *vault* above.

veer
v veer: to change direction
  The airplane *veered* off its course to avoid the thunderstorm.

veer
n veer: a change of direction
  A sharp *veer* to the left sent the passengers tumbling into the aisle.

vehement
adj ve-he-ment: forceful, violent
  His *vehement* denial surprised his family.

veil
v veil: to cover
  She *veiled* the birdcage with a light cloth to quiet the bird.

veil
n veil: a piece of light fabric as of net
  She never appears outdoors without a *veil* to protect her delicate skin.

velocity

n ve-loc-i-ty: speed

He was pedaling his bike with such *velocity* that he could not stop at the corner.

vend

v vend: to peddle, sell

To *vend* her merchandise, she had to send out a promotional letter.

vendetta

n ven-det-ta: vengeful feud

He swore to end the *vendetta* between them.

veneer

n ve-neer: covering

They reupholstered the sofa with a leather *veneer*.

veneer

v ve-neer: to cover with a thin layer of something

The factory *veneered* the chipboard with a thin slice of walnut.

vengeance

n ven-geance: revenge

He attacked the boy with *vengeance* for what had been done to his sister.

venison

n ven-i-son: deer meat

Not everyone enjoys eating *venison*.

venom

n ven-om: poison

The snake bite left *venom* in his body.

ventilate

v ven-ti-late: to circulate fresh air; discuss freely

Open the window so that we can *ventilate* the room.

He *ventilated* his views freely.

venture

n ven-ture: risky undertaking

In her business, she tries several *ventures* in a year.

venture

v ven-ture: to risk

Venture a decision about which is the correct answer to the math problem.

verbatim

adj ver-bat-im: word for word

His *verbatim* account of the accident was quite accurate.

verbose

adj ver-bose: wordy

The *verbose* presentation bored the students.

verdant

adj ver-dant: green

The forest was *verdant* and lush.

verdict

n ver-dict: decision, judgment

The jury agreed on a guilty *verdict* for the offender.

verify

v ver-if-y: to confirm

The hotel clerk *verified* their reservations for the weekend.

vermin

n ver-min: small troublesome animals

They have to keep the trash containers tightly closed so as not to attract hungry *vermin*.

vernacular

n ver-nac-u-lar: dialect or nonstandard language

I cannot understand what he says when he speaks in the *vernacular*.

versatile

adj ver-sa-tile: many-sided abilities

All that training and education has given her a *versatile* background.

versus

prep ver-sus: against

It was the green team *versus* the red team.

vertex

n ver-tex: highest point, top

They climbed to the *vertex* of the mountain.

vertigo

n ver-ti-go: dizziness

His *vertigo* makes it impossible for him to pilot the plane.

vessel

n ves-sel: boat, ship

The *vessel* carried shipments of material across the ocean.

vestibule

n ves-ti-bule: hallway, lobby

The house features a long *vestibule* from the front door to the living room.

veto

v ve-to: to reject

She *vetoed* his suggestion to go away for the weekend.

veto

n ve-to: a prohibiting order

Their suggestions for the campaign met with a *veto* from the head of the agency.

vex

v vex: to anger, provoke, annoy

They *vexed* her to the point that she started yelling at them to leave.

via

prep vi-a: by way of

They traveled to Canada *via* Michigan.

viaduct

n vi-a-duct: bridge

A *viaduct* connected one township with another.

vial

n vi-al: small bottle

He filled the *vial* with a sampling of the liquid.

vibrate

v vi-brate: to move rapidly to and fro

The dishes *vibrated* in the cupboard while he was hammering.

vice

n vice: evil habit, fault, defect

He considers smoking cigarettes to be his worst *vice*.

vicinity
n vi-cin-i-ty: nearness
> She was in the *vicinity* of her
> first house.

vicious
adj vi-cious: wicked
> The man who lives on the
> corner has a *vicious* temper.

vie
v vie: to compete, strive
> Each of the contestants *vied*
> for first place.

vigilant
adj vig-i-lant: alertly watchful
> The dog sat in *vigilant* silence
> outside of his master's door.

vigor
n vig-or: energy, power
> He claims to get his *vigor* from
> those vitamin pills.

vile
adj vile: wicked
> His *vile* behavior landed him
> in jail.

vilify
v vil-i-fy: to defame, slander
> He attempted to *vilify* the
> politician.

villa
n vil-la: a large house
> They like to spend the
> summer months at their
> *villa* near the ocean.

vindicate
v vin-di-cate: to defend, justify
> She *vindicated* her friend
> against their accusations.

viper
n vi-per: snake
> A *viper* slithered in the tall
> grass beside the pond.

virile
adj vir-ile: manly, masculine
> The boy assumed a *virile*
> manner when he addressed
> the guests.

virtue
n vir-tue: goodness
> His *virtue* was rewarded with
> a trip to the farm.

virulent
adj vir-u-lent: harmful; hostile;
toxic
> The *virulent* ingredient in the
> detergent was removed.

visa
n vi-sa: a permit on a passport
> You will need to obtain a
> *visa* before traveling to those
> countries.

viscous
adj vis-cous: thick, sticky
> The *viscous* liquid seeped
> down the path.

vital
adj vi-tal: necessary
> Eggs are a *vital* ingredient in
> that recipe.

vitals
n vi-tals: the vital organs: the
heart, brain, etc.
> They feared that the exposure
> to the cold air would harm
> his *vitals*.

vivid

adj viv-id: bright, intense

The *vivid* sunlight flooded the room.

vocation

n vo-ca-tion: occupation, career

He quit his writing job because he wished to change his *vocation* to business management.

vociferous

adj vo-cif-er-ous: loud and noisy

The people at the rear table talked in *vociferous* tones that could be heard throughout the diner.

vogue

n vogue: fashion, popularity

It is in *vogue* to wear your dress at knee length.

void

n void: an empty space

The removal of the materials left a *void* in the container.

void

v void: to make empty; render useless

The secretary *voided* her check.

volatile

adj vol-a-tile: explosive, changeable, fickle

Her *volatile* temper often got her into trouble.

volition

n vo-li-tion: willingness

He accepted our proposal of his own *volition*.

voluble

adj vol-u-ble: talking too much

He tries to avoid her *voluble* conversations on the phone.

voracious

adj vo-ra-cious: consuming greedily

Following three days of fasting, their *voracious* attack on the food was understandable.

vortex

n vor-tex: whirlpool

The combination of hot and cold winds created a *vortex* in the air.

vouch

v vouch: to assert, affirm, attest

She *vouched* for his reliability.

vow

n vow: promise

He made a *vow* to exercise every evening.

vow

v vow: to promise or declare solemnly

They *vowed* to complete her job for her when she became ill.

vulgar

adj vul-gar: coarse, unrefined

His *vulgar* language infuriated the hostess.

vulnerable

adj vul-ner-a-ble: open to attack

The roof blew off the house, leaving the occupants *vulnerable* to the storm.

W

wade

v wade: to walk through water; to go through a long and boring task

Following the storm, the kids *waded* through the puddles in the street.

wager

v wag-er: to gamble, bet

He *wagered* that he would come in first in the race.

waif

n waif: neglected child

The police took the *waif* to the orphanage.

wail

v wail: to cry

The baby *wailed* for attention.

waive

v waive: to relinquish

He *waived* his control of the stockroom and let them use it freely.

wallow

v wal-low: to flounder, roll about

The fish *wallowed* on the beach where it had been washed up.

wallow

n wal-low: an act of floundering

The *wallow* of the boat made them feel uneasy.

wan

adj wan: pale

By the end of the cold season, their faces were *wan* from lack of sun.

wane

v wane: to decline

His popularity *waned* over the years.

wanton

adj wan-ton: reckless; heartless, lewd

He is denied use of the family car because of his *wanton* way of driving.

Salome was a *wanton* young girl.

warden

n ward-en: keeper, guard

A *warden* is always on duty outside the prison.

warp

n warp: a distortion

A *warp* in the record prevented them from playing it.

warp

v warp: to bend, twist out of shape

The extreme heat *warped* the neck of the guitar.

warrant

n war-rant: guarantee; authorization to make an arrest

The new product came with a *warrant* for service.

They issued a *warrant* for his arrest.

warrant

v war-rant: to authorize, guarantee

One of the officials must *warrant* your idea before we can put it into practice.

wary
adj war-y: careful, cautious
They approached the cage
with *wary* steps.

waver
v wa-ver: to vary
His plans *wavered* when he
received additional news.

wayfarer
n way-far-er: traveler
A *wayfarer* stopped at the
motel and inquired about
rates for the night.

waylay
v way-lay: to attack, rob
He feared that someone
would *waylay* him on the
road as he traveled with
the valuable cargo.

wayward
adj way-ward: disobedient
They sent their dog to
training school to correct
his *wayward* habits.

weep
v weep: to cry
She began to *weep* when she
won the contest.

weird
adj weird: mysterious, unearthly
Neighbors gathered in the
field to look at the *weird*
object that had fallen from
the sky.

weld
v weld: to join together
He *welded* the typewriter to
the desk so that no one could
remove it.

weld
n weld: joint made by welding
This *weld* will keep the stove
in place.

wharf
n wharf: dock, pier
They dangled their legs off the
wharf into the water below.

wheedle
v whee-dle: to coax, persuade
She *wheedled* her kitten to
come down out of the tree.

wheeze
v wheeze: to breathe with
difficulty
They *wheezed* in the dust that
flew around them.

wheeze
n wheeze: a wheezing
From the sound of that *wheeze*,
I suspect that you are getting
a cold.

whet
v whet: to sharpen
Whet the knife against
this rock.

whiff
n whiff: slight smell
A *whiff* of flowers could be
detected in the air.

whiff
v whiff: to blow or puff
The bubbles *whiffed* lightly
across the lawn.

whimper

n whim-per: low, mournful sound

A *whimper* could be heard from the hospital room.

whimper

v whim-per: to cry or utter with complaint

She *whimpered* at the disappearance of her puppy.

whine

v whine: to cry complainingly

She *whined* to her father when her brother broke her doll.

whine

n whine: a complaint uttered in a whining tone

A baby's *whine* is hard to ignore.

whirl

v whirl: to spin, rotate quickly

The falling leaves *whirled* in the air before settling on the ground.

whisk

v whisk: to sweep, brush

He *whisked* the papers under the desk top.

whisk

n whisk: quick movement

A *whisk* of wind sent the seeds flying over the land.

wield

v wield: to hold and use skillfully; control

He *wielded* a paintbrush in his left hand as he studied the painting.

wilt

v wilt: to droop

By the tenth lap around the lake, they were *wilting* from all the exercising.

wily

adj wi-ly: crafty, sly

He was *wily* enough to get away with the forgery.

wince

v wince: to shrink from

He *winced* from her verbal abuse.

windfall

n wind-fall: unexpected good luck

They were delighted to receive a *windfall* of an inheritance.

wisp

n wisp: small bunch

A *wisp* of hair escaped from under her scarf.

wistful

adj wist-ful: yearning

She gazed upon her idol with a *wistful* desire to be closer to him.

wither

v with-er: to dry up, to cause to wither

The flowers *withered* under the hot sun.

witty

adj wit-ty: clever and amusing

Her *witty* remarks entertained the other diners.

woe

n woe: great grief, trouble

His friends tried to lighten his *woe* when he lost his job.

wrangle

v wran-gle: to quarrel angrily

The children *wrangled* over the morsels in the box.

wrath

n wrath: rage, anger

She reacted to their insults with extreme *wrath*.

wrest

v wrest: to pull, twist

They tried in vain to *wrest* the bone away from their dog.

wretch

n wretch: bad person

He is considered to be such a *wretch* that no one visits him.

wring

v wring: to squeeze

Wring the water out of that towel before you hand it to me.

writhe

v writhe: to twist

He *writhed* in pain from the impact of the board on his back.

writhe

n writhe: a writhing or suffering

A *writhe* of pain resulted when she pulled too hard.

wry

adj wry: twisted

His *wry* sense of humor sometimes gets him into trouble with people.

X, Y, Z

xylophone

n xy-lo-phone: musical instrument

He plays a *xylophone* in the orchestra.

yam

n yam: sweet potato

He liks *yams* served with butter and brown sugar.

yearn

v yearn: to desire, long for

She *yearned* for the days when all her children were still at home.

yelp

v yelp: to utter a short cry

The kids *yelped* when they first plunged into the cold water.

yelp

n yelp: quick, sharp cry

A *yelp* escaped from his mouth when he backed into the hot radiator.

yield

v yield: to produce, give

The crop *yielded* a large amount of vegetables.

yield

n yield: the amount yielded or produced

Their *yield* far exceeded their expectations.

yoke

n yoke: wooden frame

The *yoke* around the ox's neck was painted a bright color.

yoke

v yoke: to harness

Yoke the horse before you attempt to ride him.

zany

n za-ny: silly person

That clown is such a *zany* that all the children enjoy him.

zany

adj za-ny: of or like a zany, foolish

His *zany* antics kept the audience laughing.

zeal

n zeal: enthusiasm, desire

Her *zeal* was contagious as we all joined in to complete the job.

zenith

n ze-nith: highest point

He reached the *zenith* of his career when he was appointed chairman of the company.

zephyr

n zeph-yr: gentle wind, breeze

A *zephyr* from the ocean cooled their bodies.

zeppelin

n zep-pe-lin: dirigible, blimp

The highlight of the state fair was the ride in the *zeppelin* over the city.

zest

n zest: enjoyment, exciting quality

Her *zest* for her work is noticeable.

zither

n zith-er: musical instrument

He can play everything from piano to *zither* to violin.

zoology

n zo-ol-o-gy: science of animals

His upbringing on a farm certainly helped him with his study of *zoology*.

500+ PSAT/SAT Vocabulary List for the NEW Exams

Beginning in 2005, students will take a new version of the PSAT and SAT. Despite some major differences between the old and new tests, vocabulary continues to be most important—whether you're working on the Writing section or the Reading Comprehension section of the test. The English language is subtle; words may have many different meanings and be used in various ways. If you're not aware of these subtleties or if you don't understand a word, you just won't be able to do as well on the test as students who have more powerful vocabularies.

The following list of words has been compiled to help you improve your test-taking ability on the PSAT or SAT. There's no question that your success on these tests depends on your vocabulary knowledge. The words included here have been selected by teachers and tutors who help students prepare for these tests regularly. These words are likely to appear in one form or another on these tests.

Take your time going through them. Many may have appeared in the earlier section of this book, but these are the nitty-gritty test-preparation words that you should learn. Read the words, read the definitions so that you are able to fully understand the meanings in context, and then memorize as many as you can.

When in doubt, write the word in a pocket notebook. Try to use it in a sentence from time to time during the week. Try it out on your friends and family. The more you say it out loud and the more you use it in proper context, the more easily you will remember it. If you've read and understood the first part of the book—prefixes, suffixes, and roots—you should be able to more fully remember the words in this list.

Keep in mind the three steps to developing a more powerful vocabulary:
- read
- write
- remember

Good luck!

A

aberrant deviating from the usual; atypical

abject showing utter hopelessness or resignation

abridge to shorten

abstruse difficult to comprehend

abut to border on

adjudication a judicial decision or sentence

adroit skillful; shrewd

adversary foe; one opposed to

adversity hardship; misfortune

advocate one who maintains a cause; to support a cause

aesthetic having to do with art or beauty

affable gracious; friendly

agile moving with quick easy grace

alacrity cheerful readiness

alleviate to lighten the burden of

altruism unselfish concern for others

amalgamation consolidation or merger

ambiguous vague; having more than one meaning

ambivalence uncertainty as to which approach to follow

ameliorate to make better

amorphous without shape or form

antipathy intense dislike; hatred

apathy lack of interest

appease to calm; to pacify

approbate to approve; to sanction

appropriate to take improperly or illegally

arcane secret; mysterious

ascertain to find out

assiduous busy; persistent attention and application

assuage to ease; to pacify; to relieve

asylum a place of refuge and protection; shelter

audacious bold; adventurous; daring

augment to add to

austere harsh; severe; unadorned

autonomy the state of being self-governing; self-directed freedom

avarice greed; excessive desire for wealth

B

banal common; dull; insipid

bard poet

bastion stronghold; fortified area

behemoth something of monstrous size or power

bemuse to bewilder; to confuse

benign kind; gentle

bizarre odd; eccentric

blithe light-hearted; free-spirited

bolster to support or prop up

bombastic pretentious or inflated or pompous

C

cacophony harsh or discordant sounds

cajole to persuade with flattery

callous hardened; without sympathy for others

callow immature

candid honest; sincere; frank

capitulate to yield or acquiesce

capricious inconstant; changing unpredictably

caustic insulting; corrosive

cavalier dismissing as unimportant; disdainful

censure to criticize; to find fault with

circuitous roundabout or indirect

clandestine secret; surreptitious

coalition union; combination

coerce to force by threat

cogent valid

collaborate to work together

complacent self-satisfied; unconcerned

concise brief

concordance agreement

contempt disdain; lack of respect; intense dislike

contentious quarrelsome; belligerent

contrite grieving and penitent for sin or shortcoming

conundrum mystery; difficult problem

convoluted involved; intricate

copious abundant; large amount

cordial heartfelt; gracious

corroborate to support with evidence; to confirm

crackdown an instance of taking disciplinary action

craven cowardly; lacking courage

crop to cut off short; to trim

cryptic secret; obscure

culpable blameworthy

cursory hasty; not thorough

D

dappled characterized by patches of color different from the background

daunt to intimidate; to overwhelm; to lessen the courage of

dearth a scarcity of; inadequate supply

debacle a fiasco; a great disaster

debase to lower in quality or character

debauch to corrupt; to debase

decorum good taste in behavior; propriety

degrade to lower in status; to demote

deity god or goddess; divinity

delineate to portray; to indicate by lines drawn

demagogue a leader who uses false claims and prejudices to attain power

demarcation a separation; the act of marking limits

denigrate to belittle

denounce to criticize

deprave to make morally bad

deride to ridicule; to laugh at contemptuously

desultory random; marked by lack of definite plan

diaphanous airy; insubstantial; vague

didactic designed or intended to teach

diffident unassertive; shy; lacking in confidence

dilatory causing delay

diminutive small

discursive talkative

disdain scorn; to despise

disgruntled discontented

disparage to lower in rank; to decry

disseminate to scatter widely; to disperse throughout

divergent drawn apart; different

doggerel trivial, comic verse

dogged stubbornly determined; obstinate

dogmatic dictatorial

dubious doubtful; undecided

duplicity deceit

E

ebullience exuberance

eccentric deviating from accepted practice

eclectic coming from a variety of sources

eddy small whirlpool; contrary thought or policy

edify to improve or enlighten

efface to erase

effervesce to show liveliness or exhilaration

effrontery shameless boldness; insolence

effusive overflowing; gushing

elusive hard to comprehend or identify

embellish to decorate or enhance

emend to correct, usually textual alterations

enervate to lessen the strength of

enfranchise to set free; to give voting rights

enigma mystery; riddle; something that is difficult to understand

enmity hostility; animosity

ennui boredom

entourage one's associates; surroundings

ephemeral lasting only a short time; transient

epiphany sudden moment of insight

equanimity composure; evenness under stress

esoteric understood only by a select few

ethos distinguishing character or belief of a group

euphony pleasing or harmonious sound

euphoria feeling of well-being; elation

evanescent nonpermanent; transient

exacerbate to make worse

excoriate to censure scathingly

exhort to urge strongly

exigency urgency; demanding action

exonerate to relieve of responsibility or blame

expedite to accelerate or facilitate

expurgate to cleanse of something morally offensive

extol to praise or laud

extricate to free from; to disentangle

F

facade a false or artificial appearance

facilitate to make easier or smoother

faction a group within a group

faze to embarrass or to disturb the composure of

feckless weak; worthless; ineffectual

fecund fruitful; fertile

feign to pretend; to give a false appearance of

felicitous pleasant; delightful; fit

feral savage; wild

fervor passion; intensity of feeling

finagle to obtain by trickery

florid ornate; ruddy

flout to scorn; to scoff

foible a minor flaw or weakness in behavior

foolhardy rash; adventurous

foppish foolish; silly

forensics formal argumentation; practical application

formidable causing fear

forte strength

frenetic frantic

frivolous lacking in seriousness

frugal careful in spending money; sparing

fulsome abundant; copious; lavish

furtive secretive; surreptitious

G

gainsay to deny, to dispute

gargantuan of tremendous size or volume

garrulous talkative; rambling

gaudy tastelessly ornamental; flashy

genre a category or a kind

germane relevant; closely akin

gesticulate to make gestures

glacial devoid of warmth and cordiality

glower to frown; to stare with annoyance or anger

gravity seriousness

gregarious sociable; friendly

grovel to crawl; to wallow

gullible easily deceived or duped

H

hackneyed trite; lacking in freshness or originality

hallowed sacred; revered; consecrated

hardy robust; bold

hedonist one who seeks pleasure

heretical unorthodox; departing from accepted beliefs

hoard to hide or store a supply for oneself

honorific conveying or conferring honor

hyperbole exaggeration

hypocritical insincere

I

iconoclast one who attacks established beliefs

idiosyncratic characterized by eccentricity or peculiarity

ignominious dishonorable; humiliating; degrading

impeccable flawless

impecunious penniless; habitually having no money

impervious not allowing entrance; impenetrable

inane silly; foolish

incongruous incompatible; inconsistent within itself

inconsequential of little importance

incontrovertible indisputable; not open to question

indolent lazy

inept unfit; awkward

infallible incapable of error; certain

inimical hostile; unfriendly

inimitable matchless; not capable of being imitated

innate inborn

innocuous harmless

innovation creation; new idea; novelty

insidious treacherous, subtle

insolent impudent; insultingly contemptuous

insular isolated

insurgency uprising; revolt against a government

insurmountable incapable of overcoming

intransigent uncompromising; unyielding

inundate to flood; to overwhelm

invective insulting or abusive language

inveterate habitual

irrational lacking reason or understanding

J

jaded tired; exhausted; dulled by excess

jaunty stylish; lively

jingoism extreme chauvinism or nationalism

jubilant expressing great joy

juxtaposition placing two or more things side by side

K

kaleidoscope variegated changing pattern or appearance

kangaroo court a mock court; illegal judgment or punishment

keepsake something to be kept as a memento

kempt trim; neatly kept

keynote the central fact or idea

L

lackadaisical languid; lacking spirit

lackluster dull; lacking in vitality

laconic concise; using minimum words

languid drooping; weak; listless

lassitude fatigue; languor

laud to acclaim; to praise

lavish bestow profusely; prodigal

lethargic sluggish; apathetic

licentiousness disregard for strict rules of correctness

limber flexible; agile; nimble

loiter to dawdle; to lag behind

loquacious garrulous; talkative

lucid intelligible; clear

lucrative profitable

luminary a source of light; a brilliantly outstanding person

lunge to make a forceful movement forward

lure to entice; to tempt

lurk to move furtively; to sneak

luster radiance; brilliance

lyrical characterized by intense feeling or emotion

M

machination scheming action

magnanimous showing courageous spirit or generosity of mind

maladroit awkward; inept

malcontent a rebel; a discontented person

malevolent showing spite or hatred

malice ill will

malign to utter injurious reports about; to vilify

malinger to pretend incapacity so as to avoid duty

mar to spoil; to destroy

meander to wander aimlessly; to ramble

mediocre ordinary; of moderate or low quality

menagerie a collection of animals

mercenary greedy; one hired merely for wages

mercurial inconstant; changeable

meticulous careful; showing excessive concern for detail

milieu environment; setting

misanthrope one who hates or distrusts mankind

miser a mean grasping person; one who hoards

mitigate to lessen the severity of

mnemonics memory-aiding devices

modicum a limited quantity; a small portion

monolith an organized whole that acts as a single powerful force; a massive structure

moot debatable; disputed; purely academic

moratorium a suspension of activity

morose sullen; gloomy

moth-eaten dilapidated; outdated

motley a mixture of incongruous elements

mottled characterized by colored spots or blotches

mundane ordinary; earthly; practical

munificent lavish; liberal; generous

mutate to undergo change

N

naive unsophisticated; natural; simple

nebulous vague; indistinct

nefarious wicked; evil; vicious

nemesis a formidable opponent

notorious unfavorably known

novice a beginner

O

obdurate inflexible; unyielding

obeisance showing deference

obfuscate to confuse; to make obscure

obliterate to erase; to remove totally

oblivious forgetful; unaware

obscure hidden; vague

obsequious subservient

obsolete no longer in use; old

obstreperous unruly; characterized by aggressive noisiness

obtuse dull; insensitive; lacking sharpness

officious meddlesome; offering services where they are not needed

ominous threatening

omnipotent all powerful

opaque hard to understand or explain

opulence wealth

orthodox conventional; conforming to established doctrine

oscillation vibration; variation

ostensible apparent

ostentatious showing off; showy display

outlandish foreign; bizarre

overbearing dominant; overpowering

P

palpable perceptible; capable of being touched

paltry trivial; inferior

paradox a seemingly contradictory statement

paragon example or model of excellence

parochial provincial; narrow

parsimony stinginess

paucity smallness of number; dearth; few

pecuniary measured in money; financial

pedagogue teacher

pedantic ostentatiously learned; bookish

pedestrian unimaginative; commonplace

perfidious unfaithful; disloyal

peripheral supplementary

pithy concise

pivotal crucial; vitally important

placate to calm or pacify

plaudit enthusiastic approval

plethora excess

poignant affecting deeply; piercing

polemical controversial

polyglot speaking or writing in several languages

pontificate to sermonize

potent powerful

pragmatic practical

precarious unstable

preclude prevent

precursor forerunner

predilection in favor of something beforehand

preempt to take for oneself

prevaricate to fib; to lie

presumptuous overstepping bounds

pristine clean; uncorrupted

prodigal excessively wasteful; lavish

prodigious huge; enormous

prodigy highly talented child

profligate wildly extravagant

profundity intellectual depth; something profound

prolific fruitful; fertile; abundant

propitiate to appease; to conciliate

prosaic dull; unimaginative

protean changing; displaying great diversity

provincial narrow-minded; unsophisticated

prudent wise; discreet

pseudonym pen name; fictitious name

pugnacious warlike; belligerent

pundit a critic, a learned person

pungent causing an irritating sensation; acrid

Q

quandary a state of perplexity or doubt

quarry prey

quibble to object; to bicker

quiescent inactive; latent

quixotic foolishly idealistic; impractical

R

radical extreme

ramble to move aimlessly; to talk or write in a long-winded wandering way

rancor ill-will; hatred

rapacious greedy; ravenous

raze to demolish; to erase

reclusive solitary

recondite concealed; incomprehensible

rectitude moral integrity; righteousness

recursive characteristic of a procedure that can repeat itself indefinitely

redundant superfluous; repetitive

refine to reduce to a pure state

refuge shelter

refurbish to renovate; to freshen up

refute to disprove

regale to entertain

remorseful sorry

repatriate go back to country of birth or citizenship

repentant penitent

reprehensible culpable; blameworthy

repress to curb; to subdue

repudiate to disown; to reject as untrue

resilience the ability to recover from a misfortune or change

reticent reserved; uncommunicative

revelry noisy partying

revere to honor; to worship

revile to scold

revulsion withdrawal; a sense of utter distaste

rift fissure, crevasse

rigorous austere; strict; harsh

robust healthy; hardy; full-bodied

rotund rounded

ruse trick; deceitful act

rumple to wrinkle or crumple

rustic rural; pertaining to the country

ruthless no compassion; cruel

S

saccharine overly sweet or agreeable

sacrilege outrageous violation

sagacious discerning; shrewd

sage a wise person

salubrious promoting health or well-being

salutation greeting

sanguine ruddy; cheerful; confident

sardonic scornfully mocking

savory pleasant; palatable

scanty insufficient; meager

scrupulous careful; having moral integrity

scrutinize look over carefully

scurry to move in a brisk manner; to scamper

sentient capable of feeling; aware

sequester to set apart; to segregate

sequitur a logical consequence

serendipity finding agreeable things not sought for

servile subservient

shard a piece or fragment of a brittle substance

solace to comfort; to soothe

solicit to ask; to invite

solitude seclusion; isolation

somber grave; melancholy

somnolent sleepy; drowsy

soporific tending to cause sleep

spendthrift one who spends wastefully

sporadic infrequent; occurring occasionally

spurious false; forged; not authentic

spurn to scorn; to reject with disdain

squabble a noisy quarrel

stagnant not moving; stale; inactive

staid prim; serious

staunch faithful, substantial

stealthy secret; furtive

stoic indifferent to pain or pleasure; impassive

stolid impassive; unemotional

strident characterized by discordant sound; harsh

stultify to cause to appear foolish or illogical; to make useless

stupefy to astonish

stupor daze; a state of extreme apathy

succinct concise; not wasting words

succumb to yield

supercilious arrogant; haughty

superficial shallow; of little depth

superfluous unnecessary

supplant to take the place of

surfeit surplus; to satiate

surreptitious sly; furtive; secretive

tacit implied but not actually expressed

taciturn silent; uncommunicative

tactful diplomatic; showing sensitive perception

tactile capable of being touched

taunt to ridicule; to mock

temerity rashness or recklessness

tempest tumult; uproar

tenuous thin; having little substance

tepid lukewarm

terse concise

tether to fasten or restrain by a chain or rope

torpid sluggish; lethargic

tractable obedient; docile

trademark distinguishing characteristic or feature

transient short-lived; fleeting

transitory of brief duration; tending to pass away

trifling frivolous; lacking in significance or worth

trite stale; overused

trivial commonplace; ordinary

truncate to cut off; to shorten

truculent cruel; belligerent

U

unadulterated pure; unmixed

undermine to weaken; to take away support of

unpretentious free from affectation; modest

unrelenting hard; stern; not letting up

untenable cannot be defended

upbraid to scold; to find fault with

urbane very polite; polished

usurp to seize by force

V

vacillate to hesitate; to waver in deciding

vacuous empty; stupid

vagrant a homeless person

vapid dull; tasteless; flavorless

variegated varied

vehement powerful; impassioned

venerable revered

verbose wordy

verdant green

veritable authentic

vigor active strength or force

vilify to malign; to portray someone as a villain

vindicate to clear of blame

vindictive vengeful; spiteful

virtuoso one who excels in the arts

virulent harmful; malignant

visage appearance or aspect of a person

vitality physical or mental vigor

vituperate to scold; to berate

vivacious lively

vociferous loud; clamorous, boisterous

volatile explosive; unstable

voluble talkative

voluminous of great volume; large

vulnerable capable of being injured or harmed

W

wan sickly, pale, feeble

wanderlust impulse toward wandering

wield to hold and use skillfully, control

wither to dry up

wrest to pull, twist

wry twisted

X, Y, Z

xylophone musical instrument

yam sweet potato

yearn to desire, long for

yield to produce, give

zany silly person

zeal enthusiasm, desire

zenith highest point

zephyr gentle wind, breeze

zest enjoyment

Abbreviations

a or @
at
to

A1
first class

A
ace, argon

A
angstrom unit

AA
Alcoholics Anonymous
anti-aircraft

AAA
Agricultural Adjustment
Administration
American Automobile
Association

AAAL
American Academy of
Arts and Letters

AAAS
American Association
for the Advancement
of Science

A and M
agricultural and
mechanical
ancient and modern

AAR
against all risks

AAU
Amateur Athletic Union

AAUP
American Association of
University Professors

AAUW
American Association of
University Women

AB
able-bodied seaman
airman basic
Alberta, (*artium
baccalaureus*) bachelor
of arts

ABA
American Bankers
Association
American Bar
Association
American Basketball
Association
American Booksellers
Association

abbr
abbreviation

ABC
American Bowling
Congress
American Broadcasting
Company
Australian Broadcasting
Company

ABCD
accelerated business
collection and delivery

abd or abdom
abdomen
abdominal

abl
ablative

abn
airborne

abr
abridged
abridgment

abs
absolute
abstract

ABS
American Bible Society

abstr
abstract

ac
account
acre

AC
air-conditioning
alternating current
(*ante Christum*) before
Christ

acad
academic, academy

AC and U
Association of Colleges
and Universities

acc
accusative

accel
accelerando

acct
account
accountant

accus
accusative

ACE
American Council on
Education

ack
acknowledge
acknowledgment

ACLU
American Civil Liberties
Union

ACP
American College of
Physicians

acpt
acceptance

ACS
American Chemical
Society
American College of
Surgeons

act
active
actor
actual

ACT
American College Test
Association of Classroom
Teachers
Australian Capital
Territory

actg
acting

AD
active duty
after date
(*anno Domini*) in the year
of our Lord

ADA
American Dental
Association
average daily attendance

ADC
aide-de-camp
Air Defense Command

ADD
American Dialect
Dictionary

addn
addition

addnl
additional

ADF
automatic direction
finder

ADH
antidiuretic hormone

ad int
ad interim

ADIZ
air defense identification
zone

adj
adjective
adjunct
adjustment
adjutant

ad loc
(*ad locum*) to or at
the place

adm
administration
administrative

admin
administration

admrx
administratrix

ADP
automatic data
processing

adv
adverb
(*adversus*) against

ad val
ad valorem

advt
advertisement

AEC
Atomic Energy
Commission

AEF
American Expeditionary
Force

aeq
(*aequalis*) equal

aero
aeronautical
aeronautics

aet or aetat
(*aetatis*) of age
aged

af
affix

AF
air force
audio frequency

AFB
air force base

AFC
American Football
Conference
automatic frequency
control

aff
affirmative

afft
affidavit

AFL-CIO
American Federation of
Labor and Congress of
Industrial
Organizations

aft
afternoon

AFT
American Federation of
Teachers
automatic fine tuning

AFTRA
American Federation of
Television and Radio
Artists

AG
adjutant general
attorney general

agcy
agency

AGR
advanced gas-cooled
reactor

agr or agric
agricultural
agriculture

agt
agent

AH
ampere-hour
(*anno hegiræ*) in the year
of the Hegira (the
flight of Mohammed
from Mecca to
Medina, 622 AD)

AHL
American Hockey
　League

AI
ad interim
artificial insemination
artificial intelligence

AID
Agency for International
　Development

AIDS
acquired immune (or
　immuno-) deficiency
　syndrome

AIM
American Indian
　Movement

AK
Alaska

aka
also known as

AKC
American Kennel Club

AL
Alabama
American League
American Legion

Ala
Alabama

ALA
American Library
　Association

alc
alcohol

alk
alkaline

allo
allegro

alt
alternate
altitude

Alta
Alberta

alw
allowance

Am
America
American

AM
(*ante meridiem*) before
　midday
(*artium magister*) master
　of arts

AMA
American Medical
　Association

Amer
America
American

Amer Ind
American Indian

Amn
airman

amp
ampere

amp hr
ampere-hour

AMS
Agricultural Marketing
　Service

AMU
atomic mass unit

AMVETS
American Veterans (of
　World War I)

AN
airman (Navy)

ANA
American Newspaper
　Association
American Nurses
　Association

anat
anatomical
anatomy

Angl
Anglican

anhyd
anhydrous

ann
annals
annual

anon
anonymous

ANOVA
analysis of variance

AO
account of

AP
additional premium
antipersonnel
Associated Press
author's proof

APB
all points bulletin

APC
armored personnel
　carrier

API
air position indicator

APO
army post office

appl
applied

approx
approximate
approximately

appt
appoint
appointed
appointment

apptd
appointed

Apr
April

APR
annual percentage rate

apt
apartment
aptitude

aq
aqua
aqueous

AR
accounts receivable
acknowledgment of
receipt
all risks
Arkansas

ARC
American Red Cross

arch
archaic
architect
architecture

Arch
Archbishop

arg
argent
argument

arith
arithmetical

Ariz
Arizona

Ark
Arkansas

ARP
air-raid precautions

arr
arranged
arrival
arrive

art
article
artificial

AS
after sight
American Samoa
Anglo-Saxon

ASA
American Standards
Association

ASAP
as soon as possible

asb
asbestos

ASCAP
American Society of
Composers, Authors
and Publishers

ASCU
Association of State
Colleges and
Universities

ASE
American Stock
Exchange

ASEAN
Association of Southeast
Asian Nations

ASI
airspeed indicator

ASL
American Sign Language

ASR
airport surveillance
radar
air-sea rescue

assn
association

assoc
associate
associated
association

ASSR
Autonomous Soviet
Socialist Republic

asst
assistant

Assyr
Assyrian

astrol
astrologer
astrology

astron
astronomer
astronomy

ASV
American Standard
Version

Atl
Atlantic

atm
atmosphere
atmospheric

attn
attention

atrib
attributive
attributively

aud
audit
auditor

Aug
August

Aus
Austria
Austrian
Australia
Australian

AUS
Army of the United
States

Austral
Australia

auth
authentic
authorized

auto
automatic

av
avenue
average
avoidupois

AV
ad valorem
audiovisual
Authorized Version

AVC
automatic volume
control

avdp
avoirdupois

ave
avenue

avg
average

AWACS
airborne warning and
control system

AYC
American Youth
Congress

AYD
American Youth for
Democracy

AZ
Arizona

B

BA
bachelor of arts

BAEd
bachelor of arts in
education

BAg
bachelor of agriculture

bal
balance

B and B
bed-and-breakfast

b and w
black and white

Bapt
Baptist

bar
barometer
barometric

BAr
bachelor of architecture

Bart
baronet

BBC
British Broadcasting
Corporation

bbl
barrel
barrels

BC
before Christ
British Columbia

BCD
binary-coded decimal

BCh
bachelor of chemistry

bcn
beacon

BCSE
Board of Civil Service
Examiners

bd ft
board foot

bdl or bdle
bundle

bdrm
bedroom

BE
bachelor of education
bachelor of engineering
bill of exchange

BEC
Bureau of Employees'
Compensation

BEd
bachelor of education

BEF
British Expeditionary
Force

beg
begin
beginning

Belg
Belgian
Belgium

BEM
British Empire Medal

BEngr
bachelor of engineering

BFA
bachelor of fine arts

BG or B Gen
brigadier general

BH
bill of health

bhd
bulkhead

BHE
Bureau of Higher
Education

bhp
bishop

BIA
bachelor of industrial
arts
Braille Institute
of America
Bureau of Indian Affairs

bib
Bible
biblical

biog
biographer
biographical
biography

biol
biologic
biological
biologist
biology

bk
bank
book

Bk
berkelium

bkg
banking
bookkeeping
breakage

bkgd
background

bks
barracks

bkt
basket
bracket

bl
bale
barrel
block

BL
bachelor of law
bachelor of letters
bill of lading
breadth/length

bldg
building

bldr
builder

BLitt or BLit
(*baccalaureus litterarum*)
  bachelor of letters
bachelor of literature

blk
black
block
bulk

blvd
boulevard

BMR
basal metabolic rate

BNDD
Bureau of Narcotics and
  Dangerous Drugs

BO
back order
body odor
branch office
buyer's option

BOD
biochemical oxygen
  demand
biological oxygen
  demand

bor
borough

bot
botanical
botanist
botany
bottle
bottom
bought

BP
bills payable
blood pressure
blue print
boiling point

BPD
barrels per day

bpi
bits per inch
bytes per inch

Br
Britain
British

BR
bills receivable

brig
brigade
brigadier

Brig Gen
brigadier general

Brit
Britain
British

brl
barrel

bro
brother
brothers

bros
brothers

BS
bachelor of science
balance sheet
bill of sale
British standard

BSA
Boy Scouts of America

BSI
British Standards
  Institution

bskt
basket

Bt
baronet

btry
battery

Btu
British thermal unit

bu
bureau
bushel

bur
bureau

bus
business

BV
Blessed Virgin

BW
bacteriological warfare
biological warfare
black and white

BWI
British West Indies

BYO
bring your own

C

ca
circa

CA
California
chartered accountant
chief accountant

CAB
Civil Aeronautics Board

CAD
computer-aided design

CAF
cost and freight

CAGS
Certificate Advanced
  Graduate Study

CAI
computer-aided
  instruction
computer-associated
  instruction

cal
calendar
caliber
calorie
small calorie

Cal
California
large calorie

calc
calculate
calculated

Calif
California

CAM
computer-aided
manufacturing

can
canceled
cancellation

Can or Canad
Canada
Canadian

canc
canceled

C and F
cost and freight

C and W
country and western

cap
capacity
capital
capitalize

CAP
Civil Air Patrol

caps
capitals
capsule

Capt
captain

card
cardinal

CAS
certificate of advanced
study

cat
catalog
catalyst

cath
cathedral
cathode

CATV
community antenna
television

caus
causative

cav
cavalry
cavity

Cb
columbium

CBC
Canadian Broadcasting
Corporation

CBD
cash before delivery

CBI
computer-based
instruction
Cumulative Book Index

CBS
Columbia Broadcasting
System

CBW
chemical and biological
warfare

cc
cubic centimeter

CC
carbon copy
chief clerk

CCF
Cooperative
Commonwealth
Federation (of
Canada)

cckw
counterclockwise

CCTV
closed-circuit television

CCU
cardiac care unit
coronary care unit
critical care unit

ccw
counterclockwise

cd
candela

CD
carried down
certificate of deposit
civil defense
compact disk

CDD
certificate of disability
for discharge

cdg
commanding

CDR
commander

CDT
central daylight time

ce
chemical engineer
civil engineer

CEA
College English
Association
Council of Economic
Advisors

CED
Committee for Economic
Development

cem
cement

cent
centigrade
central
centium
century

Cent
Central

CENTO
Central Treaty
Organization

CEO
chief executive officer

CER
conditioned emotional
  response

cert
certificate
certified

CETA
Comprehensive
  Employment and
  Training Act

cf
(*confer*) compare

CF
carried forward
cost and freight
cystic fibrosis

CFI
cost, freight and
  insurance

cfm
cubic feet per minute

cfs
cubic feet per second

cg or cgm
centigram

CG
center of gravity
coast guard
commanding general

ch
chain
chapter
church

CH
clearinghouse
courthouse
customhouse

chan
channel

chap
chapter

chem
chemical
chemist
chemistry

chg
change
charge

chm
chairman
checkmate

Chmn
chairman

chron
chronicle
chronological
chronology

Ci
curie

CI
certificate of insurance
cost and insurance

CIA
Central Intelligence
  Agency

CID
Criminal Investigation
  Department

cie
(*compagnie*) company

CIF
cost, insurance and
  freight

C in C
commander in chief

CIP
Cataloging in Publication

cir
circle
circuit
circumference

circ
circular

cit
citation
cited
citizen

civ
civil
civilian

CJ
chief justice

ck
cask
check

cl
centiliter
class

CL
center line
civil law
common law

cld
called
cleared

Clev
Cleveland

clin
clinical

clk
clerk

clr
clear
clearance

CLU
chartered life underwriter

cm
centimeter
cumulative

CMA
certified medical assistant

cmd
command

cmdg
commanding

cmdr
commander

CMG
Companion of the Order
of St. Michael and
St. George

cml
commercial

CMSgt
chief master sergeant

CN
credit note

CNO
chief of naval operations

CNS
central nervous system

co
company
county

CO
cash order
Colorado
commanding officer
conscientious objector

c/o
care of

cod
codex

COD
cash on delivery

C of S
chief of staff

col
color
colored
column

col or coll
collateral
college

Col
colonel
Colorado

COL
colonel
cost of living

collat
collateral

colloq
colloquial

Colo
Colorado

comb
combination
combined

comd
command

comdg
commanding

comdr
commander

comdt
commandant

COMECON
Council for Mutual
Economic Assistance

coml
commercial

comm
command
commerce
commission
committee
communication

commo
Commodore

comp
compare
complex

compd
compound

comr
commissioner

conc
concentrate
concentrated

conf
conference
confidential

Confed
Confederate

cong
congress
congressional

Conn
Connecticut

consol
consolidated

cont
containing
contents
continent
continued

contd
continued

contg
containing

contrib
contribution
contributor

CORE
Congress of Racial
Equality

corp
corporal
corporation

corr
correct
corrected
corresponding

cos
cosine

COS
cash on shipment
chief of staff

cp
compare
coupon

CP
candlepower
charter party
communist party

CPA
certified public
accountant

CPB
Corporation for Public
  Broadcasting

CPCU
chartered property and
  casualty underwriter

cpd
compound

CPFF
cost plus fixed fee

CPI
consumer price index

Cpl
corporal

CPO
chief petty officer

CPOM
master chief petty officer

CPOS
senior chief petty officer

CPS
characters per second
cycles per second

CPT
captain

cpu
central processing unit

CR
carrier's risk
cathode ray

CRC
Civil Rights Commission

cresc
crescendo

crim
criminal

crit
critical
criticism
criticized

CRT
cathode-ray tube

cryst
crystalline
crystallized

CS
capital stock
chief of staff
Christian Science
civil service

C/S
cycles per second

CSA
Confederate States
  of America

CSC
Civil Service
  Commission

CSM
command sergeant
  major

CST
central standard time

ct
carat
cent
count
county
court

CT
central time
certificated teacher
Connecticut

CTC
centralized traffic control

ctf
certificate

ctg or ctge
cartage

ctn
carton

cto
concerto

C to C
center to center

ctr
center
counter

cu
cubic
cumulative

CU
close-up

cum
cumulative

cur
currency
current

CV
cardiovascular
curriculum vitae

cvt
convertible

cw
clockwise

CW
chemical warfare
chief warrant officer

CWO
cash with order
chief warrant officer

cwt
hundred weight

CY
calendar year

cyl
cylinder

CYO
Catholic Youth
  Organization

CZ
Canal Zone

D

d
deceased

D
Democrat
deuterium

da
deka-

DA
days after acceptance
deposit account
district attorney

DAB
Dictionary of American
  Biography

dag
dekagram

dal
dekaliter

dam
dekameter

DAR
Daughters of the
  American Revolution

dat
dative

DAV
Disabled American
  Veterans

db
debenture

db or dB
decibel

DB
daybook

DBE
Dame Commander of
  the Order of the
  British Empire

dbl
double

DBMS
data base management
  system

DC
direct current
District of Columbia

dd
dated
delivered

DD
days after date
demand draft
dishonorable discharge
due date

DDC
Dewey Decimal
  Classification

DDD
direct distance dialing

DDS
doctor of dental science
doctor of dental surgery

DE
Delaware

deb
debenture

dec
deceased
declaration
declared
decorative
decrease

Dec
December

def
defendant
defense
deferred
defined
definite

deg
degree

del
delegate
delegation
delete

Del
Delaware

dely
delivery

dem
demonstrative
demurrage

Dem
Democrat
Democratic

Den
Denmark

dent
dental
dentist
dentistry

dep
depart
department
departure
deposit
depot
deputy

dept
department

der or deriv
derivation
derivative

DEW
distant early warning

DF
damage free
direction finder

DFC
Distinguished Flying
  Cross

DFM
Distinguished Flying
  Medal

dft
defendant
draft

dg
decigram

DG
director general
(*Dei gratia*) by the
grace of God

dia
diameter

diag
diagonal
diagram

dial
dialect

diam
diameter

dict
dictionary

dim
diminutive

dip
diploma

dir
director

disc
discount

dist
distance
district

distr
distribute
distribution

div
dividend
division

DJ
disc jockey
district judge
doctor of jurisprudence

DJIA
Dow Jones Industrial
Average

dkg
dekagram

dkl
dekaliter

dkm
dekameter

dl
deciliter

DLitt or DLit
(*doctor litterarum*) doctor
of letters
doctor of literature

DLO
dead letter office
dispatch loading only

dm
decimeter

DM
deutsche mark

DMZ
demilitarized zone

dn
down

DNB
Dictionary of National
Biography

do
ditto

DOA
dead on arrival

DOB
date of birth

doc
document

DOD
Department of Defense

DOE
Department of Energy

dol
dollar

DOM
(*Deo optimo maximo*)
to God, the best and
greatest

DOS
disk operating system

DOT
Department of
Transportation

doz
dozen

DP
data processing
dew point

DPH
department of public
health

dr
dram

Dr
doctor

DR
dead reckoning

DSM
Distinguished Service
Medal

DSO
Distinguished Service
Order

DSP
(*decessit sine prole*) died
without issue

DST
daylight saving time

dup
duplex
duplicate

DV
(*Deo volente*) God willing

DW
deadweight

dwt
deadweight ton
pennyweight

DX
distance

dy
delivery
deputy
duty

dynam
dynamics

dz
dozen

E

ea
each

E and OE
errors and omissions
excepted

EB
eastbound

eccl
ecclesiastic
ecclesiastical

ECG
electrocardiogram

ECM
European Common
Market

ecol
ecological
ecology

econ
economics
economist
economy

ed
edited
edition
editor
education

EDP
electronic data processing

EDT
eastern daylight time

educ
education
educational

EEC
European Economic
Community

EEG
electroencephalogram
electroencephalograph

EENT
eye, ear, nose, and throat

EEO
equal employment
opportunity

eff
efficiency

EFT or EFTS
electronic funds transfer
(system)

e.g.
(*exempli gratia*) for
example

EHF
extremely high frequency

EHP
effective horsepower
electric horsepower

EHV
extra high voltage

elec
electric
electrical
electricity

elem
elementary

elev
elevation

ELF
extremely low frequency

ELSS
extravehicular life
support system

EM
electromagnetic
electron microscope

emer
emeritus

emf
electromotive force

emp
emperor
empress

enc or encl
enclosure

ENE
east-northeast

eng
engine
engineer
engineering

Eng
England
English

ENS
ensign

env
envelope

EO
executive order

EOM
end of month

EP
extended play

EPA
Environmental
Protection Agency

eq
equal
equation

equip
equipment

equiv
equivalency
equivalent

ESE
east-southeast

ESL
English as a second
language

esp
especially

Esq
esquire

est
established
estimate
estimated

EST
eastern standard time

esu
electrostatic unit

ESV
earth satellite vehicle

ET
eastern time
extra-terrestrial

ETA
estimated time of arrival

et al.
et alii (masc.)
et aliae (fem.) or *et alia*
(neut.) and others

etc
et cetera, and so forth

ETD
estimated time of
departure

ETO
European theater of
operations

et seq
(*et sequens*) and the
following one

et ux
(*et uxor*) and wife

Eur
Europe
European

EVA
extravehicular activity

ex
example
exchange
excluding
executive
express
extra

exch
exchange
exchanged

exec
executive

exhbn
exhibition

exor
executor

expy
expressway

ext
extension
exterior
external

F

f
Fahrenheit
farad
faraday
and the following one

FA
field artillery
fielding average
football association

FAA
Federal Aviation
Administration
free of all average

fac
facsimile
faculty

FADM
fleet admiral

fam
familiar
family

F and A
fore and aft

FAO
Food and Agriculture
Organization of the
United Nations

FAQ
fair average quality
frequently asked
question

far
farthing

FAS
free alongside ship

fath
fathom

FBI
Federal Bureau of
Investigation

FCA
Farm Credit
Administration

FCC
Federal
Communications
Commission

fcp
foolscap

FDA
Food and Drug
Administration

FDIC
Federal Deposit
Insurance Corporation

Feb
February

fec
(*fecit*) he made it

fed
federal
federation

fem.
female
feminine

FERA
Federal Emergency
Relief Administration

ff
folios
and the following ones
fortissimo

FHA
Federal Housing
  Administration

fict
fiction
fictitious

FIFO
first in, first out

fig
figurative
figuratively
figure

fin
finance
financial
finish

FIO
free in and out

fir
firkin

fl
floor

FL
Florida

Fla
Florida

fl oz
fluid ounce

FLSA
Fair Labor Standards Act

fm
fathom

FM
field manual

FMB
Federal Maritime Board

FMCS
Federal Mediation and
  Conciliation Service

fn
footnote

fo or fol
folio

FO
foreign office

FOB
free on board

FOC
free of charge

fp
freezing point

FPA
Foreign Press
  Association
free of particular
  average

FPC
Federal Power
  Commission

fps
feet per second
foot-pound-second
frames per second

fr
father
franc
from

freq
frequency

Fri
Friday

FRS
Federal Reserve System

frt
freight

frwy
freeway

FS
Foreign Service

FSLIC
Federal Savings and
  Loan Insurance
  Corporation

FSP
Food Stamp Program

ft
feet
foot

FTC
Federal Trade
  Commission

fth
fathom

ft lb
foot-pound

fur
furlong

fut
future

fwd
foreword
forward

FWD
front-wheel drive

FX
foreign exchange

FY
fiscal year

FYI
for your information

fz
(*forzando, forzato*)
  accented

G

g
acceleration of gravity
gram
gravity

Ga
Georgia

GA
general assembly
general average
Georgia

gal
gallery
gallon

galv
galvanized

GAO
General Accounting
  Office

gar
garage

GATT
General Agreement on
  Tariffs and Trade

GAW
guaranteed annual wage

gaz
gazette

GB
Great Britain

GCA
ground-controlled
  approach

GCB
Knight Grand Cross of
  the Bath

GDR
German Democratic
  Republic

GE
gilt edges

gen
general
genitive
genus

Gen AF
general of the air force

genl
general

geog
geographic
geographical
geography

geol
geologic
geological
geology

geom
geometric
geometrical
geometry

ger
gerund

GGPA
graduate grade-point
  average

GHQ
general headquarters

gi
gill

GI
gastrointestinal
general issue
government issue

GM
general manager
grand master
guided missile

GMT
Greenwich mean time

GMW
gram-molecular weight

gn
guinea

GNI
Gross national income

GNP
gross national product

GO
general order

GOP
Grand Old Party
  (Republican)

gov
government
governor

govt
government

gp
group

GP
general practice

GPD
gallons per day

GPH
gallons per hour

GPM
gallons per minute

GPO
general post office
Government Printing
  Office

GPS
gallons per second

gr
grade
grain
gram
gravity
gross

grad
graduate
graduated

gram
grammar
grammatical

gro
gross

gr wt
gross weight

GSA
General Services
  Administration
Girl Scouts of America

GSC
general staff corps

GSO
general staff officer

GSV
guided space vehicle

GT
gross ton

Gt Brit
Great Britain

gtd
guaranteed

gyn
gynecology

H

ha
hectare

hab corp
habeas corpus

Hb
hemoglobin

hc
(*honoris case*) for the sake of honor

HC
Holy Communion
House of Commons

HCF
highest common factor

hd
head

HD
heavy duty

hdbk
handbook

HE
Her Excellency
His Excellency

HEW
Department of Health, Education and Welfare

hf
half

HF
high frequency

hg
hectogram

HH
Her Highness
His Highness
His Holiness

HI
Hawaii

Hind
Hindustani

hist
historian
historical
history

hl
hectoliter

HL
House of Lords

hld
hold

HLS
(*hoc loco situs*) laid in this place
holograph letter signed

hlt
halt

hm
hectometer

HM
Her Majesty
Her Majesty's
His Majesty
His Majesty's

HMC
Her Majesty's Customs
His Majesty's Customs

HMS
Her Majesty's Ship
His Majesty's Ship

HN
head nurse

hon
honor
honorable
honorary

hor
horizontal

hort
horticultural
horticulture

hosp
hospital

HP
high pressure
hire purchase
horsepower

HQ
headquarters

hr
hour

HR
House of Representatives

HRH
Her Royal Highness
His Royal Highness

hrzn
horizon

HS
high school

HSGT
high-speed ground transport

HST
Hawaiian standard time

ht
height

HUD
Department of Housing and Urban Development

HV
high velocity
high-voltage

hvy
heavy

HWM
high-water mark

hwy
highway

Hz
hertz

Ia or IA
Iowa

IAAF
International Amateur
Athletic Federation

IABA
International Amateur
Boxing Association

IAEA
International Atomic
Energy Agency

IALC
instrument approach
and landing chart

IATA
International Air
Transport Association

ib or ibid
(*ibidem*) in the same
place

IBM
intercontinental ballistic
missile

IBRD
International Bank for
Reconstruction and
Development

ICA
International Cooperation
Administration
International Cooperative
Alliance

ICAO
International Civil
Aviation Organization

ICBM
intercontinental ballistic
missile

ICC
Indian Claims
Commission
International Chamber
of Commerce
Interstate Commerce
Commission

ICFTU
International
Confederation of
Free Trade Unions

ICJ
International Court of
Justice

ICRC
International Committee
of the Red Cross

ICU
intensive care unit

id
idem

ID
Idaho
identification

i.e.
(*id est*) that is

IFC
International Finance
Corporation

IG
inspector general

illust or illus
illustrated
illustration
illustrator

IL
Illinois

ILO
International Labor
Organization

ILS
instrument landing
system

IMF
International Monetary
Fund

immun
immunity
immunization

imp
imperative
imperfect
import

in
inch

IN
Indiana

inc
including
incorporated
increase

incl
including
inclusive

incog
incognito

ind
independent
industrial
industry

Ind
Indian
Indiana

inf
infantry
infinitive

inq
inquire

INRI
(*Iesus Nazarenus Rex
Iudaeorum*) Jesus of
Nazareth, King of
the Jews

ins
inches
insurance

INS
Immigration and
Naturalization Service

int or intnl
international

intrans
intransitive

in trans
(*in transitu*) in transit

intsv
intensive

IOC
International Olympic
  Committee

ipm
inches per minute

IPPF
International Planned
  Parenthood
  Federation

ips
inches per second

iq
(*idem quod*) the same as

IR
infrared
inland revenue
intelligence ratios
internal revenue

IRA
Irish Republican Army

IRBM
intermediate range
  ballistic missile

irreg
irregular

IRS
Internal Revenue Service

ISBN
International Standard
  Book Number

ISC
interstate commerce

ISSN
International Standard
  Serial Number

ital
italic
italicized

ITO
International Trade
  Organization

IU
international unit

IV
intravenous
intravenously

IWW
Industrial Workers of
  the World

J

j
joule

JA
joint account
judge advocate

JAG
judge advocate general

Jan
January

JBS
John Birch Society

JCS
joint chiefs of staff

jct
junction

JD
justice department
juvenile delinquent
(*juris doctor*) doctor of
  jurisprudence
doctor of law

JP
justice of the peace

Jr
junior

jt or jnt
joint

jun
junior

Jun
June

junc
junction

juv
juvenile

K

k
karat
kilogram

K
Kelvin

Kan or Kans
Kansas

kb or kbar
kilobar

KB
kilobyte

KC
Kansas City
King's Counsel
Knights of Columbus

kcal
kilocalorie
kilogram calorie

KCB
Knight Commander of
  the Order of the Bath

kc/s
kilocycles per second

KD
knocked down

kg
kilogram

KG
Knight of the Order of
  the Garter

KGB
(*Komitet Gosudarstvennoi
  Bezopasnosti*) (Soviet)
  State Security
  Committee

kHz
kilohertz

KIA
killed in action

KJV
King James Version

KKK
Ku Klux Klan

kl
kiloliter

km
kilometer

kmps
kilometers per second

kn
knot

K of C
Knights of Columbus

kph
kilometers per hour

Kr
Krypton

KS
Kansas

kt
karat
knight

kv
kilovolt

kw
kilowatt

kwhr or kwh
kilowatt-hour

Ky or KY
Kentucky

L

La
Louisiana

LA
law agent
Los Angeles
Louisiana

Lab
Labrador

lam
laminated

lang
language

lat
latitude

Lat
Latin
Latvia

LAT
local apparent time

lb
(*libra*) pound

LB
Labrador

lc
lowercase

LC
landing craft
letter of credit
Library of Congress

lcd
least common
    denominator

LD
lethal dose

LDC
less developed country

ldg
landing
loading

LDS
Latter-day Saints

lect
lecture
lecturer

leg
legal
legislative
legislation

legis
legislation
legislative
legislature

LF
low frequency

lg
large
long

LH
left hand

LI
Long Island

lib
liberal
librarian

lieut
lieutenant

LIFO
last in
first out

lin
lineal
linear

ling
linguistics

liq
liquid
liquor

lit
liter
literal
literally
literary
literature

lith
lithographic
lithography

LL
limited liability

LM
Legion of Merit
lunar module

LMT
local mean time

lndg
landing

LNG
liquefied natural gas

loc cit
(*loco citato*) in the
place cited

LP
low pressure

LPG
liquefied petroleum gas

LPGA
Ladies Professional Golf
Association

LS
(*locus sigilli*) place of
the seal

LSS
lifesaving station
life-support system

Lt
lieutenant

LT
long ton

LTC or Lt Col
lieutenant colonel

Lt Comdr
lieutenant commander

ltd
limited

LTG or Lt Gen
lieutenant general

lt gov
lieutenant governor

LTJG
lieutenant, junior grade

lub
lubricant
lubricating

LVT
landing vehicle, tracked

LWM
low-water mark

LWV
League of Women Voters

LZ
landing zone

M

m
much
meter
(*mille*) thousand

M
monsieur

ma or mA
milliampere

MA
Massachusetts
(*magister artium*) master
of arts

MAD
mutual assured
destruction

MAE or MA Ed
master of arts in
education

mag
magnesium
magnetism
magnitude

Maj
major

Maj Gen
major general

man
manual

Man
Manitoba

manuf
manufacture
manufacturing

MAP
modified American plan

mar
maritime

Mar
March

masc
masculine

MASH
mobile army surgical
hospital

Mass
Massachusetts

math
mathematical
mathematician

matric
matriculated
matriculation

max
maximum

mb
millibar

MB
bachelor of medicine
Manitoba
megabyte

MBA
master of business
administration

mbd
million barrels per day

MBE
Member of the Order of
the British Empire

MBS
Mutual Broadcasting
System

mc
megacycle
millicurie

MC
Member of Congress

mcf
thousand cubic feet

mcg
microgram

MCPO
master chief petty officer

Md
Maryland

MD
Maryland
(*medicinae doctor*) doctor
of medicine

mdse
merchandise

MDT
mountain daylight time

Me
Maine
methyl

ME
Maine

meas
measure

mech
mechanical
mechanics

med
medicine
medieval
medium

Med
Mediterranean

MEd
master of education

met
meteorological
meteorology
metropolitan

METO
Middle East Treaty
Organization

Mex
Mexican
Mexico

MF
medium frequency
mezzo forte
microfiche

mfd
manufactured

mfg
manufacturing

MFN
most favored nation

mfr
manufacturer

mg
milligram

mgd
million gallons per day

mgr
manager
monseigneur
monsignor

mgt
management

MH
medal of honor
mobile home

MHz
megahertz

mi
mile
mileage
mill

MI
Michigan
military intelligence

MIA
missing in action

Mich
Michigan

mid
middle

midn
midshipman

mil
military
million

min
minimum
minute

Minn
Minnesota

misc
miscellaneous

Miss
Mississippi
mistress (unmarried
woman)

Mk
Mark

mks
meter-kilogram-second

mktg
marketing

Ml
milliliter

MLA
Member of the
Legislative Assembly

MLD
median lethal dose
minimum lethal dose

MLF
multilateral force

Mlle
mademoiselle

Mlles
mademoiselles

mm
millimeter

MM
messieurs
mutatis mutandis

Mme
madame

MN
Minnesota

mo
month

Mo
Missouri

MO
mail order
medical officer
Missouri
modus operandi
money order

mod
moderate
modern
modification
modified
module
modulus

modif
modification

mol
molecular
molecule

MOL
Manned Orbiting
  Laboratory

Mont
Montana

MP
melting point
member of parliament
metropolitan police
military police
military policeman

mpg
miles per gallon

mph
miles per hour

MR
map reference
mentally retarded

Mr
mister

mRNA
messenger RNA

Mrs
mistress (married
  woman)

ms
millisecond

MS
manuscript
master of science
military science
Mississippi
motorship
multiple sclerosis

Ms
mistress (woman, marital
  status unmarked)

MSc
master of science

msec
millisecond

msg
message

MSG
master sergeant
monosodium glutamate

msgr
monseigneur
monsignor

MSgt
master sergeant

MSS
manuscripts

MST
mountain standard time

mt
mount
mountain

MT
Montana
mountain time

mtg
meeting
mortgage

mtge
mortgage

mun or munic
municipal

mus
museum
music
musical
musician

mv or mV
millivolt

MV
motor vessel

MVA
Missouri Valley
  Authority

MW
megawatt

MWe
megawatts electric

mxd
mixed

N

n
neuter
neutron
north
northern
noun
number

N
newton

NA
no account
North America
not applicable

NAACP
National Association
  for the Advancement
  of Colored People

NAB
New American Bible

NACU
National Association of
  Colleges and
  Universities

NAMH
National Association for
  Mental Health

NAS
National Academy of
  Sciences
naval air station

NASA
National Aeronautics and
  Space Administration

nat
national native
natural

NATO
North Atlantic Treaty
  Organization

naut
nautical

NB
New Brunswick
northbound
nota bene

NBA
National Basketball
  Association
National Boxing
  Association

NBC
National Broadcasting
  Company

NBS
National Bureau of
  Standards

NC
no charge
no credit
North Carolina

NCAA
National Collegiate
  Athletic Association

ncv
no commercial value

ND
North Dakota

N Dak
North Dakota

NE
Nebraska
New England
northeast

NEA
National Education
  Association

Neb or Nebr
Nebraska

NEB
New English Bible

neg
negative

nem con
(*nemine contrudicente*) no
  one contradicting

nem diss
(*nemine dissentiente*) no
  one dissenting

neut
neuter

Nev
Nevada

New Eng
New England

NF
Newfoundland
no funds

NFC
National Football
  Conference

NFL
National Football League

Nfld
Newfoundland

NFS
not for sale

ng
nanogram

NG
national guard
no good

NH
New Hampshire

NHL
National Hockey League

NHP
nominal horsepower

NIH
National Institutes of
  Health

NJ
New Jersey

NL
National League
new line
(*non licet*) it is not
  permitted

NLF
National Liberation
  Front

NLRB
National Labor Relations
  Board

NLT
night letter

NM
nautical mile
New Mexico
no mark

N Mex
New Mexico

NMI
no middle initial

NMR
nuclear magnetic
  resonance

NNE
north-northeast

NNW
north-northwest

no
north
northern
(*numero*) number

nom
nominative

non seq
(*non sequitur*) it does not
 follow

NOP
not otherwise
 provided for

Nor
Norway
Norwegian

NORAD
North American Air
 Defense Command

norm
normal

nos
numbers

NOS
not otherwise specified

Nov
November

NPR
National Public Radio

nr
near

NRA
National Recovery
 Administration
National Rifle
 Association

NRC
National Research
 Council
Nuclear Regulatory
 Commission

NS
new style
not specified
not sufficient
Nova Scotia

NSA
National Security
 Agency

NSC
National Security Council

NSW
New South Wales

NT
New Testament
Northern Territory
Northwest Territories

NTP
normal temperature and
 pressure

nt wt or n wt
net weight

NV
Nevada
nonvoting

NW
northwest

NWT
Northwest Territories

NY
New York

NYA
National Youth
 Administration

NYC
New York City

NYSE
New York Stock
 Exchange

NZ
New Zealand

O

o
ohm

O
Ohio

o/a
on or about

OAS
Organization of
 American States

OAU
Organization of African
 Unity

ob
(*obit*) he died, she died

OBE
Officer of the Order of
 the British Empire

obj
object
objective

OCR
optical character reader
optical character
 recognition

oct
octavo

Oct
October

OD
on demand
overdose
overdrawn

OE
Old English

OECD
Organization for
 Economic
 Cooperation and
 Development

OED
Oxford English
 Dictionary

OF
outfield

off
office
officer
official

offic
official

OH
Ohio

OHMS
on Her Majesty's service
on His Majesty's service

OIT
Office of International
   Trade

OK
Oklahoma

Okla
Oklahoma

OM
order of merit

On or ONT
Ontario

OP
out of print

op cit
(*opere citato*) in the
   work cited

OPEC
Organization of
   Petroleum Exporting
   Countries

Opp
opposite

opt
optical
optician

OR
Oregon
owner's risk

orch
orchestra

ord
order
ordinance

Ore or Oreg
Oregon

org
organic
organization
organized

orig
original
originally
originator

OS
old style
ordinary seaman
out of stock

OT
occupational therapy
Old Testament
overtime

OTC
over-the-counter

OTS
officers' training school

OW
one-way

Oxon
(*Oxonia*) Oxford

oz
(*onza*) ounce
ounces

P

p
page
penny
peseta
peso

Pa
Pennsylvania

PA
particular average
Pennsylvania
per annum
personal appearance
power of attorney
press agent
private account

p and h
postage and handling

P and L
profit and loss

par
paragraph
parallel

part
participle
particular

pass
passenger
passive

pat
patent

path or pathol
pathological
pathology

PAU
Pan American Union

PAYE
pay as you earn
pay as you enter

payt
payment

PB
power brakes

PBS
Public Broadcasting
   Service

PBX
private branch exchange

PC
Peace Corps
percent
percentage
personal computer
postcard

pct
percent
percentage

pd
paid

PD
per diem
police department

PDD
past due date

PDT
Pacific daylight time

PE
physical education
printer's error
probable error

P/E
price/earnings

pen
peninsula

PEN
International Association
of Poets, Playwrights,
Editors, Essayists and
Novelists

Penn
Pennsylvania

per
period
person

perf
perfect
perforated
performance

perh
perhaps

perm
permanent

perp
perpendicular

pers
person
personal
personnel

pert
pertaining

pfd
preferred

PGA
Professional Golfers'
Association

ph
phase

PH
public health
Purple Heart

phar
pharmacy

pharm
pharmaceutical
pharmacist
pharmacy

PhB
(*philosophiae baccalaureus*)
bachelor of
philosophy

PhD
(*philosophiae doctor*)
doctor of philosophy

phon
phonetics

photog
photographic
photography

phr
phrase

phys
physics

pinx
(*pinxit*) he painted it, she
painted it

pk
park
peak
peck
pike

PK
psychokinesis

pkg
package

pkng
packaging

pkt
packet
pocket

pkwy
parkway

pl
place
plate
plural

PL
partial loss
private line

plat
plateau
platoon

plf
plaintiff

PLO
Palestine Liberation
Organization

PLSS
portable life-support
system

pm
phase modulation
premium

PM
paymaster
permanent magnet
police magistrate
postmaster
(*post meridien*) after
midday
postmortem
prime minister
provost marshal

pmk
postmark

pmt
payment

PN
promissory note

PO
petty officer
postal order
post office
purchase order

POC
port of call

POD
pay on delivery
post office department

POE
port of embarkation
port of entry

poly
polytechnic

POO
post office order

pop
popular
population

por
portrait

POR
pay on return

Port
Portugal
Portuguese

pos
position
positive

poss
possessive

PP
pages
(*per procurationem*) by
   proxy

PP
parcel post
past participle
postpaid
prepaid

ppd
post paid
prepaid

ppm
parts per million

PPS
(*post postscriptum*) an
   additional postscript

ppt
parts per thousand
parts per trillion

pptn
precipitation

PQ
previous question
Province of Quebec

pr
pair
price
printed

PR
payroll
proportional
   representation
public relations

PRC
People's Republic of
   China

prec
preceding

pred
predicate

pref
preface
preferred
prefix

prem
premium

prep
preparatory
preposition

pres
present
president

Presb
Presbyterian

prev
previous
previously

prf
proof

prim
primary
primitive

prin
principal
principle

priv
private
privately
privative

PRN
(*pro re nata*) for the
   emergency, as needed

PRO
public relations officer

prob
probable
probably
probate
problem

proc
proceedings

prod
product
production

prof
professional
professor

prom
promontory

pron
pronoun
pronounced
pronunciation

prop
property
proposition
proprietor

pros
prosody

Prot
Protestant

prov
province
provincial
provisional

PS
(*postscriptum*) postscript

pseud
pseudonym
pseudonymous

psi
pounds per square inch

PST
Pacific standard time

psych
psychology

psychol
psychologist
psychology

pt
part
payment
pint
point
port

PT
Pacific time
part-time
physical therapy
physical training

pta
peseta

PTA
Parent-Teacher
    Association

ptg
printing

PTO
Parent-Teacher
    Organization
please turn over

pub
public
publication
published
publisher
publishing

publ
publication
published
publisher

PUD
pickup and delivery

PVA
polyvinyl acetate

PVC
polyvinyl chloride

pvt
private

PVT
pressure, volume,
    temperature

PW
prisoner of war

pwr
power

pwt
pennyweight

PX
please exchange
post exchange

Q

q
quart
quartile
quarto
query
question

QB
queen's bench

QC
quality control
queen's counsel

QED
(*quod erat demonstrandum*)
    which was to be
    demonstrated

QEF
(*quod erat faciendum*)
    which was to be done

QEI
(*quod erat inveniendum*)
    which was to be
    found out

QMG
quartermaster general

qp or q pl
(*quantum placet*) as much
    as you please

qq
questions

qr
quarter
quire

qs
(*quantum sufficit*) as
    much as suffices

qt
quantity
quart

qtd
quartered

qto
quarto

qty
quantity

qu or ques
question

quad
quadrant

qual
qualitative
quality

quant
quantitative

quar
quarterly

Que
Quebec

quot
quotation

qv
(*quod vide*) which see

R

r
radius
repeat
Republican
ruble
rupee

R
radical
registered trademark

RA
regular army
Royal Academician
Royal Academy

RAAF
Royal Australian
  Air Force

rad
radical
radian
radiator
radio
radius
radix

RAF
Royal Air Force

RAM
random access memory

R & B
rhythm and blues

R & D
research and
  development

R & R
rest and recreation
rest and recuperation

RBC
red blood cells
red blood count

RBE
relative biological
  effectiveness

RC
Red Cross
Roman Catholic

RCAF
Royal Canadian Air Force

RCMP
Royal Canadian
  Mounted Police

RCN
Royal Canadian Navy

rct
recruit

rd
road
rod
round

RD
refer to drawer

RDA
recommended daily
  allowance
recommended dietary
  allowance

RDF
radio direction finder
radio direction finding

rec
receipt
record
recording
recreation

recd
received

recip
reciprocal
reciprocity

rec sec
recording secretary

rect
receipt
rectangle
rectangular
rectified

red
reduce
reduction

ref
reference
referred
refining
reformed
refunding

refl
reflex
reflexive

refirig
refrigerating
refrigeration

reg
region
register
registered
registration
regular

regd
registered

regt
regiment

rel
relating
relative
released
religion
religious

relig
religion

rep
report
representative
republic

Rep
Republican

repl
replace
replacement

req
request
require
required
requisition

reqd
required

res
research
reservation
reserve
residence
resolution

resp
respective
respectively

retd
retained
retired
returned

rev
revenue
reverse
review
reviewed
revised
revision
revolution

Rev
reverend

rf
refunding

RF
radio frequency

rh
relative humidity

rhet
rhetoric

RI
refractive index
Rhode Island

RIP
(*requiescat in pace*) may
    he rest in peace, may
    she rest in peace

rit
ritardando

riv
river

rm
ream
room

RMS
Royal Mail Service
Royal Mail Steamship

RN
registered nurse
Royal Navy

rnd
round

ROG
receipt of goods

ROI
return on investment

Rom
Roman
Romance
Romania
Romanian

ROM
read-only memory

ROP
record of production

rot
rotating
rotation

ROTC
Reserve Officers
    Training Corps

RP
Received Pronunciation
reply paid
reprint
reprinting

RPM
revolutions per minute

RPO
railways post office

RPS
revolutions per second

rpt
repeat
report

RR
railroad

RS
Royal Society

RSV
Revised Standard Version

RSVP
(*répondez s'il vous plait*)
    please reply

RSWC
right side up with care

rt
right

RT
radiotelephone
room temperature

rte
route

rtw
ready-to-wear

RV
recreational vehicle

rwy or ry
railway

S

s
saint
schilling
senate
shilling
sine
singular
small
south
southern

SA
Salvation Army
seaman apprentice
(*sine anno* without year)
    without dates
South Africa
South America
South Australia

SAC
Strategic Air Command

SAE
self-addressed envelope
stamped addressed
  envelope

SALT
Strategic Arms
  Limitation Talks

SAM
surface-to-air missile

S & M
sadism and masochism

sanit
sanitary
sanitation

SASE
self-addressed stamped
  envelope

Sask
Saskatchewan

sat
saturate
saturated
saturation

Sat
Saturday

satd
saturated

S Aust
South Australia

sb
substantive

SBA
Small Business
  Administration

SBN
Standard Book Number

sc
scale
scene
science
(*sculpsit*) he carved it,
  she carved it, he
  engraved it, she
  engraved it

SC
Scots
small capitals
South Carolina
supreme court

sch
school

sci
science
scientific

SCP
single-cell protein

SCPO
senior chief petty officer

sct
scout

SD
South Dakota
special delivery
stage direction

SDA
specific dynamic action

S Dak
South Dakota

SDI
Strategic Defense
  Initiative

SDR
special drawing rights

SE
southeast
Standard English
stock exchange

SEATO
Southeast Asia Treaty
  Organization

sec
second
secretary
(*secundum*) according to

sect
section
sectional

secy
secretary

sed
sediment
sedimentation

sel
selected
selection

sen
senate
senator
senior

sep
separate
separated

Sep
September

sepd
separated

Sept
September

seq
(*sequens*) the following

serg or sergt
sergeant

serv
service

sf or sfz
sforzando

SF
science fiction
sinking fund

SFC
sergeant first class

SG
sergeant
solicitor general
specific gravity

sgd
signed

Sgt
sergeant

Sgt Maj
sergeant major

sh
share

shipt
shipment

shpt
shipment

sht
sheet

shtg
shortage

SI
(*Système International d'Unités*) International System of Units

SIDS
sudden infant death syndrome

sig
signal
signature
signor

SIG
special interest group

sin
sine

sing
singular

SJ
Society of Jesus

SK
Saskatchewan

sl
slightly
slow

SL
salvage loss
sea level
south latitude

SLBM
submarine-launched ballistic missile

sld
sailed
sealed
sold

SLR
single lens reflex

SMaj
sergeant major

SMSgt
senior master sergeant

SMV
slow-moving vehicle

SNG
substitute natural gas
synthetic natural gas

so
south
southern

SO
seller's option
strikeout

soc
social
society

sociol
sociologist
sociology

soln
solution

soph
sophomore

sp
species
specific
specimen
spelling

SP
self-propelled
shore patrol

SPCA
Society for the Prevention of Cruelty to Animals

SPCC
Society for the Prevention of Cruelty to Children

spec
special
specifically

specif
specific
specifically

sp gr
specific gravity

SPOT
satellite positioning and tracking

SPQR
(*senatus populusque Romanus*) the senate and the people of Rome

sq
squadron
square

Sr
senior
señor
sister

Sra
señora

SRO
standing room only

Srta
señorita

SS
saints
same size
Social Security
steamship

SSA
Social Security Administration

SSE
south-southeast

SSG or SSgt
staff sergeant

SSM
staff sergeant major

SSW
south-southwest

st
stanza
state
street

St
saint
stratus

ST
short ton
single throw
standard time

sta
station
stationary

stat
(*statim*) immediately

stbd
starboard

std
standard

Ste
(*sainte*) saint (*fem.*)

ster or stg
sterling

stge
storage

stk
stock

STOL
short takeoff and
landing

stor
storage

STP
standard temperature
and pressure

STV
subscription television

sub
subaltern
subtract
suburb

subj
subject
subjunctive

suff
sufficient
suffix

Sun
Sunday

supp or suppl
supplement
supplementary

supr
supreme

supt
superintendent

sur
surface

surg
surgeon
surgery
surgical

surv
survey
surveying
surveyor

sv
sailing vessel
saves
(*sub verbo* or *sub voce*)
under the word

svgs
savings

sw
switch

SW
shortwave
southwest

sym
symbol
symmetrical

syn
synonym
synonymous

syst
system

T

TA
teaching assistant

TAC
Tactical Air Command

tan
tangent

tb
tablespoon
tablespoonful

TB
trial balance
tubercle bacillus

tbs or tbsp
tablespoon
tablespoonful

tchr
teacher

TD
touchdown
Treasury Department

TDN
total digestible nutrients

tech
technical
technically
technician
technological
technology

TEFL
teaching English as a
foreign language

tel
telegram
telegraph
telephone

teleg
telegraphy

temp
temperance
temperature
template
temporal
temporary

Tenn
Tennessee

TESL
teaching English as a
second language

TESOL
Teachers of English
to speakers of other
languages

Test
Testament

Tex
Texas

TG
transformational
grammar
type genus

Th
Thursday

Thurs or Thu
Thursday

tk
tank
truck

tkt
ticket

TL
total loss
truckload

TLC
tender loving care

TLO
total loss only

tlr
tailor
trailer

TM
trademark
transcendental
meditation

TMO
telegraph money order

tn
ton
town
train

TN
Tennessee
true north

tng
training

tnpk
turnpike

topog
topography

tot
total

tpk or tpke
turnpike

tps
townships
troops

tr
translated
translator
transpose

trans
transaction
transitive
translated
translation
translator

transl
translated
translation

transp
transportation

trib
tributary

trop
tropic
tropical

ts
tensile strength

tsp
teaspoon
teaspoonsful

TT
telegraphic transfer
Trust Territories

Tu
Tuesday

TU
trade union
transmission unit

TUC
Trades Union Congress

Tue or Tues
Tuesday

TV
television
terminal velocity
transvestite

TX
Texas

U

U
university

UAE
United Arab Emirates

UAR
United Arab Republic

UC
undercharge
uppercase

ugt
urgent

UHF
ultrahigh frequency

UK
United Kingdom

ult
ultimate
ultimo

UN
United Nations

unan
unanimous

UNESCO
United Nations
Educational, Scientific,
and Cultural
Organization

UNICEF
United Nations
International
Children's Emergency
Fund

univ
universal
university

UNRWA
United Nations Relief
and Works Agency

uns
unsymmetrical

UPC
Universal Product Code

UPI
United Press International

USA
United States Army
United States of America

USAF
United States Air Force

USCG
United States Coast
Guard

USDA
United States Department
of Agriculture

USIA
United States Information
Agency

USM
United States Mail

USMC
United States Marine
Corps
United States Maritime
Corps

USN
United States Navy

USO
United Service
Organizations

USPS
United States Postal
Service

USS
United States ship

USSR
Union of Soviet Socialist
Republics

usu
usual
usually

UT
Universal time
Utah

util
utility

UV
ultraviolet

UW
underwriter

ux
wife

UXB
unexploded bomb

V

v
vector
verb
versus
very
volt
voltage
vowel

Va
Virginia

VA
Veterans Administration
vice admiral
Virginia
visual aid
volt-ampere

vac
vacuum

VADM
vice admiral

val
value
valued

var
variant
variety
various

VAT
value-added tax

vb
verb
verbal

VC
veterinary corps
vice-chancellor
vice-consul
Victoria Cross
Vietcong

VD
vapor density
venereal disease

VDT
video display terminal

VDU
visual display unit

veg
vegetable

vel
vellum
velocity

vert
vertebrate
vertical

VFD
volunteer fire
department

VG
very good
vicar-general

VHF
very high frequency

vi
verb intransitive

VI
Virgin Islands
viscosity index
volume indicator

vic
vicinity

Vic
Victoria

vil
village

vis
visibility
visual

VISTA
Volunteers in Service to
America

viz
videlicet (that is to say)

VLF
very low frequency

VOA
Voice of America

voc
vocational
vocative

vocab
vocabulary

vol
volcano
volume
volunteer

VOLAR
volunteer army

VOM
volt ohm meter

VP
variable pitch
various places
verb phrase
vice president

VRM
variable rate mortgage

vs
verse
versus

VS
veterinary surgeon

vss
verses
versions

V/STOL
vertical short takeoff and
landing

Vt
Vermont

VT
vacuum tube
variable time
Vermont

VTOL
vertical takeoff and
landing

VTR
video tape recorder
video tape recording

VU
volume unit

Vulg
Vulgate

vv
verses
vice versa

W

WA
Washington
Western Australia

war
warrant

W Aust
Western Australia

WC
water closet
without charge

Wed
Wednesday

WFTU
World Federation of
Trade Unions

WH
watt-hour

WHA
World Hockey
Association

whf
wharf

WHO
World Health
Organization

whr
watt-hour

whs or whse
warehouse

whsle
wholesale

wi
when issued

WI
West Indies
Wisconsin

WIA
wounded in action

wid
widow
widower

wk
week
work

wkly
weekly

WL
waterline
wavelength

WNW
west-northwest

WO
warrant officer

w/o
without

W/O
water-in-oil

WOC
without compensation

WP
without prejudice

WPM
words per minute

wpn
weapon

WR
warehouse receipt

WRAC
Women's Royal Army
  Corps

WRAF
Women's Royal Air Force

WRNS
Women's Royal Naval
  Service

wrnt
warrant

WSW
west-southwest

wt
weight

WT
watertight
wireless telegraphy

WV or W Va
West Virginia

WVS
Women's Voluntary
  Services

WW
warehouse warrant
with warrants
world war

w/w
wall-to-wall

WY or Wyo
Wyoming

X

x
cross
ex
experimental
extra

XC
ex coupon

XD or x div
ex dividend

XI or x in or x int
ex interest

XL
extra large
extra long

Y

y
yard
year
yen

YB
yearbook

yd
yard

YO
year old

YOB
year of birth

yr
year
younger
your

yrbk
yearbook

Yug
Yugoslavia

Z

z
zero
zone

ZPG
zero population growth

Chemical Abbreviations

A

Ac
Actinium

Ag
Silver

Al
Aluminum

Am
Americium

Ar
Argon

As
Arsenic

At
Astatine

Au
Gold

B

B
Boron

Ba
Barium

Be
Beryllium

Bh
Bohrium

Bi
Bismuth

Bk
Berkelium

Br
Bromine

C

C
Carbon

Ca
Calcium

Cd
Cadmium

Ce
Cerium

Cf
Californium

Cl
Chlorine

Cm
Curium

Co
Cobalt

Cr
Chromium

Cs
Cesium

Cu
Copper

D

Db
Dubnium

Dy
Dysprosium

E

Er
Erbium

Es
Einsteinium

Eu
Europium

F

F
Fluorine

Fe
Iron

Fm
Fermium

Fr
Francium

G

Ga
Gallium

Gd
Gadolinium

Ge
Germanium

H

H
Hydrogen

He
Helium

Hf
Hafnium

Hg
Mercury

Ho
Holmium

Hs
Hassium

I

I
Iodine

In
Indium

Ir
Iridium

K

K
Potassium

Kr
Krypton

L

La
Lanthanum

Li
Lithium

Lr
Lawrencium

Lu
Lutetium

M

Md
Mendelevium

Mg
Magnesium

Mn
Manganese

Mo
Molybdenum

Mt
Meitnerium

N

N
Nitrogen

Na
Sodium

Nb
Niobium

Nd
Neodymium

Ne
Neon

Ni
Nickel

No
Nobelium

Np
Neptunium

O

O
Oxygen

Os
Osmium

P

P
Phosphorus

Pa
Protactinium

Pb
Lead

Pd
Palladium

Pm
Promethium

Po
Polonium

Pr
Praseodymium

Pt
Platinum

Pu
Plutonium

R

Ra
Radium

Rb
Rubidium

Re
Rhenium

Rf
Rutherfordium

Rh
Rhodium

Rn
Radon

Ru
Ruthenium

S

S
Sulfur

Sb
Antimony

Sc
Scandium

Se
Selenium

Sg
Seaborgium

Si
Silicon

Sm
Samarium

Sn
Tin

Sr
Strontium

T

Ta
Tantalum

Tb
Terbium

Tc
Technetium

Te
Tellurium

Th
Thorium

Ti
Titanium

Tl
Thallium

Tm
Thulium

U

U
Uranium

V

V
Vanadium

W

W
Tungsten

X

Xe
Xenon

Y

Y
Yttrium

Yb
Ytterbium

Z

Zn
Zinc

Zr
Zirconium

Fun with Words

*For Those Who Enjoy Language (or Severe Distortions Thereof)
These are just for fun. Enjoy them.*

Those who jump off a bridge in Paris are in Seine.

A backward poet writes inverse.

A man's home is his castle, in a manor of speaking.

Dijon vu—the same mustard as before.

Practice safe eating—always use condiments.

Shotgun wedding: A case of wife or death.

A hangover is the wrath of grapes.

Dancing cheek-to-cheek is really a form of floor play.

Does the name Pavlov ring a bell?

Reading while sunbathing makes you well red.

When two egotists meet, it's an I for an I.

A bicycle can't stand on its own because it is two tired.

What's the definition of a will? (It's a dead giveaway.)

Time flies like an arrow. Fruit flies like a banana.

In democracy, your vote counts. In feudalism, your count votes.

She was engaged to a boyfriend with a wooden leg but broke it off.

A chicken crossing the road is poultry in motion.

If you don't pay your exorcist, you get repossessed.

With her marriage, she got a new name and a dress.

When a clock is hungry, it goes back four seconds.

The man who fell into an upholstery machine is fully recovered.

You feel stuck with your debt if you can't budge it.

Local Area Network in Australia: the LAN down under.

He often broke into song because he couldn't find the key.

Every calendar's days are numbered.

A lot of money is tainted. It taint yours and it taint mine.

A boiled egg in the morning is hard to beat.

He had a photographic memory that was never developed.

A plateau is a high form of flattery.

A midget fortune-teller who escapes from prison is a small medium at large.

Those who get too big for their britches will be exposed in the end.

Once you've seen one shopping center, you've seen a mall.

Bakers trade bread recipes on a knead-to-know basis.

Santa's helpers are subordinate clauses.

Acupuncture is a jab well done.